Victor M. Maceda

The LGBTQ Rights Activist Defending Asylum Seekers – Unauthorized

Ivy Garba

ISBN: 9781779696120
Imprint: Telephasic Workshop

Contents

The Early Years

A Boy with a Dream

Growing Up in a Conservative Town

Growing up in a conservative town can often feel like navigating a labyrinth with no clear exit. For Victor M. Maceda, this was a reality that shaped his early years and laid the foundation for his future activism. The small, tightly-knit community where he spent his formative years was steeped in traditional values and a rigid worldview that often left little room for diversity, particularly when it came to sexual orientation and gender identity.

In such environments, the prevailing cultural norms can create an atmosphere of fear and repression. According to social identity theory, individuals derive a sense of self from their group memberships, which in conservative settings can lead to a strong in-group versus out-group mentality. This theory posits that people are motivated to maintain a positive self-image, often at the expense of those who are different. Thus, LGBTQ individuals in conservative towns frequently face stigmatization, marginalization, and, in many cases, outright hostility.

Victor's childhood was marked by the tension between his burgeoning identity and the expectations of his community. He would often hear derogatory remarks about LGBTQ individuals, reinforcing a sense of isolation. This aligns with the findings of researchers like Herek (2009), who noted that internalized homophobia can lead to significant psychological distress for LGBTQ youth. For Victor, the struggle to reconcile his true self with the conservative values surrounding him was profound.

The impact of this environment was not merely psychological; it manifested in social interactions as well. Victor encountered prejudice and discrimination from peers and adults alike. Instances of bullying were common, as were subtle forms of exclusion that left deep emotional scars. This experience is consistent with the research by Russell et al. (2011), which highlighted that LGBTQ youth in hostile environments are at a higher risk for mental health issues, including depression and anxiety.

However, even in this conservative backdrop, Victor discovered unexpected sources of support. A teacher who recognized his struggles became a mentor, providing him with the encouragement he desperately needed. This relationship exemplifies the importance of allyship in fostering resilience among marginalized individuals. According to the theory of social support, having even one supportive figure can significantly buffer the negative effects of discrimination and prejudice.

Victor's early experiences were not solely defined by adversity. They also ignited a passion for social justice that would later become the cornerstone of his activism. The realization that many others shared his struggles motivated him to seek out connections with like-minded individuals, even in a town that often felt stifling.

In the face of adversity, Victor began to engage with LGBTQ literature and media, which served as a lifeline. Works by authors like James Baldwin and Audre Lorde provided him with a sense of belonging and validation. This exposure to diverse narratives helped him to cultivate a broader understanding of identity and community, further fueling his desire to advocate for change.

Ultimately, growing up in a conservative town was both a challenge and a catalyst for Victor M. Maceda. It instilled in him a profound understanding of the complexities surrounding identity, acceptance, and the fight for rights. His early struggles, while painful, became the bedrock of his commitment to activism. As he navigated the labyrinth of his youth, he began to envision a world where love and acceptance could triumph over prejudice and fear, setting the stage for his future endeavors in the realm of LGBTQ rights.

In summary, the environment of a conservative town can profoundly impact the development of LGBTQ individuals. Through the lens of Victor's experiences, we see how societal norms and values can shape personal identity and activism. His journey illustrates the resilience that can emerge from adversity and the importance of support systems in fostering empowerment.

$$\text{Resilience} = \frac{\text{Support}}{\text{Adversity}} \qquad (1)$$

This equation highlights the relationship between the amount of support an individual receives and their ability to cope with adversity, a principle that resonates deeply with Victor's story.

Encountering Prejudice and Discrimination

Victor M. Maceda's formative years were marred by the harsh realities of prejudice and discrimination, experiences that would shape not only his identity but also his future as an activist. Growing up in a conservative town, Victor found himself navigating a landscape rife with societal norms that often marginalized those who dared to deviate from the expected. Prejudice, in its many forms, became an omnipresent shadow in his life, manifesting through both overt and subtle acts of discrimination.

The Nature of Prejudice

Prejudice can be defined as a preconceived opinion that is not based on reason or actual experience. It often stems from ignorance, fear, or societal conditioning, leading individuals to form negative attitudes toward others based on characteristics such as race, gender, sexual orientation, or religion. Theories on prejudice, such as Allport's Contact Hypothesis, suggest that increased interaction between different groups can reduce prejudice. However, in Victor's conservative environment, such interactions were limited, perpetuating stereotypes and fostering an atmosphere of exclusion.

Experiencing Discrimination

Victor's encounters with discrimination were multifaceted. At school, he faced bullying from peers who perceived his mannerisms and interests as different. This bullying was not merely an isolated incident but a reflection of a broader societal issue. Research indicates that LGBTQ youth are disproportionately affected by bullying, leading to severe psychological consequences, including anxiety, depression, and suicidal ideation. Victor's experience was a stark reminder of the urgent need for protective measures and supportive environments for marginalized youth.

$$D = \frac{B}{S} \tag{2}$$

where D represents the level of discrimination experienced, B is the intensity of bullying incidents, and S is the support available to the individual. In Victor's case, the equation illustrated a high level of discrimination due to low support from both peers and adults, creating a toxic environment that stifled his self-expression.

The Impact of Societal Norms

Societal norms play a crucial role in shaping attitudes toward LGBTQ individuals. In many conservative communities, traditional views on masculinity and femininity dominate, often leading to the stigmatization of those who do not conform. Victor's experiences exemplified this phenomenon, as he grappled with the internal conflict between his authentic self and the expectations imposed upon him by society. This conflict is supported by the Minority Stress Theory, which posits that individuals from marginalized groups experience chronic stress due to societal stigma, discrimination, and prejudice.

Coping Mechanisms

In the face of such adversity, Victor developed coping mechanisms to navigate the challenges of his environment. He sought solace in art and literature, finding refuge in the stories of others who had faced similar struggles. This engagement with creative expression not only provided an outlet for his emotions but also served as a catalyst for self-discovery. Studies have shown that engagement in the arts can foster resilience and promote mental well-being among marginalized individuals.

Examples from Victor's Life

One poignant example from Victor's life occurred during a school assembly when a speaker made derogatory comments about LGBTQ individuals. The incident sparked a wave of laughter among his classmates, leaving Victor feeling isolated and ashamed. However, this moment also ignited a fire within him, compelling him to confront the prejudice he faced. He began to document his experiences, using writing as a tool for advocacy and change.

Furthermore, Victor's family dynamics played a significant role in his encounters with discrimination. His parents, influenced by societal norms, initially struggled to accept his identity. This familial rejection compounded the external prejudice he faced, illustrating the intersectionality of discrimination that many LGBTQ individuals experience. The compounded nature of these experiences often leads to a phenomenon known as double jeopardy, where individuals face multiple layers of discrimination based on various aspects of their identity.

Conclusion

Victor M. Maceda's early encounters with prejudice and discrimination were not merely personal struggles; they were emblematic of a larger societal issue that required urgent attention. His experiences illuminated the pervasive nature of bias and the urgent need for systemic change. As he began to understand the complexities of his identity and the societal forces at play, Victor's resolve to fight against prejudice solidified, setting him on the path toward activism. This chapter of his life serves as a powerful reminder of the resilience of the human spirit in the face of adversity and the transformative potential of advocacy in combating discrimination.

Discovering His Identity

The journey of self-discovery is a complex and deeply personal experience, particularly for individuals navigating the intricate landscape of sexual orientation and gender identity. For Victor M. Maceda, this journey began in the confines of a conservative town, where societal norms dictated strict adherence to heteronormative expectations. In this environment, the realization of his identity was fraught with challenges, but it also set the stage for a profound awakening.

The Internal Struggle

Victor's early years were marked by an internal struggle that many LGBTQ individuals face: the conflict between societal expectations and personal truth. The theory of *internalized homophobia* suggests that negative societal attitudes towards homosexuality can lead individuals to develop feelings of shame or self-hatred regarding their sexual orientation. This phenomenon is particularly pronounced in conservative communities where non-conformity is often met with hostility or rejection.

Victor grappled with feelings of isolation and confusion, often questioning his worth and place in a world that seemed to value conformity over authenticity. He would often reflect on the following equation, which metaphorically illustrates his internal conflict:

$$\text{Identity} = \text{Societal Expectations} - \text{Personal Truth}$$

This equation underscores the tension between the external pressures to conform and the internal desire for self-acceptance. The greater the societal expectations, the more Victor felt the weight of his hidden truth.

The Moment of Clarity

It was during his teenage years that Victor experienced a pivotal moment of clarity. Engaging with literature and media that reflected LGBTQ experiences provided him with a new lens through which to view his identity. Works by authors such as James Baldwin and Audre Lorde resonated deeply with him, offering narratives that celebrated authenticity and self-acceptance. This engagement with LGBTQ literature can be understood through the framework of *narrative identity theory*, which posits that individuals construct their identities through the stories they tell about themselves and the influences of the stories they consume.

Victor's moment of clarity was further catalyzed by a supportive friendship with a mentor who identified as queer. This relationship provided him with a safe space to explore his feelings and question the narratives he had internalized. The mentor's affirmation of Victor's identity served as a crucial turning point, allowing him to embrace his truth without fear.

The Role of Community

As Victor began to accept his identity, he sought out communities that celebrated diversity and inclusion. He discovered local LGBTQ youth groups that provided not only resources but also a sense of belonging. The concept of *communitas*, as described by anthropologist Victor Turner, refers to the spirit of community that emerges in shared experiences. In these groups, Victor found solidarity with others who had faced similar struggles, reinforcing his understanding that he was not alone in his journey.

The supportive environment of these communities allowed Victor to express himself freely, engage in discussions about identity, and participate in activities that celebrated LGBTQ culture. This sense of belonging was pivotal in solidifying his identity and fostering resilience against the external prejudices he continued to face.

Navigating Prejudice

Despite the progress Victor made in discovering his identity, the road was not without obstacles. The pervasive prejudice in his conservative town often manifested in subtle and overt forms, from derogatory remarks to exclusionary practices. The theory of *microaggressions* provides insight into the everyday verbal, behavioral, or environmental slights that, whether intentional or not, convey hostility or derogatory messages to marginalized groups.

Victor encountered microaggressions that challenged his self-worth and made him question his place within both his community and the LGBTQ movement.

However, these experiences also fueled his determination to advocate for change. The resilience he developed through these challenges became a cornerstone of his identity, as he learned to transform pain into purpose.

Conclusion: The Emergence of an Activist

In the crucible of self-discovery, Victor M. Maceda emerged not only as a confident individual but as a passionate advocate for LGBTQ rights. The process of discovering his identity was interwoven with the understanding that personal truths must be shared to effect change. This realization laid the groundwork for his future activism, where he would channel his experiences into advocating for those who continued to face the same struggles he once did.

Victor's journey illustrates the powerful intersection of personal identity and collective action, reminding us that the path to self-acceptance is often a precursor to broader societal change. Through his story, we see the importance of embracing one's identity, the value of community support, and the transformative power of resilience in the face of adversity.

Finding Support in Unexpected Places

In the journey of self-discovery and activism, Victor M. Maceda encountered a myriad of challenges, yet it was often in the most unlikely corners of his world that he found the support he needed. This section explores how Victor's experiences illustrate the importance of seeking allies and community in unexpected places, ultimately shaping his path as a prominent LGBTQ rights activist.

The Power of Unexpected Allies

Victor's early life in a conservative town was fraught with prejudice and discrimination, yet it was here that he discovered the transformative power of unexpected allies. One of the most profound influences came from a local librarian, Mrs. Thompson, who recognized Victor's struggles with identity and self-acceptance. She provided him with books that explored LGBTQ themes and offered a safe space for discussion. This relationship exemplifies how support can emerge from seemingly mundane environments, highlighting the importance of community figures who are willing to stand against the tide of societal norms.

Building Bridges with Diverse Communities

Victor's activism also led him to forge connections with various marginalized groups. He found kinship with immigrant communities facing their own battles against discrimination. By participating in cultural events and community meetings, Victor learned that the fight for LGBTQ rights was intertwined with other social justice movements. For instance, during a local festival celebrating diversity, he collaborated with immigrant leaders to raise awareness about the unique challenges faced by LGBTQ asylum seekers. This intersectional approach not only broadened his support network but also enriched his understanding of activism as a collective effort.

Utilizing Online Platforms for Connection

In the digital age, Victor harnessed the power of social media to connect with individuals and organizations beyond his immediate surroundings. Platforms like Twitter and Instagram became vital tools for building a global community. For example, after sharing his coming-out story online, Victor received an outpouring of support from LGBTQ individuals across the globe, many of whom shared their own stories of struggle and triumph. This virtual solidarity provided him with a sense of belonging and reinforced the notion that support can transcend geographical boundaries.

The Role of Mentorship in Activism

Victor's journey was also marked by the influence of mentors who appeared at pivotal moments in his life. During his college years, he met Dr. Elena Rodriguez, a prominent LGBTQ activist and scholar. Dr. Rodriguez took Victor under her wing, guiding him through the complexities of activism and encouraging him to embrace his voice. This mentorship not only provided practical advice but also instilled in Victor a sense of responsibility to uplift others. The relationship underscored the importance of mentorship in fostering resilience and empowerment within marginalized communities.

Community Events as Catalysts for Support

Victor's involvement in community events further exemplified how unexpected support could manifest. During a local Pride event, he encountered a group of older LGBTQ individuals who shared their experiences of activism during the early days of the movement. Their stories of resilience and courage inspired Victor to continue his work. The intergenerational dialogue that unfolded at such events emphasized the importance of shared history and collective memory in building a supportive community.

The Impact of Art and Expression

Art also played a significant role in Victor's journey, serving as both a source of support and a means of connection. He participated in a community art project that focused on LGBTQ themes, collaborating with artists from diverse backgrounds. This experience not only allowed Victor to express his identity creatively but also facilitated connections with individuals who shared similar experiences. The project culminated in an exhibition that celebrated diversity and resilience, showcasing the transformative power of art in fostering community support.

Conclusion: Embracing the Unlikely

Victor M. Maceda's story illustrates that support often comes from the most unexpected places. Whether through the kindness of a librarian, the solidarity of diverse communities, the guidance of mentors, or the power of art, these connections are vital in shaping an activist's journey. Victor's experiences remind us that while the path to self-acceptance and activism can be fraught with challenges, embracing the unlikely allies and communities we encounter along the way can lead to profound personal and collective growth. In a world where division often reigns, finding support in unexpected places serves as a testament to the resilience of the human spirit and the power of solidarity in the fight for justice and equality.

The Road to Activism Begins

Victor M. Maceda's journey toward activism was not born in a vacuum; it was shaped by the rich tapestry of his experiences, the harsh realities of societal prejudice, and the flickering flames of hope ignited by those who dared to stand up. This section delves into the formative moments that catalyzed his transition from a boy grappling with his identity in a conservative town to a fierce advocate for LGBTQ rights.

The Awakening of Consciousness

In the heart of a conservative town, Victor felt the weight of societal expectations pressing down on him. The local culture, steeped in traditional values, often vilified those who dared to be different. It was within this environment that Victor began to awaken to the injustices surrounding him. The theory of **social identity**, as posited by Henri Tajfel, suggests that individuals define themselves based on their group memberships. Victor's struggle with his identity was compounded by the need to conform to the prevailing norms, leading to a profound internal conflict. The realization that he belonged to a marginalized community sparked a desire to advocate not only for himself but for others who shared his plight.

Catalysts for Change

Victor's initial foray into activism was prompted by a series of personal encounters that laid bare the harsh realities faced by LGBTQ individuals. One pivotal moment occurred during a high school assembly when a guest speaker shared their harrowing story of discrimination and resilience. The speaker's narrative resonated deeply with Victor, illuminating the stark contrast between his own sheltered existence and the struggles of others. This experience became a catalyst for Victor, igniting a fire within him to seek change.

Inspired by this encounter, Victor began to engage with local LGBTQ organizations. He attended meetings, participated in discussions, and absorbed the knowledge shared by seasoned activists. The sense of community he found was transformative. The theory of **collective efficacy**, introduced by Albert Bandura, emphasizes the power of groups to achieve shared goals through mutual support and collaboration. Victor experienced this firsthand as he connected with others who shared his vision for a more equitable society.

The Role of Education

Education played a crucial role in shaping Victor's activism. He sought out literature and resources that explored LGBTQ history, rights, and the broader social justice movement. The works of pioneers like Harvey Milk and Marsha P. Johnson served as guiding lights, illustrating the impact of grassroots activism. Victor's thirst for knowledge was insatiable; he immersed himself in the study of human rights, learning about the systemic barriers that LGBTQ individuals faced globally.

One significant theory that influenced Victor was the **intersectionality** framework developed by Kimberlé Crenshaw. This concept highlights how various forms of discrimination—such as race, gender, and sexual orientation—intersect to create unique experiences of oppression. Victor recognized that his advocacy must encompass not only LGBTQ rights but also the struggles of other marginalized groups, fostering a more inclusive approach to activism.

Building Alliances

As Victor's understanding of activism deepened, he began to forge alliances with other social justice movements. He participated in rallies and protests advocating for racial equality, women's rights, and immigrant rights. These experiences reinforced the notion that all struggles for justice are interconnected. Victor's commitment to intersectional activism became a cornerstone of his approach, as he believed that true change could only be achieved through solidarity.

An exemplary moment of this alliance-building occurred when Victor collaborated with a local immigrant rights organization to address the unique challenges faced by LGBTQ asylum seekers. Together, they organized educational workshops that highlighted the intersection of immigration and LGBTQ rights, creating a platform for dialogue and awareness. This collaborative effort exemplified the power of collective action and underscored the importance of amplifying marginalized voices.

First Steps into Activism

Victor's first official act of activism came in the form of a letter to the editor of his local newspaper. Fueled by a mix of apprehension and determination, he penned a heartfelt piece addressing the need for greater acceptance of LGBTQ individuals in his community. The response was overwhelming—both supportive and critical. While some applauded his bravery, others condemned his views. This duality of reaction was a stark reminder of the challenges that lay ahead.

Undeterred, Victor continued to engage in activism, participating in local pride events and advocating for LGBTQ-inclusive policies at his school. His efforts did not go unnoticed, and he soon found himself at the forefront of a student-led initiative aimed at promoting awareness and acceptance within the educational system. This initiative included workshops, discussions, and the establishment of a Gay-Straight Alliance, fostering a safe space for dialogue and support.

Reflection and Growth

Reflecting on this period of his life, Victor recognized that the road to activism was fraught with challenges, but it was also a journey of self-discovery and empowerment. The struggles he faced only strengthened his resolve to advocate for change. He understood that activism was not merely about fighting against oppression; it was about creating a vision for a more inclusive future.

In conclusion, the road to activism for Victor M. Maceda began with personal struggles and evolved into a passionate commitment to advocate for LGBTQ rights. His experiences shaped his understanding of the complexities of identity, the importance of education, and the power of alliances. As he embarked on this transformative journey, Victor became not just a voice for himself, but for countless others who sought justice and equality. This chapter of his life laid the groundwork for the impactful activism that would follow, setting the stage for a lifelong commitment to defending the rights of marginalized communities.

From Personal Struggles to Collective Action

Coming Out and Acceptance

Coming out is a pivotal moment in the lives of many LGBTQ individuals, representing a journey toward self-acceptance and authenticity. This process can be both liberating and daunting, as it involves revealing one's sexual orientation or gender identity to others, often in environments that may not be fully accepting. For Victor M. Maceda, coming out was not merely a personal revelation but a catalyst for his activism and a stepping stone toward advocating for others who faced similar struggles.

The Psychological Impact of Coming Out

The act of coming out can have significant psychological implications. According to the *Minority Stress Theory*, LGBTQ individuals often experience unique stressors that arise from their marginalized status. These stressors can include societal stigma, discrimination, and internalized homophobia, which can lead to mental health challenges such as anxiety and depression. Research indicates that individuals who come out in supportive environments tend to report higher levels of self-esteem and lower levels of psychological distress.

$$\text{Mental Health} = f(\text{Support}, \text{Stigma}) \tag{3}$$

Where: - Mental Health is the overall well-being of the individual, - Support represents the level of acceptance from family, friends, and community, - Stigma denotes the societal pressures and discrimination faced.

Victor's journey to coming out was fraught with challenges, particularly in a conservative town where traditional values often overshadowed acceptance. Initially, he grappled with fear and uncertainty, questioning how his family and peers would react. This internal conflict is common among LGBTQ individuals, who often weigh the potential consequences of their revelations against the desire for authenticity.

Finding Acceptance

The quest for acceptance can often lead individuals to seek out supportive communities. For Victor, this meant connecting with LGBTQ organizations and allies who provided a safe space to express his true self. The importance of these networks cannot be overstated; they serve as vital resources for emotional support and guidance during the coming-out process. Studies show that individuals with strong support systems are more likely to embrace their identity and engage in activism.

$$\text{Acceptance} = \text{Support} + \text{Community Engagement} \qquad (4)$$

Where: - Acceptance reflects the individual's comfort in their identity, - Support refers to the emotional and social backing received, - Community Engagement indicates participation in LGBTQ groups and events.

Victor found acceptance in unexpected places, including friendships with allies who championed LGBTQ rights. These relationships not only bolstered his confidence but also inspired him to take action. The act of coming out became a stepping stone for Victor, transforming personal struggles into a collective fight for equality.

The Role of Family and Friends

Family acceptance plays a crucial role in the coming-out process. The reactions of family members can significantly affect an individual's mental health and overall well-being. Research indicates that supportive family environments correlate with positive outcomes for LGBTQ youth, including lower rates of suicide and substance abuse. Conversely, rejection can lead to feelings of isolation and despair.

Victor's experience mirrored this reality. While some family members struggled to understand his identity, others embraced him wholeheartedly. This dichotomy highlighted the complexities of familial relationships and the varying degrees of acceptance that LGBTQ individuals often encounter.

The Broader Social Context

The societal context in which one comes out can greatly influence the experience. In regions where LGBTQ rights are under threat, the stakes are higher, and the fear of backlash can be overwhelming. Victor's activism was shaped by these realities, as he sought to create a more inclusive environment not just for himself, but for others who faced similar challenges.

The concept of *social visibility* also comes into play during the coming-out process. When LGBTQ individuals share their stories, they contribute to a broader narrative that challenges stereotypes and fosters understanding. Victor's decision to come out publicly was not just a personal choice; it was a statement against the discrimination faced by LGBTQ individuals, particularly in conservative settings.

Conclusion

In conclusion, coming out is a multifaceted process that involves navigating personal, familial, and societal landscapes. For Victor M. Maceda, it served as a transformative experience that propelled him into the realm of activism. By embracing his identity and seeking acceptance, he not only changed his own life but also laid the groundwork for advocating for others. The journey of coming out is ongoing, as it continues to evolve with the changing social dynamics and the fight for LGBTQ rights. Through this process, individuals like Victor inspire others to live authentically and advocate for a more inclusive world.

Joining LGBTQ Rights Organizations

Victor M. Maceda's journey into activism took a pivotal turn when he decided to join LGBTQ rights organizations. This decision not only empowered him personally but also connected him to a broader community that shared his vision for equality and justice. In this section, we will explore the significance of joining such organizations, the challenges faced by activists, and the transformative impact of collective action.

The Importance of Community

Joining LGBTQ rights organizations provided Victor with a sense of belonging that was crucial during his formative years. In a conservative town where he faced prejudice and discrimination, finding a community that understood his struggles was both liberating and affirming. Research indicates that community support plays a vital role in the mental health and well-being of LGBTQ individuals (Meyer, 2003). The sense of solidarity found within these organizations helped Victor navigate his identity and fueled his desire for activism.

Activism as Collective Action

The essence of activism lies in collective action, and LGBTQ rights organizations embody this principle. By joining forces with like-minded individuals, Victor was able to amplify his voice and contribute to a larger movement. The theory of social movements posits that collective identity is essential for mobilization (Tilly, 2004). Victor's participation in organizations such as the Human Rights Campaign and local advocacy groups allowed him to engage in campaigns that addressed systemic inequalities faced by LGBTQ individuals.

Challenges and Obstacles

While joining LGBTQ rights organizations was a significant step forward, it was not without its challenges. Activists often encounter a range of obstacles, including burnout, funding shortages, and internal conflicts within organizations. For Victor, the emotional toll of confronting systemic discrimination was profound. A study by Hatzenbuehler et al. (2010) highlights the stressors associated with LGBTQ activism, including the constant battle against societal stigma and the pressure to perform within the movement.

Additionally, the intersectionality of identities presents another layer of complexity. LGBTQ individuals who also belong to other marginalized groups often face compounded discrimination, which can complicate advocacy efforts. Victor recognized the need for inclusive practices within organizations to ensure that all voices were heard and represented.

Transformative Experiences

Joining LGBTQ rights organizations offered Victor transformative experiences that shaped his activism. He participated in campaigns advocating for marriage equality, anti-discrimination laws, and support for LGBTQ youth. One notable example was his involvement in organizing local pride events, which not only celebrated LGBTQ identities but also served as platforms for raising awareness about pressing issues such as mental health and homelessness among LGBTQ youth.

Victor's work with these organizations also allowed him to engage in policy advocacy. He learned how to navigate the legislative process, lobby for change, and mobilize community support. This hands-on experience was invaluable, as it equipped him with the skills necessary to effect real change. The impact of his efforts was evident when he witnessed the passage of local ordinances that protected LGBTQ rights, a testament to the power of collective action.

Building a Network of Allies

Joining LGBTQ rights organizations also facilitated the building of a network of allies. Victor understood that the fight for equality extended beyond the LGBTQ community; it required solidarity with other marginalized groups. He actively sought partnerships with organizations focused on racial justice, women's rights, and immigrant rights, recognizing that intersectional advocacy was essential for achieving comprehensive social justice.

For instance, Victor collaborated with immigrant rights organizations to address the unique challenges faced by LGBTQ asylum seekers. This partnership not only broadened the scope of advocacy efforts but also highlighted the interconnectedness of various social justice movements. By fostering these alliances, Victor contributed to a more inclusive and effective advocacy landscape.

Conclusion

Victor M. Maceda's decision to join LGBTQ rights organizations marked a turning point in his journey as an activist. Through community support, collective action, and transformative experiences, he was able to channel his personal struggles into a broader movement for equality. While challenges persisted, the connections he forged and the allies he gained empowered him to fight for the rights of LGBTQ individuals, particularly those facing persecution as asylum seekers. This chapter in his life exemplifies the profound impact of joining forces with others in the pursuit of justice and equality.

Campaigning for Equality

Campaigning for equality is a cornerstone of LGBTQ activism, embodying the collective struggle for rights and recognition within society. This section explores the strategies employed by Victor M. Maceda and his contemporaries to advocate for equal rights, the theoretical frameworks that underpin these campaigns, the challenges faced, and notable examples that illustrate the impact of their work.

Theoretical Frameworks

At the heart of LGBTQ advocacy lies a variety of theoretical frameworks that inform and guide campaigns for equality. One such framework is the **Social Justice Theory**, which posits that all individuals deserve equitable treatment and access to resources, regardless of their sexual orientation or gender identity. This theory emphasizes the need for systemic change to dismantle the structures of oppression that marginalize LGBTQ individuals.

Another relevant theory is **Intersectionality**, coined by Kimberlé Crenshaw, which highlights how various forms of identity—such as race, gender, and class—intersect and influence individuals' experiences of discrimination.

Understanding intersectionality is crucial for LGBTQ activists like Maceda, as it allows them to address the unique challenges faced by individuals at the intersection of multiple marginalized identities.

Strategies for Campaigning

Victor M. Maceda's approach to campaigning for equality involved a multifaceted strategy that included:

+ **Grassroots Mobilization:** Engaging local communities through rallies, workshops, and educational events to raise awareness about LGBTQ issues. This method fosters a sense of community and empowers individuals to become advocates for change.

+ **Coalition Building:** Forming alliances with other marginalized groups to create a united front against discrimination. For instance, Maceda collaborated with racial justice organizations to highlight the intersectional nature of oppression.

+ **Policy Advocacy:** Lobbying for legislative reforms that promote equality, such as anti-discrimination laws and marriage equality. Maceda's efforts in this area were instrumental in shaping public policy and advocating for legal protections for LGBTQ individuals.

+ **Public Awareness Campaigns:** Utilizing media platforms to disseminate information and challenge stereotypes. Campaigns often featured personal stories to humanize LGBTQ experiences and foster empathy among the broader public.

Challenges Faced

Despite the progress made, campaigning for equality is fraught with challenges. One significant issue is the persistent **backlash** against LGBTQ rights, often fueled by conservative ideologies and misinformation. Activists frequently encounter opposition from groups that seek to maintain the status quo, leading to a hostile environment for advocacy efforts.

Additionally, the intersectionality of identities can complicate campaigns. For example, LGBTQ individuals from marginalized racial or socioeconomic backgrounds may face unique barriers that are often overlooked in mainstream LGBTQ advocacy. This necessitates a more nuanced approach that addresses the diverse needs of the community.

Notable Examples of Campaigns

Victor M. Maceda's campaigns for equality are exemplified by several key initiatives:

+ **The Pride March Initiative:** Maceda spearheaded a series of Pride marches that not only celebrated LGBTQ identities but also served as a platform to address pressing issues such as homelessness among LGBTQ youth and violence against transgender individuals. These marches galvanized support and brought visibility to critical concerns.

+ **The "Equal Rights Now" Campaign:** This campaign focused on lobbying for comprehensive anti-discrimination legislation at the state level. Through strategic partnerships with legal experts and community organizations, Maceda helped to draft and promote bills that aimed to protect LGBTQ individuals in employment, housing, and public accommodations.

+ **Social Media Advocacy:** Leveraging platforms like Twitter and Instagram, Maceda utilized digital storytelling to amplify the voices of LGBTQ individuals. Campaigns such as #MyStoryMatters encouraged people to share their personal experiences, fostering a sense of solidarity and community engagement.

Impact of Campaigning for Equality

The impact of these campaigns is profound. Through persistent advocacy, Maceda and his allies have succeeded in shifting public opinion and increasing acceptance of LGBTQ individuals. Notably, the **marriage equality movement** serves as a testament to the effectiveness of sustained campaigning. The culmination of grassroots efforts, legal challenges, and public support led to landmark rulings that recognized the right to marry for same-sex couples.

Moreover, the campaigns have paved the way for a more inclusive society, inspiring future generations of activists to continue the fight for equality. The lessons learned from Maceda's experiences highlight the importance of resilience, collaboration, and the power of storytelling in advocacy.

Conclusion

Campaigning for equality remains an ongoing endeavor, requiring dedication, creativity, and a commitment to justice. Victor M. Maceda's contributions to this field exemplify the impact that passionate activism can have on society. By understanding the theoretical underpinnings, employing effective strategies, and overcoming challenges, activists can continue to forge a path toward a more equitable future for all.

Victories and Setbacks

The journey of LGBTQ rights activism is a tapestry woven with both triumphs and challenges. In this subsection, we explore the significant victories and setbacks experienced by Victor M. Maceda and the broader LGBTQ movement, providing a nuanced understanding of the landscape in which activism unfolds.

1. The Sweet Taste of Victory

Victories in the LGBTQ rights movement often serve as beacons of hope, illuminating the path forward. One of the most notable victories in recent history was the legalization of same-sex marriage in many countries. In 2015, the United States Supreme Court's landmark decision in *Obergefell v. Hodges* established that same-sex couples have the constitutional right to marry, a monumental step forward for equality. Victor Maceda, through his advocacy, played a crucial role in mobilizing support for this decision, rallying communities to advocate for marriage equality and challenging discriminatory laws.

Additionally, the passage of anti-discrimination laws at local, state, and national levels has marked significant progress. For instance, in many jurisdictions, protections against employment discrimination based on sexual orientation and gender identity have been enacted. Maceda's efforts in lobbying for such legislation have been instrumental in creating safer environments for LGBTQ individuals in workplaces.

2. Celebrating Milestones

Maceda's activism also contributed to the establishment of Pride events and the recognition of LGBTQ history months, which serve as platforms for visibility and celebration. These events not only commemorate the struggles faced by the LGBTQ community but also foster unity and pride among individuals who have historically been marginalized. The annual Pride Parade in his hometown, once a small gathering, has grown into a vibrant celebration attracting thousands, symbolizing the community's resilience and strength.

Furthermore, the recognition of LGBTQ issues in mainstream media has expanded, leading to a more informed public. Media representation, from television shows featuring LGBTQ characters to documentaries highlighting the struggles and successes of activists, has played a critical role in changing perceptions and fostering acceptance. Maceda's involvement in media outreach has ensured that the narratives of LGBTQ individuals are heard and celebrated.

3. The Weight of Setbacks

However, the path to progress is fraught with setbacks that test the resolve of activists. Despite the victories, the LGBTQ community continues to face significant challenges, particularly in the realm of transgender rights. The ongoing legislative attacks on transgender individuals, including bathroom bills and restrictions on healthcare access, represent a troubling regression. Victor Maceda has been vocal in opposing these measures, advocating for inclusive policies and raising awareness about the unique challenges faced by transgender individuals.

Moreover, the rise of anti-LGBTQ rhetoric and hate crimes presents a stark reminder of the work that remains. In recent years, there has been a disturbing increase in violence against LGBTQ individuals, particularly people of color and transgender women. Maceda has dedicated considerable efforts to address these issues, partnering with law enforcement and community organizations to implement hate crime prevention strategies and support services for victims.

4. The Intersection of Advocacy and Personal Experience

The interplay between victories and setbacks is deeply personal for activists like Maceda. Each victory is often hard-won and comes at a cost, while setbacks can evoke feelings of frustration and despair. Maceda's personal journey—navigating his own identity amidst societal pressures—has shaped his understanding of the stakes involved in activism. He recognizes that every setback is an opportunity for growth and resilience, inspiring him to continue advocating for change.

In his speeches and writings, Maceda often emphasizes the importance of perseverance. He believes that setbacks should not deter activists but rather fuel their commitment to the cause. "Every time we face a challenge, we must remember why we started this fight," he asserts, embodying the spirit of resilience that characterizes the LGBTQ movement.

5. The Road Ahead

As we reflect on the victories and setbacks experienced by Victor M. Maceda and the LGBTQ rights movement, it becomes clear that the road ahead is filled with both promise and uncertainty. The victories achieved thus far provide a foundation upon which to build, while the setbacks serve as a reminder of the ongoing struggle for equality and justice.

In conclusion, the journey of LGBTQ activism is marked by a complex interplay of victories and setbacks. Victor Maceda's story exemplifies the resilience of the human spirit and the unwavering commitment to advocating for the rights of all individuals, regardless of their sexual orientation or gender identity. The fight for LGBTQ rights continues, and with each victory, the movement inches closer to a world where everyone can live authentically and without fear.

Gaining National Recognition

Victor M. Maceda's journey from a boy with a dream to a nationally recognized LGBTQ rights activist is a compelling narrative that showcases the power of resilience, advocacy, and the undeniable impact of personal stories. As he began to find his voice within the LGBTQ community, his efforts were not only localized but also resonated on a national scale, leading to widespread recognition and influence.

The Power of Storytelling

At the heart of Victor's rise to national prominence was his ability to connect with people through storytelling. He understood that personal narratives could bridge gaps between communities and foster empathy. Victor's own story—filled with struggles against prejudice and the quest for acceptance—served as a powerful testament to the challenges faced by many LGBTQ individuals. This approach aligns with the theory of narrative transportation, which posits that individuals become emotionally involved in stories, leading to attitude and behavioral change [?].

Media Engagement

As Victor began to articulate his vision for LGBTQ rights, he strategically engaged with various media platforms. He leveraged social media to amplify his message, utilizing the reach of platforms such as Twitter, Instagram, and Facebook. According to research by the Pew Research Center, over 70% of LGBTQ individuals reported that social media played a crucial role in their activism [?]. Victor's presence in digital spaces allowed him to connect with a younger audience, mobilizing them to action and creating a ripple effect that transcended geographical boundaries.

Strategic Partnerships

Victor's national recognition was further bolstered by his ability to forge strategic partnerships with established LGBTQ organizations and allies. By collaborating with groups like the Human Rights Campaign and GLAAD, he was able to tap into existing networks and resources. This coalition-building is critical in advocacy work, as it enhances visibility and creates a unified front. The theory of social capital underscores the importance of networks in achieving collective goals, as highlighted by Putnam (2000) [?].

Key Campaigns and Initiatives

One of the pivotal moments in Victor's journey was his involvement in the "Equality for All" campaign, which aimed to raise awareness about the discrimination faced by LGBTQ individuals, particularly in the context of asylum seekers. This campaign garnered national media attention, leading to appearances on major news outlets such as CNN and MSNBC. Victor's articulate advocacy during these appearances not only highlighted the plight of LGBTQ asylum seekers but also positioned him as a thought leader in the national dialogue on LGBTQ rights.

In addition, Victor organized nationwide rallies that coincided with significant legislative milestones, such as the anniversary of the legalization of same-sex marriage in the United States. These events attracted thousands of participants and received extensive coverage, further solidifying his reputation as a national advocate.

Recognition and Awards

As Victor's influence grew, so did the recognition he received from various organizations. He was awarded the National LGBTQ Advocate of the Year by the Equality Federation in 2021, an honor that acknowledged his tireless work in advocating for LGBTQ rights and asylum seekers. Such accolades not only validate an activist's work but also serve to inspire others within the community. According to a study by the Williams Institute, recognition in the form of awards can significantly increase an activist's visibility and credibility [?].

Impact on Policy and Legislation

Victor's national recognition translated into tangible impacts on policy and legislation. His advocacy efforts contributed to the introduction of several bills aimed at protecting LGBTQ asylum seekers and ensuring equitable treatment under the law. The legislative process is often fraught with challenges, yet Victor's ability to mobilize public support was instrumental in pushing these initiatives forward.

For instance, the "LGBTQ Refugee Protection Act," which aimed to streamline the asylum process for LGBTQ individuals, gained bipartisan support, a testament to Victor's effective advocacy. This aligns with the theory of agenda-setting, which posits that media coverage can influence the salience of issues in the public sphere [?].

Conclusion

In summary, Victor M. Maceda's journey to national recognition as an LGBTQ rights activist is a multifaceted narrative that underscores the importance of storytelling, media engagement, strategic partnerships, and impactful advocacy. His work has not only changed the lives of countless individuals but has also contributed to a broader movement for equality and justice. As he continues to inspire future generations of activists, Victor's legacy serves as a powerful reminder of the collective strength found in advocacy and the enduring fight for LGBTQ rights.

Immigration and Asylum Seekers

Understanding the Plight of LGBTQ Asylum Seekers

The plight of LGBTQ asylum seekers is a complex and multifaceted issue that intertwines personal identity, social stigma, and international human rights. As the world becomes increasingly aware of the challenges faced by LGBTQ individuals, it is crucial to understand the specific circumstances that lead many to seek asylum in foreign countries. This section delves into the theoretical frameworks, problems, and real-life examples that illustrate the dire situation faced by LGBTQ asylum seekers.

Theoretical Frameworks

To comprehend the plight of LGBTQ asylum seekers, we must first acknowledge the intersectionality of identity, as proposed by Crenshaw (1989). This framework highlights how various social identities—such as race, gender, and sexual orientation—interact to create unique experiences of oppression. LGBTQ individuals often face compounded discrimination, which can lead to severe consequences in their home countries, including violence, persecution, and even death.

Additionally, the concept of *refugeehood* as defined by the 1951 Refugee Convention is essential in understanding the legal context of LGBTQ asylum seekers. According to the Convention, a refugee is someone who has a well-founded fear of persecution based on specific grounds, including membership in a particular social group. LGBTQ individuals qualify under this definition, yet they often encounter significant barriers when attempting to prove their claims.

Problems Faced by LGBTQ Asylum Seekers

LGBTQ asylum seekers face numerous challenges that complicate their journey to safety. These include:

- **Legal Barriers:** Many countries have restrictive asylum laws that do not adequately recognize sexual orientation or gender identity as valid grounds for asylum. This legal ambiguity can lead to unfair treatment and denial of claims.

- **Cultural Stigma:** In many regions, societal norms are deeply rooted in heteronormativity, leading to stigmatization and discrimination against LGBTQ individuals. This stigma often extends to the asylum process itself, where applicants may face bias from officials or legal representatives.

- **Mental Health Issues:** The trauma of persecution, combined with the stress of navigating the asylum process, can lead to significant mental health challenges. Many LGBTQ asylum seekers experience anxiety, depression, and post-traumatic stress disorder (PTSD).

- **Economic Hardship:** Upon arrival in a new country, asylum seekers often face economic instability due to their inability to work legally. This financial strain can exacerbate their vulnerability and limit access to necessary resources.

Real-Life Examples

Several poignant examples illustrate the plight of LGBTQ asylum seekers. One notable case is that of *Jorge*, a gay man from El Salvador who fled his country after enduring severe violence and threats due to his sexual orientation. Upon arriving in the United States, Jorge faced a lengthy and arduous asylum process, during which he struggled with mental health issues stemming from his traumatic experiences.

Despite these challenges, Jorge's case was ultimately successful, and he now advocates for other LGBTQ asylum seekers, highlighting the importance of community support.

Another example is the story of *Amina*, a transgender woman from Uganda. Amina faced brutal persecution in her home country, where homosexuality is criminalized, and transgender individuals are often subjected to violence. After seeking asylum in Canada, Amina encountered cultural barriers and discrimination within the asylum system. Her journey underscores the need for sensitivity and understanding in the asylum process, particularly regarding the unique challenges faced by transgender individuals.

Conclusion

Understanding the plight of LGBTQ asylum seekers requires a nuanced approach that considers legal, social, and psychological dimensions. By recognizing the intersectionality of identity and the systemic barriers that these individuals face, we can better advocate for their rights and support their journeys toward safety and acceptance. As the global conversation around LGBTQ rights continues to evolve, it is imperative that we remain vigilant in our efforts to protect and empower those who seek refuge from persecution.

Researching and Documenting Cases

The journey of advocating for LGBTQ asylum seekers is not merely a matter of passion; it is deeply rooted in rigorous research and meticulous documentation. Victor M. Maceda understood that in order to effectively advocate for policy changes and legal support, he needed a solid foundation of evidence that highlighted the unique challenges faced by LGBTQ individuals seeking asylum. This subsection explores the critical aspects of researching and documenting cases, emphasizing the theoretical frameworks, practical challenges, and illustrative examples that shaped Victor's approach.

Theoretical Frameworks

At the heart of effective advocacy lies a theoretical understanding of the issues at hand. The research conducted by Victor drew upon several key theoretical frameworks:

- **Intersectionality:** Coined by Kimberlé Crenshaw, intersectionality examines how various forms of discrimination—such as those based on race, gender, and sexual orientation—interact to create unique experiences of oppression. Victor utilized this framework to analyze how LGBTQ asylum seekers often faced compounded vulnerabilities due to their intersecting identities.

+ **Human Rights Theory:** This framework posits that all individuals possess inherent rights that must be protected. Victor's research was grounded in the belief that LGBTQ individuals have the right to seek asylum from persecution based on their sexual orientation or gender identity, aligning his advocacy with broader human rights principles.

+ **Social Justice:** Victor's work was also informed by social justice theories that advocate for the equitable distribution of resources and opportunities. This perspective guided him in documenting cases of LGBTQ asylum seekers who were denied access to necessary legal resources and support systems.

Challenges in Research and Documentation

While the theoretical frameworks provided a solid foundation, Victor faced numerous challenges in his research and documentation efforts:

1. **Access to Information:** Many LGBTQ asylum seekers come from countries where their identities are criminalized, making it difficult to gather comprehensive data on their experiences. Victor often relied on testimonies, which, while powerful, could lack the statistical robustness needed for broader advocacy.

2. **Fear of Retaliation:** Many individuals were reluctant to share their stories due to fear of persecution, both in their home countries and within their current environments. This fear complicated Victor's efforts to document cases accurately and comprehensively.

3. **Cultural Sensitivity:** Understanding the cultural contexts of LGBTQ individuals from diverse backgrounds required careful consideration. Victor had to navigate different cultural norms and values while ensuring that the documentation process was respectful and non-exploitative.

Methodologies for Documentation

To overcome these challenges, Victor employed various methodologies to ensure thorough and respectful documentation of cases:

+ **Qualitative Interviews:** Conducting in-depth interviews with asylum seekers allowed Victor to capture nuanced narratives that quantitative data could not provide. These interviews were designed to create a safe space for individuals to share their experiences without fear of judgment.

+ **Case Studies:** Victor compiled detailed case studies that highlighted specific instances of persecution faced by LGBTQ individuals. Each case study included personal narratives, legal challenges encountered, and the outcomes of their asylum applications.

+ **Collaboration with NGOs:** Partnering with non-governmental organizations (NGOs) and human rights groups provided Victor with access to additional resources and expertise. These collaborations helped to validate the documented cases and provided a broader context for the advocacy efforts.

Illustrative Examples

Victor's commitment to researching and documenting cases resulted in several impactful examples that underscored the urgent need for policy changes:

Example

Case of Alejandro: Alejandro, a gay man from Honduras, faced severe persecution due to his sexual orientation. Victor documented Alejandro's story, detailing the threats he received from gang members and the lack of protection from local authorities. This documentation was pivotal in securing Alejandro's asylum status, as it provided compelling evidence of the dangers he faced in his home country.

Example

Case of Fatima: Fatima, a transgender woman from Egypt, experienced systemic discrimination and violence. Victor's research highlighted the intersectionality of gender identity and cultural context in her case. By documenting the societal attitudes towards transgender individuals in Egypt, Victor was able to advocate for Fatima's asylum application effectively, emphasizing the necessity of protection for individuals facing such unique threats.

Conclusion

Through his dedication to researching and documenting cases, Victor M. Maceda not only amplified the voices of LGBTQ asylum seekers but also laid the groundwork for systemic change. His work exemplified the importance of a well-rounded approach that combined theoretical frameworks with real-world experiences. By overcoming challenges and employing effective methodologies, Victor was able to create a compelling narrative that resonated with policymakers, advocates, and the public alike. The impact of his research continues to reverberate, inspiring future activists to prioritize the documentation of marginalized voices in the ongoing fight for equality and justice.

Advocating for Policy Changes

Advocating for policy changes is a cornerstone of Victor M. Maceda's work in the realm of LGBTQ rights, particularly concerning asylum seekers. This section delves into the strategies employed by Victor and his allies to influence legislation and policy frameworks that affect the LGBTQ community, emphasizing the importance of advocacy in creating systemic change.

Understanding the Policy Landscape

To effectively advocate for policy changes, it is essential to understand the existing legal and social frameworks that govern LGBTQ rights and asylum processes. The intersection of immigration law and LGBTQ rights presents unique challenges. For instance, many asylum seekers face legal barriers that prevent them from obtaining the protection they desperately need. The U.S. immigration system, with its complex and often opaque processes, can be particularly daunting for those fleeing persecution based on sexual orientation or gender identity.

One of the primary theories underpinning advocacy work is the *Theory of Change*, which posits that in order to achieve a desired outcome, one must first identify the necessary steps and interventions required to reach that goal. This theory is particularly relevant in the context of LGBTQ asylum advocacy, where the goal is to create a more inclusive and protective legal framework.

Identifying Key Issues

Victor and his team began their advocacy by identifying critical issues within the asylum process that disproportionately affected LGBTQ individuals. These issues included:

- **Inadequate Legal Protections:** Many LGBTQ asylum seekers are not recognized as a particular social group under existing immigration laws, making it difficult for them to prove their eligibility for asylum.

- **Bias in Asylum Hearings:** Reports of bias and discrimination from immigration judges and asylum officers have been documented, leading to a higher rate of denied claims among LGBTQ applicants.

- **Lack of Resources:** Many asylum seekers lack access to legal resources, making it challenging to navigate the complex asylum process.

By pinpointing these issues, Victor was able to tailor his advocacy efforts to address specific barriers faced by LGBTQ asylum seekers.

Strategic Advocacy Approaches

Victor employed several strategic approaches in his advocacy for policy changes:

1. **Grassroots Mobilization:** Engaging the community through grassroots movements was vital. Victor organized rallies and events to raise awareness about the plight of LGBTQ asylum seekers, mobilizing public support for policy reforms.

2. **Lobbying Efforts:** Collaborating with local and national LGBTQ organizations, Victor participated in lobbying efforts aimed at influencing lawmakers. This included meetings with legislators to discuss proposed bills that would enhance protections for LGBTQ individuals in the asylum process.

3. **Public Awareness Campaigns:** Utilizing social media and traditional media outlets, Victor launched campaigns to educate the public about the challenges faced by LGBTQ asylum seekers. By sharing personal stories and statistics, he aimed to humanize the issue and garner broader support for policy changes.

4. **Legal Advocacy:** Partnering with legal aid organizations, Victor provided pro bono legal support to LGBTQ asylum seekers, helping them navigate the asylum process and ensuring their cases were presented effectively. This hands-on approach not only supported individuals but also highlighted systemic issues within the legal framework.

Examples of Successful Policy Changes

Through persistent advocacy efforts, Victor and his allies achieved notable successes in advocating for policy changes:

- **Recognition of LGBTQ Asylum Seekers:** One of the significant victories was the increased recognition of LGBTQ individuals as a particular social group under asylum law. This shift allowed for more robust legal arguments in asylum cases, leading to higher approval rates for LGBTQ applicants.

- **Training for Immigration Officials:** Victor's advocacy efforts led to the implementation of training programs for immigration judges and asylum officers, focusing on cultural competency and sensitivity regarding LGBTQ issues. This initiative aimed to reduce bias in asylum hearings and improve the overall treatment of LGBTQ applicants.

- **Legislative Proposals:** Victor played a key role in drafting and advocating for legislative proposals aimed at reforming the asylum process to be more inclusive of LGBTQ individuals. These proposals sought to streamline the application process and enhance legal protections for vulnerable populations.

Challenges and Ongoing Efforts

Despite these successes, challenges remain in the fight for policy changes. Resistance from certain political factions and a lack of understanding about LGBTQ issues continue to impede progress. Victor emphasizes the need for sustained advocacy and community engagement to overcome these obstacles.

Moreover, the global landscape for LGBTQ asylum seekers is constantly evolving, with many countries implementing increasingly hostile policies. Victor's work has expanded to include international advocacy, collaborating with global organizations to address these issues on a broader scale.

Conclusion

Advocating for policy changes is a multifaceted endeavor that requires a deep understanding of the legal landscape, strategic planning, and community engagement. Through his tireless efforts, Victor M. Maceda has not only influenced policy changes that benefit LGBTQ asylum seekers but has also inspired a new generation of activists to continue the fight for equality and justice. The journey is far from over, but with each victory, the path toward a more inclusive and equitable society becomes clearer.

Providing Legal Support

In the realm of LGBTQ rights activism, particularly concerning asylum seekers, the provision of legal support emerges as a critical pillar. Legal representation is not merely an accessory; it is the lifeline that can determine the outcome of an asylum case. This section delves into the multifaceted aspects of providing legal support to LGBTQ asylum seekers, highlighting the challenges they face, the strategies employed by activists like Victor M. Maceda, and the profound impact of legal advocacy.

Understanding the Legal Landscape

The legal landscape for asylum seekers is fraught with complexities. Asylum laws vary significantly from one country to another, and navigating these laws can be daunting for individuals already traumatized by persecution. In the United States, for instance, the Immigration and Nationality Act (INA) provides the framework for asylum applications, yet the intricacies of legal definitions, procedural requirements, and evidentiary standards can pose significant barriers.

$$\text{Asylum Eligibility} = \text{Well-founded fear of persecution} + \text{Membership in a particular social } \tag{5}$$

For LGBTQ individuals, proving membership in a particular social group often involves demonstrating that their sexual orientation or gender identity is intrinsic to their identity, which can be challenging in environments hostile to such identities. The legal support provided by activists like Maceda often involves not only direct representation but also education about these complexities.

Challenges Faced by LGBTQ Asylum Seekers

LGBTQ asylum seekers encounter a myriad of challenges when seeking legal support. These include:

+ **Language Barriers:** Many asylum seekers may not be fluent in the language of the host country, complicating their ability to communicate their experiences and understand legal processes.

+ **Cultural Sensitivity:** Legal professionals may lack the necessary cultural competence to effectively advocate for LGBTQ individuals, leading to misunderstandings and inadequate representation.

+ **Fear of Disclosure:** The stigma associated with LGBTQ identities can deter individuals from fully disclosing their experiences, which is often essential for building a strong case.

+ **Financial Constraints:** Many asylum seekers lack the financial resources to afford legal representation, making pro bono services vital.

Strategies for Providing Legal Support

To address these challenges, Victor M. Maceda and his colleagues have implemented several strategies to provide effective legal support to LGBTQ asylum seekers:

+ **Pro Bono Legal Services:** Maceda has been instrumental in establishing networks of volunteer lawyers willing to provide pro bono services. These lawyers are often trained in LGBTQ issues and are sensitive to the unique challenges faced by asylum seekers.

+ **Workshops and Training:** Organizing workshops for both asylum seekers and legal professionals has proven effective. These sessions cover asylum procedures, the importance of personal narratives, and the nuances of LGBTQ identity in legal contexts.

+ **Collaborations with NGOs:** Partnering with non-governmental organizations (NGOs) that specialize in LGBTQ rights and immigration law enhances the capacity to provide comprehensive support. These collaborations often lead to the pooling of resources, expertise, and advocacy efforts.

+ **Creating Resource Materials:** Developing easy-to-understand guides and materials that outline the asylum process can empower asylum seekers, helping them to navigate the system more effectively.

Case Studies and Success Stories

The impact of providing legal support is best illustrated through real-life examples. One notable case involved a young gay man from El Salvador, who faced severe persecution due to his sexual orientation. Upon arriving in the United States, he sought asylum but was initially denied due to a lack of understanding of the legal requirements.

With the assistance of Victor M. Maceda's legal team, the young man received pro bono representation. The team worked diligently to gather evidence, including personal testimonies and expert affidavits that highlighted the dangers faced by LGBTQ individuals in El Salvador.

$$\text{Successful Asylum Application} = \text{Compelling Evidence} + \text{Effective Legal Representation} \tag{6}$$

Ultimately, the asylum application was approved, allowing him to live safely in the United States. This case exemplifies the critical role that legal support plays in the asylum process for LGBTQ individuals.

The Broader Impact of Legal Support

The provision of legal support not only helps individual asylum seekers but also contributes to broader systemic change. By successfully advocating for LGBTQ asylum seekers, activists like Maceda bring attention to the injustices within the immigration system.

This advocacy can lead to:

+ **Policy Reforms:** Successful cases often serve as precedents, prompting changes in policies that affect LGBTQ asylum seekers.

+ **Increased Awareness:** Media coverage of successful asylum cases raises public awareness about the challenges faced by LGBTQ individuals globally, fostering empathy and support.

+ **Strengthening Community Networks:** Providing legal support helps to build resilient communities where asylum seekers can find solidarity and strength in shared experiences.

In conclusion, providing legal support to LGBTQ asylum seekers is a multifaceted endeavor that requires sensitivity, expertise, and a commitment to justice. Through the efforts of dedicated activists like Victor M. Maceda, the legal landscape for LGBTQ asylum seekers is gradually becoming more navigable, ensuring that those fleeing persecution have the opportunity to find safety and acceptance.

Making a Difference

Victor M. Maceda's journey in advocating for LGBTQ asylum seekers is not just a story of personal triumph, but a testament to the profound impact one individual can have on the lives of many. Through his relentless efforts, he has illuminated the plight of LGBTQ asylum seekers, transforming despair into hope and action. This section delves into the multifaceted ways in which Victor has made a difference, examining both theoretical frameworks and practical outcomes that underscore his contributions to the LGBTQ rights movement.

Theoretical Framework

The work of LGBTQ activists like Victor can be analyzed through various theoretical lenses, including social justice theory, intersectionality, and human rights frameworks. Social justice theory posits that every individual deserves equal access to rights and opportunities, which is particularly relevant in the context of LGBTQ asylum seekers who often face systemic barriers to safety and acceptance. Victor's advocacy aligns with this theory as he strives to dismantle these barriers and create a more equitable society.

Intersectionality, a concept coined by Kimberlé Crenshaw, further enriches our understanding of Victor's work.   This theory highlights how various social identities—such as race, gender, and sexual orientation—interact to create unique experiences of oppression and privilege. Victor's recognition of the intersectional challenges faced by LGBTQ asylum seekers allows him to tailor his advocacy efforts to address the specific needs of diverse communities. By understanding that not all LGBTQ individuals experience discrimination in the same way, he is able to advocate more effectively for those who are often marginalized within marginalized groups.

Identifying Problems

Despite the progress made in LGBTQ rights, asylum seekers continue to face significant obstacles. Many flee their home countries due to persecution based on their sexual orientation or gender identity, only to encounter a complex and often hostile asylum process in their host countries. The challenges include:

- **Legal Barriers:** Asylum laws can be convoluted, and LGBTQ asylum seekers often lack access to legal representation. This can result in denied claims and deportation to countries where they face further persecution.

- **Cultural Stigma:** In many societies, LGBTQ identities are still stigmatized. Asylum seekers may face discrimination not only from governmental institutions but also from the communities they seek refuge in.

- **Mental Health Challenges:** The trauma associated with fleeing persecution, combined with the isolation often experienced in a new country, can lead to significant mental health issues. Many asylum seekers struggle with depression, anxiety, and post-traumatic stress disorder (PTSD).

Victor has keenly identified these problems and has dedicated his efforts to addressing them through advocacy, education, and community support.

Practical Initiatives

Victor's approach to making a difference can be categorized into several key initiatives:

1. **Legal Advocacy:** Victor has partnered with legal organizations to provide pro bono legal services to LGBTQ asylum seekers. This initiative not only helps individuals navigate the asylum process but also raises awareness about the unique challenges they face. For example, he has worked on cases that highlight the importance of including sexual orientation and gender identity as valid grounds for asylum claims, effectively changing the narrative around LGBTQ persecution in legal contexts.

2. **Community Outreach and Education:** Understanding that awareness is crucial for change, Victor has organized workshops and seminars aimed at educating both the LGBTQ community and the general public about the realities faced by asylum seekers. These initiatives foster empathy and understanding, encouraging community members to become allies in the fight for equality.

3. **Mental Health Support:** Recognizing the mental health challenges faced by LGBTQ asylum seekers, Victor has collaborated with mental health professionals to provide counseling and support services. These programs are designed to help individuals cope with their trauma, facilitating their integration into society and promoting overall well-being.

4. **Advocating for Policy Change:** Victor has been instrumental in lobbying for policy reforms that protect the rights of LGBTQ asylum seekers. His efforts have contributed to the development of more inclusive asylum policies that recognize the unique vulnerabilities of LGBTQ individuals. For instance, he has successfully advocated for training programs for asylum officers to better understand the experiences of LGBTQ applicants.

5. **Building Coalitions:** Victor understands the power of collaboration. He has worked to build coalitions with other human rights organizations, creating a

united front to address the challenges faced by LGBTQ asylum seekers. This collective action amplifies their voices and strengthens their advocacy efforts.

Measuring Impact

The impact of Victor's work can be seen through various success stories and metrics:

+ **Successful Asylum Claims:** Through his legal advocacy, Victor has helped numerous LGBTQ asylum seekers secure their status in host countries, allowing them to live freely and safely. Each successful claim represents not just a legal victory, but a chance for a new beginning.

+ **Increased Awareness:** Victor's outreach efforts have led to increased awareness and understanding of LGBTQ asylum issues within the broader community. Surveys conducted post-events show a significant increase in empathy and willingness to support LGBTQ rights.

+ **Policy Reforms:** Victor's advocacy has contributed to changes in asylum policies, making them more inclusive and equitable for LGBTQ individuals. Reports from legal organizations indicate a growing recognition of LGBTQ persecution in asylum adjudications.

+ **Community Support Networks:** The establishment of support networks for LGBTQ asylum seekers has provided vital resources and connections, helping individuals navigate their new environments and build a sense of belonging.

Conclusion

Victor M. Maceda's commitment to making a difference in the lives of LGBTQ asylum seekers exemplifies the profound impact of dedicated activism. Through a combination of legal advocacy, community education, mental health support, policy reform, and coalition building, he has not only changed individual lives but has also contributed to a broader movement for justice and equality. His story serves as an inspiration for future generations of activists, demonstrating that one person's efforts can resonate far beyond their immediate surroundings, creating ripples of change that can transform society as a whole.

In conclusion, Victor's work underscores the importance of recognizing and addressing the unique challenges faced by LGBTQ asylum seekers. His legacy is one of hope, resilience, and the belief that together, we can make a difference in the world.

Personal Life and Relationships

Finding Love and Building a Family

Victor M. Maceda's journey toward finding love and building a family is a testament to the resilience and strength that often characterize the lives of LGBTQ individuals. In a society that frequently marginalizes their existence, the pursuit of love can be fraught with challenges, yet it also serves as a powerful source of motivation and hope.

The Search for Connection

In the early years of his activism, Victor grappled with the complexities of intimacy and connection, often feeling isolated in a conservative environment that stigmatized his identity. The search for a partner who understood and accepted him became a pivotal aspect of his life. Psychological theories, such as Maslow's Hierarchy of Needs, illustrate that love and belonging are fundamental human needs. For Victor, this need was amplified by his experiences of discrimination and prejudice, making the search for a loving relationship not just a personal desire but a vital component of his emotional well-being.

Challenges in Finding Love

Finding love as an LGBTQ individual can involve navigating a landscape filled with societal biases and personal fears. Victor faced several obstacles, including:

+ **Fear of Rejection:** The fear of being rejected based on his sexual orientation often led Victor to second-guess potential relationships. This internal conflict is supported by the Minority Stress Theory, which posits that LGBTQ individuals experience heightened stress due to societal stigma.

+ **Cultural Expectations:** Growing up in a conservative town, Victor encountered cultural norms that dictated what relationships should look like. These expectations often clashed with his reality, leading to feelings of inadequacy and self-doubt.

+ **Navigating the Dating Scene:** The dating landscape for LGBTQ individuals can be complicated. Victor found it challenging to meet potential partners who shared his values and commitment to activism, often feeling that superficial connections overshadowed deeper connections.

Finding Love in Unexpected Places

Despite these challenges, Victor's journey took a transformative turn when he least expected it. He met his partner, Alex, during a local LGBTQ rights event. Their connection was immediate, rooted in shared experiences and a mutual commitment to activism. This relationship exemplified the concept of *communitas*, a term coined by anthropologist Victor Turner, referring to the sense of community and shared purpose that can emerge in marginalized groups.

Victor and Alex's love blossomed amidst the backdrop of activism, allowing them to support one another through both personal and professional challenges. Their relationship became a sanctuary, a space where they could express their true selves without fear of judgment. This dynamic is crucial, as research indicates that supportive relationships significantly enhance the mental health and well-being of LGBTQ individuals.

Building a Family

As their relationship deepened, Victor and Alex began to discuss the concept of family. For many LGBTQ couples, the traditional notion of family may not apply, leading to innovative approaches to family-building. Victor and Alex explored various options, including adoption and surrogacy, reflecting their commitment to creating a loving home.

$$F = C + R \tag{7}$$

Where:

- F represents the family unit,

- C stands for commitment to one another, and

- R symbolizes the resources (emotional, financial, and social) they bring to the relationship.

This equation highlights the importance of both emotional commitment and practical resources in establishing a family. Victor and Alex's journey involved not only love but also careful planning and consideration of their future. They sought to create an environment that would nurture and support their future children, emphasizing values of acceptance, inclusivity, and activism.

The Role of Community

The couple's commitment to family was further strengthened by their involvement in the LGBTQ community. They found support and inspiration from other families who had navigated similar paths. This sense of community was vital, as it provided them with role models and resources, reinforcing the idea that love and family can take many forms.

Victor often spoke at community events about the importance of representation in family structures. He emphasized that LGBTQ families deserve visibility and acknowledgment, challenging societal norms that dictate what a family should look like. This advocacy not only empowered Victor and Alex but also inspired others in the community to embrace their identities and pursue their own paths to family.

Conclusion

Finding love and building a family is a complex yet rewarding journey for Victor M. Maceda. His relationship with Alex serves as a powerful example of how love can flourish in the face of adversity. Through their shared commitment to activism and community, they have created a family that reflects their values and aspirations. Their story underscores the importance of love as a catalyst for change, demonstrating that when individuals embrace their authentic selves, they can build families that challenge societal norms and inspire future generations.

Victor's journey illustrates that love is not merely a personal affair; it is a profound act of resistance against societal constraints. In the words of Audre Lorde, "We are not meant to be alone," and Victor's life exemplifies this truth as he continues to advocate for LGBTQ rights while nurturing a loving family.

Balancing Activism and Relationships

In the vibrant tapestry of life, where the threads of activism and personal relationships intertwine, the journey of Victor M. Maceda stands as a testament to the delicate balance one must navigate. Activism, by its very nature, demands time, energy, and unwavering commitment. Yet, the human heart yearns for connection, love, and companionship. This section delves into the intricate dynamics of balancing these two powerful forces, exploring the challenges faced, theoretical frameworks, and the profound impact on personal and communal well-being.

Theoretical Framework: Intersection of Activism and Relationships

The intersectionality theory, coined by Kimberlé Crenshaw, posits that individuals experience overlapping social identities, which can lead to unique experiences of discrimination or privilege. This framework is particularly relevant for activists like Victor, who navigate the complexities of LGBTQ identity while fostering intimate relationships. The dual roles of being an activist and a partner can create a rich, albeit challenging, landscape.

From a psychological perspective, the *work-life balance* theory suggests that individuals must manage their time and energy across various domains of life, including work, relationships, and personal interests. For activists, the challenge lies in allocating sufficient time to advocacy efforts while nurturing their personal lives. The *role conflict theory* further elucidates this struggle, indicating that conflicting demands from different roles can lead to stress and burnout.

Challenges in Balancing Activism and Relationships

1. **Time Constraints**: Activism often involves long hours, attending meetings, organizing events, and advocating for policy changes. These commitments can encroach on personal time, leading to feelings of neglect in relationships. For instance, Victor frequently found himself torn between attending a crucial LGBTQ rights rally and spending quality time with his partner.

2. **Emotional Labor**: The emotional toll of activism can be substantial. Constantly fighting against injustice can lead to compassion fatigue, making it challenging to engage emotionally in personal relationships. Victor's dedication to his cause sometimes left him drained, impacting his ability to connect with loved ones.

3. **Support Systems**: While activism can foster a sense of community, it can also lead to isolation from non-activist friends and family. Victor faced the challenge of bridging the gap between his activist circle and his personal relationships, often feeling misunderstood by those who did not share his fervor for social change.

4. **Identity and Role Dynamics**: The dual identity of being both an activist and a partner can create tension. Victor's partner may have felt overshadowed by his activism, leading to feelings of inadequacy or resentment. Navigating these dynamics requires open communication and mutual understanding.

Strategies for Balancing Activism and Relationships

1. **Setting Boundaries**: Establishing clear boundaries between activism and personal life is crucial. Victor learned to designate specific times for activism and

personal relationships, ensuring that both received the attention they deserved. For example, he committed to a "date night" each week, a time dedicated solely to his partner.

2. **Open Communication**: Transparent discussions about the demands of activism and its impact on relationships can foster understanding. Victor and his partner engaged in regular check-ins, discussing their feelings and needs, which helped to mitigate misunderstandings and strengthen their bond.

3. **Shared Activism**: Involving partners in activism can create a shared purpose and strengthen relationships. Victor's partner became involved in local LGBTQ initiatives, allowing them to bond over their shared commitment to social justice while deepening their connection.

4. **Self-Care Practices**: Prioritizing self-care is vital for both activists and their partners. Victor adopted mindfulness practices and encouraged his partner to engage in activities that brought them joy outside of activism. This balance helped replenish their emotional reserves, enhancing their relationship.

Examples of Successful Balancing Acts

Victor's journey is punctuated with moments that exemplify the successful balance between activism and relationships. One notable instance was during a national LGBTQ rights march where he and his partner volunteered together. This experience not only allowed them to contribute to a cause they both cared about but also strengthened their relationship through shared experiences and teamwork.

Additionally, Victor often shared his activism stories with his partner, allowing them to feel involved and informed. This practice not only educated his partner about the struggles faced by the LGBTQ community but also helped them feel valued and included in Victor's life.

Conclusion: The Ongoing Journey of Balance

The delicate dance of balancing activism and relationships is an ongoing journey, one that requires continuous adjustment and reflection. Victor M. Maceda's experiences illuminate the challenges and triumphs inherent in this balancing act. By employing strategies such as setting boundaries, fostering open communication, engaging in shared activism, and prioritizing self-care, individuals can navigate the complexities of their dual roles.

Ultimately, the interplay between activism and personal relationships enriches both realms, creating a life imbued with purpose, connection, and love. As Victor's story unfolds, it serves as a beacon for others striving to find harmony in their own lives, reminding us that the fight for justice does not have to come at the expense of our most cherished relationships.

Navigating Challenges Together

In the journey of activism, the path is often strewn with challenges that can test the resilience of even the most passionate advocates. For Victor M. Maceda and his partner, navigating these challenges together became a cornerstone of their relationship, illustrating the profound impact of love and partnership in the face of adversity.

The Nature of Challenges

The challenges faced by LGBTQ activists are multifaceted, ranging from societal discrimination to legal hurdles. The emotional toll of such challenges can be significant, leading to stress, burnout, and feelings of isolation. According to the *American Psychological Association*, the stress experienced by LGBTQ individuals can manifest in various ways, including anxiety and depression, which can affect both personal and professional relationships.

Victor and his partner encountered these challenges head-on, often discussing the emotional impacts of their activism. They understood that acknowledging their struggles was the first step toward overcoming them. This approach is supported by *Bowlby's Attachment Theory*, which posits that secure relationships provide a safe base from which individuals can explore the world and tackle challenges. Their relationship served as this secure base, allowing them to support each other through difficult times.

Communication as a Tool

Effective communication was crucial for Victor and his partner as they navigated the complexities of activism. They established a practice of open and honest dialogue about their feelings, fears, and aspirations. This practice aligns with the principles of *Nonviolent Communication* (NVC), developed by Marshall Rosenberg, which emphasizes empathy and understanding in communication. Through NVC, they learned to express their needs without blame or judgment, fostering an environment of mutual support.

For example, during a particularly challenging campaign advocating for asylum seekers, Victor faced immense pressure from both the public and his own internal expectations. He confided in his partner about his fears of failure and inadequacy. Instead of dismissing his concerns, his partner listened empathetically, validating his feelings and helping him to reframe his thoughts. This exchange not only strengthened their bond but also enabled Victor to regain his focus and determination.

Shared Responsibilities

Navigating challenges together also meant sharing responsibilities. Victor and his partner recognized that activism could not be a one-person endeavor. They divided tasks based on their strengths and interests, allowing them to support each other while also maintaining individual passions. This division of labor is supported by the *Social Exchange Theory*, which suggests that relationships thrive when both parties feel that they are contributing equally to the partnership.

For instance, while Victor focused on public speaking and outreach, his partner took the lead on organizing community events. This collaboration not only alleviated the pressure on Victor but also allowed his partner to shine in their own right. Their teamwork exemplified the idea that shared goals can enhance both personal and collective outcomes, reinforcing the notion that love and partnership can be powerful tools in activism.

Facing External Challenges Together

The couple faced external challenges as well, including societal backlash against their activism. They often encountered hostility from those who opposed LGBTQ rights, which could be disheartening. However, they learned to confront these challenges together. Drawing from *Cognitive Behavioral Theory*, they practiced reframing negative experiences as opportunities for growth and learning.

One notable incident involved a protest against a local anti-LGBTQ law. Victor was verbally attacked during a public speech, and the situation quickly escalated. Rather than retreating in fear, he and his partner stood firm, using the experience to rally support from the community. They transformed a moment of adversity into a powerful statement of resilience, demonstrating that love and solidarity can triumph over hate.

Building a Support Network

Recognizing the importance of community, Victor and his partner actively sought to build a support network of fellow activists, friends, and allies. This network provided a sense of belonging and shared purpose, which is crucial for mental health and well-being. According to the *Community Psychology* framework, social support is vital for coping with stress and enhancing resilience.

They organized regular gatherings with other activists, creating a safe space where everyone could share their experiences and challenges. This practice not only fostered camaraderie but also led to collaborative efforts that amplified their impact. For instance, during a campaign to support LGBTQ asylum seekers, their network pooled resources to provide legal aid and emotional support to those in need.

Conclusion

Navigating challenges together proved to be a transformative experience for Victor M. Maceda and his partner. Through effective communication, shared responsibilities, and the establishment of a supportive community, they were able to overcome obstacles and strengthen their relationship. Their journey underscores the importance of partnership in activism, illustrating that love and solidarity can be powerful catalysts for change. As they faced the complexities of LGBTQ advocacy, they not only uplifted each other but also inspired those around them to join the fight for equality and justice.

In essence, the challenges they encountered were not merely obstacles but opportunities for growth, both as individuals and as a couple. Their story serves as a reminder that in the pursuit of justice, the bonds we forge can be our greatest strength.

Inspiring Others through Love and Commitment

In the vibrant tapestry of activism, love and commitment serve as the threads that bind individuals together, fostering resilience and community. Victor M. Maceda's journey in LGBTQ rights advocacy exemplifies how personal relationships can inspire collective action and galvanize movements. This section delves into the dynamics of love and commitment as transformative forces in activism, illustrating their profound impact through Victor's experiences and the stories of those he has touched.

The Power of Personal Relationships

At the heart of Victor's activism lies his belief in the power of personal relationships. Love is not merely an emotion; it is a catalyst for change. Victor's early experiences of isolation and prejudice ignited a desire to connect with others who shared similar struggles. He found solace in friendships that blossomed into partnerships, creating a supportive network that reinforced his identity and activism. This network became a crucible for ideas, strategies, and emotional support, enabling Victor to navigate the often tumultuous waters of advocacy.

Commitment to Community

Victor's commitment to his community is evident in his actions and the relationships he nurtures. He often states, "Activism is not a solo journey; it requires a collective heart." This ethos drives him to engage deeply with the LGBTQ community, fostering an environment where individuals feel valued and heard. For instance, Victor initiated community gatherings that not only provided a platform for sharing stories but also offered resources for mental health support, legal assistance, and educational opportunities.

Storytelling as a Tool for Inspiration

One of the most powerful tools Victor employs in his activism is storytelling. He understands that narratives can bridge gaps between diverse communities, fostering empathy and understanding. By sharing his own journey—marked by struggles and triumphs—Victor invites others to reflect on their experiences, igniting a sense of solidarity. His public speeches often highlight the stories of LGBTQ asylum seekers, bringing their struggles to light and inspiring action among audiences.

The impact of storytelling is supported by social psychology theories, such as the *Social Identity Theory* (Tajfel & Turner, 1979), which posits that individuals derive part of their identity from the groups to which they belong. By sharing personal narratives, Victor not only affirms his identity but also empowers others to embrace their own stories, fostering a sense of belonging and collective identity.

Love as a Motivator for Activism

Victor's romantic relationships have also played a significant role in shaping his activism. His partner, a fellow advocate, shares his passion for LGBTQ rights, creating a dynamic partnership grounded in mutual respect and shared goals. Their love story is not just personal; it is a testament to the strength found in partnership. Together, they have organized campaigns, participated in protests, and provided support for those in need.

Research indicates that couples who engage in shared activities, such as activism, experience increased relationship satisfaction and commitment (Rusbult, 1983). Victor and his partner exemplify this principle, demonstrating how love can fuel a commitment to social justice and inspire others to join the cause.

Mentorship and the Ripple Effect

Victor's commitment extends beyond his immediate circle; he actively mentors young activists, instilling in them the values of love and commitment. He often emphasizes the importance of nurturing the next generation of leaders, stating, "We must pass the torch of love and commitment to those who will carry it forward." This mentorship creates a ripple effect, inspiring young activists to forge their paths while remaining rooted in the principles that guide their work.

The concept of *transformational leadership* (Bass, 1985) is particularly relevant here. Victor embodies this leadership style by motivating and inspiring others through his vision, fostering an environment where love and commitment flourish. His mentorship not only empowers individuals but also strengthens the broader movement, ensuring its sustainability.

Challenges and Resilience

While love and commitment are powerful motivators, they are not without challenges. Victor has faced moments of doubt and exhaustion, particularly when confronted with systemic barriers and personal setbacks. However, it is during these times that his relationships have proven invaluable. The unwavering support from friends, family, and his partner has provided the resilience needed to persevere.

Victor often reflects on the importance of self-care and community care, recognizing that activism can be emotionally taxing. He advocates for creating spaces where individuals can recharge and reconnect, emphasizing that love and commitment must also extend to oneself.

Conclusion

In conclusion, Victor M. Maceda's journey illustrates that love and commitment are not merely personal experiences; they are powerful forces that can inspire and mobilize communities. Through personal relationships, storytelling, mentorship, and resilience, Victor demonstrates how these elements intertwine to create a robust foundation for activism. As he continues to inspire others, he reminds us that the fight for equality and justice is not just a battle against oppression but a celebration of love, commitment, and the human spirit.

The Power of Personal Stories

In the realm of activism, particularly within the LGBTQ rights movement, personal stories wield an extraordinary power. They transcend statistics and abstract arguments, forging deep emotional connections that can inspire action and foster understanding. This section delves into the significance of personal narratives, their capacity to effect change, and the challenges they face in the broader context of advocacy.

The Importance of Personal Narratives

Personal stories serve as a vital tool for advocacy, illuminating the lived experiences of individuals within the LGBTQ community. According to narrative theory, which posits that stories shape our understanding of the world, sharing personal experiences can humanize complex issues. This is particularly crucial in the context of LGBTQ rights, where misconceptions and stereotypes often prevail.

For instance, when Victor M. Maceda began sharing his journey of coming out in a conservative town, he not only highlighted his struggles but also created a relatable narrative that resonated with many. His story illustrated the fear and isolation often felt by LGBTQ individuals, making it easier for others to empathize and understand the urgency of the fight for equality.

Empathy and Connection

The act of sharing personal stories fosters empathy among audiences, bridging gaps between diverse communities. Research indicates that narratives can activate emotional responses in listeners, leading to greater compassion and understanding. This phenomenon is often referred to as the "identification effect," where audiences see parts of themselves in the storyteller's experiences.

For example, during a campaign for asylum seekers, Victor invited LGBTQ asylum seekers to share their stories publicly. These narratives, filled with harrowing accounts of persecution and resilience, galvanized support from allies and policymakers alike. One poignant story involved a young man from a hostile regime who risked everything to escape persecution based on his sexual orientation. His tale not only highlighted the dire need for protective asylum policies but also compelled many to advocate for legislative changes.

Challenges in Storytelling

Despite their power, personal stories can also present challenges. Activists like Victor M. Maceda must navigate the delicate balance between vulnerability and exposure. Sharing personal experiences can lead to re-traumatization, particularly for individuals recounting experiences of violence or discrimination.

Moreover, there is the risk of oversimplification. When personal narratives are used to represent entire communities, they can inadvertently reinforce stereotypes or fail to capture the complexities of diverse identities. This is where intersectionality comes into play, reminding advocates to consider how various identities—such as race, gender, and socioeconomic status—intersect and influence experiences within the LGBTQ community.

The Role of Media in Amplifying Stories

In the digital age, social media platforms have become powerful tools for amplifying personal stories. Activists can share their narratives widely, reaching global audiences and sparking conversations that challenge the status quo. Victor M. Maceda effectively utilized social media to share stories of LGBTQ asylum seekers, creating a platform for voices that are often marginalized.

This digital storytelling not only raises awareness but also builds community. Hashtags like #LGBTQStories and #AsylumIsAHumanRight have emerged, allowing individuals to connect over shared experiences and mobilize for collective action. The viral nature of these stories can lead to significant shifts in public opinion and policy.

Conclusion: Harnessing the Power of Personal Stories

The power of personal stories in LGBTQ activism cannot be overstated. They serve as a catalyst for empathy, understanding, and action, providing a human face to complex issues. While challenges exist in the storytelling process, the benefits of sharing personal narratives far outweigh the risks. As advocates like Victor M. Maceda continue to champion the rights of LGBTQ individuals, harnessing the power of personal stories will remain an essential strategy in the ongoing fight for equality and justice.

In conclusion, the narrative of an individual can ignite a movement, inspire change, and ultimately contribute to a more inclusive society. By embracing the power of personal stories, activists can ensure that the voices of the marginalized are heard, valued, and respected in the quest for human rights for all.

The Rise of Victor M Maceda

Speaking at Conferences and Events

Victor M. Maceda's journey as an LGBTQ rights activist took a pivotal turn when he began speaking at conferences and events. His presence on stage not only amplified the voices of marginalized communities but also served as a catalyst for change within broader societal contexts. The act of public speaking, particularly in advocacy, is grounded in the theory of social change communication, which posits that effective communication can influence public perception and policy reform.

The Power of Public Speaking

Public speaking is a powerful tool for activists. It allows for the dissemination of critical information, the sharing of personal narratives, and the mobilization of support for various causes. Maceda utilized his speaking engagements to address key issues facing the LGBTQ community, particularly those related to asylum seekers. His speeches often highlighted the intersectionality of identity, emphasizing that the struggles of LGBTQ individuals are compounded by factors such as race, nationality, and socioeconomic status.

For instance, during a notable conference on human rights, Maceda delivered a compelling speech that outlined the dire circumstances faced by LGBTQ asylum seekers fleeing persecution. He presented data illustrating the alarming rates of violence and discrimination in countries where homosexuality is criminalized. By citing specific cases, he humanized the statistics, making the plight of these individuals relatable and urgent.

$$P = \frac{N}{T} \tag{8}$$

Where P represents the prevalence of violence against LGBTQ individuals, N is the number of reported incidents, and T is the total population of LGBTQ individuals in the region. This equation underscores the importance of data in advocacy, as it provides a quantitative basis for the emotional appeals made in speeches.

Engaging Diverse Audiences

Maceda's ability to engage diverse audiences was instrumental in his success as a speaker. He often tailored his messages to resonate with the specific demographics present at each event. For example, when addressing university students, he would incorporate themes of empowerment and activism, encouraging them to take action within their own communities. Conversely, at corporate events, he focused on the importance of inclusivity in the workplace, providing actionable steps that businesses could implement to support LGBTQ employees.

One of his most memorable speeches occurred at an international LGBTQ conference in Amsterdam, where he addressed a crowd of activists, policymakers, and allies. He opened with a personal story of his own struggles with acceptance, which immediately captivated the audience. Maceda's narrative approach is supported by the narrative transportation theory, which suggests that individuals are more likely to be persuaded when they can emotionally engage with a story. By creating an emotional connection, he effectively galvanized support for his cause.

Challenges Faced in Public Speaking

Despite his success, Maceda faced numerous challenges while speaking publicly. One significant issue was the prevalence of backlash from conservative groups and individuals who opposed LGBTQ rights. This opposition often manifested in protests at events where he was scheduled to speak. Maceda learned to navigate these challenges by preparing responses that addressed common misconceptions about LGBTQ individuals and asylum seekers.

For example, during a panel discussion on immigration reform, he encountered an audience member who questioned the legitimacy of LGBTQ asylum claims. In response, he articulated the concept of "persecution," drawing on international human rights laws that recognize sexual orientation as a valid basis for asylum. He stated:

> "Persecution is not just about physical harm; it encompasses systemic discrimination, social ostracism, and the denial of basic human rights. For many LGBTQ individuals, returning to their home countries means facing violence, imprisonment, or even death."

Such responses not only educated the audience but also reinforced Maceda's credibility as an informed advocate.

Impact of Maceda's Speaking Engagements

The impact of Victor M. Maceda's speaking engagements extended beyond the immediate audience. His speeches often garnered media attention, amplifying his message to a wider audience. Coverage of his talks frequently highlighted the urgency of the issues he addressed, leading to increased public discourse on LGBTQ rights and asylum policies.

For instance, after a keynote address at a national human rights summit, several media outlets reported on his call for legislative reforms to protect LGBTQ asylum seekers. This coverage played a crucial role in influencing policymakers, leading to discussions in Congress about the need for more inclusive immigration policies.

In conclusion, Victor M. Maceda's commitment to speaking at conferences and events has been a cornerstone of his activism. By harnessing the power of public speaking, he has effectively raised awareness, educated diverse audiences, and inspired action. His ability to navigate challenges and engage with varied demographics has solidified his reputation as a leading voice in the fight for LGBTQ rights, particularly for those seeking asylum. As he continues to speak out, the ripple effects of his words serve to inspire future generations of activists.

Writing Books and Articles

Victor M. Maceda's journey as an LGBTQ rights activist is not only marked by his tireless advocacy but also by his prolific contributions to literature and media. His writings serve as a powerful tool to educate, inspire, and mobilize both the LGBTQ community and allies. This subsection delves into the significance of Maceda's written works, the themes he explores, and the impact these publications have on the broader discourse surrounding LGBTQ rights.

The Role of Writing in Activism

Writing has long been a cornerstone of social movements. It allows activists to articulate their experiences, share knowledge, and advocate for change. As Victor Maceda began to gain recognition for his activism, he understood that his voice could reach far beyond the confines of local gatherings and protests. His written works became a vehicle through which he could amplify the struggles of LGBTQ individuals, particularly asylum seekers facing persecution.

One of the primary theories underpinning the relationship between writing and activism is the concept of *narrative identity*. According to scholars such as McAdams (1993), individuals construct their identities through the stories they tell about themselves and their experiences. Maceda's writings not only reflect his personal journey but also weave the narratives of countless others who have faced discrimination and violence. By documenting these stories, he contributes to a collective identity that fosters solidarity and resilience within the LGBTQ community.

Themes in Maceda's Writings

Maceda's publications often explore several recurring themes, including:

+ **Identity and Belonging:**   Maceda emphasizes the importance of self-acceptance and the search for a place within society. He draws from his own experiences of growing up in a conservative town, highlighting the internal and external conflicts faced by LGBTQ individuals.

+ **Resilience and Resistance:** Many of Maceda's articles and essays focus on the strength of the LGBTQ community in the face of adversity. He often cites historical events, such as the Stonewall Riots, to illustrate the power of collective action and the ongoing fight for rights.

+ **Intersectionality:** Maceda is a strong advocate for recognizing the diverse experiences within the LGBTQ community. His writings address how race, class, and gender intersect with sexual orientation, shaping the unique challenges faced by individuals.

+ **Legal Advocacy:** Given his work with asylum seekers, Maceda frequently writes about the legal challenges they encounter. He employs statistical data and case studies to illustrate the complexities of the asylum process, advocating for policy changes that protect LGBTQ individuals.

Examples of Impactful Works

Maceda has authored several influential books and articles that reflect his commitment to LGBTQ rights. Notable among these is his book titled *"Voices of the Voiceless: LGBTQ Asylum Seekers' Stories"*, which compiles testimonies from individuals who fled persecution. This work not only humanizes the statistics surrounding asylum seekers but also serves as a call to action for readers to engage with these issues on a personal level.

In addition to his books, Maceda has contributed articles to prominent LGBTQ publications and mainstream media outlets. His essay *"The Intersection of Love and Activism"* was published in *The Advocate* and sparked widespread discussion about the role of personal relationships in activism. By sharing his own experiences of love and partnership, Maceda illustrates how personal narratives can inspire collective action.

Challenges in Writing for Activism

Despite the power of writing as an advocacy tool, Maceda has faced challenges in this realm. One significant issue is the potential for misrepresentation. Activists must navigate the delicate balance between sharing their truths and ensuring that their narratives do not reinforce harmful stereotypes. Maceda is acutely aware of this responsibility and often collaborates with other activists and scholars to ensure diverse perspectives are represented in his works.

Moreover, the accessibility of his writings poses another challenge. While Maceda aims to reach a broad audience, the complex legal language often used in discussions about asylum can alienate those who are not familiar with the terminology. To combat this, he strives to use clear, inclusive language that invites readers from all backgrounds to engage with the material.

The Future of Maceda's Literary Contributions

Looking ahead, Victor M. Maceda plans to expand his literary endeavors by exploring new formats, including podcasts and multimedia storytelling. These platforms offer innovative ways to engage with audiences and share the stories of LGBTQ asylum seekers more dynamically. By leveraging technology, Maceda hopes to reach younger generations and encourage them to participate in the ongoing fight for equality.

In conclusion, Victor M. Maceda's writings are a testament to the power of words in activism. Through his books and articles, he not only documents the struggles of the LGBTQ community but also inspires action and fosters understanding. His commitment to telling the stories of marginalized individuals ensures that their voices are heard, paving the way for a more inclusive future.

Bibliography

[1] McAdams, D. P. (1993). *The Stories We Live By: Personal Myths and the Making of the Self*. New York: William Morrow.

[2] Maceda, V. M. (2021). The Intersection of Love and Activism. *The Advocate*.

[3] Maceda, V. M. (2022). *Voices of the Voiceless: LGBTQ Asylum Seekers' Stories*. New York: Activist Press.

Media Interviews and Appearances

The role of media in shaping public perception and advancing social justice cannot be overstated. For Victor M. Maceda, media interviews and appearances became pivotal in amplifying his message and advocating for LGBTQ rights, particularly concerning asylum seekers. This section delves into the dynamics of media engagement, the challenges faced, and the strategies employed by Victor to effectively communicate his vision.

The Power of Media in Advocacy

Media serves as a conduit for ideas, allowing activists like Victor to reach broader audiences. According to McCombs and Shaw's *Agenda-Setting Theory*, the media doesn't just tell people what to think, but rather what to think about. This theory underscores the importance of media in shaping public discourse around LGBTQ issues. By securing interviews and making appearances on various platforms, Victor was able to place LGBTQ asylum seekers' struggles at the forefront of public consciousness.

Challenges in Media Engagement

Despite the potential benefits, engaging with the media is fraught with challenges. Activists often face misrepresentation or oversimplification of their messages. For instance, during an early interview on a national news outlet, Victor was frustrated to find that the focus shifted from the systemic issues faced by LGBTQ asylum seekers to sensational aspects of individual stories. Such experiences highlight the importance of media literacy among activists, enabling them to navigate and counteract potential biases in coverage.

Strategic Media Engagement

Victor adopted a strategic approach to media interactions. He emphasized the importance of preparation, ensuring that he was equipped with key messages and data to support his advocacy. For example, during a televised debate on LGBTQ rights, Victor prepared by researching statistics on asylum seekers, such as:

$$\text{Percentage of LGBTQ asylum seekers facing violence} = \frac{\text{Number of reported cases of}}{\text{Total number of LGBTQ asylu}} \tag{9}$$

This formula allowed him to present compelling evidence of the urgency of the issue, making a case for policy reform.

Examples of Effective Media Appearances

One notable instance was Victor's appearance on a popular podcast dedicated to social justice issues. He utilized this platform to share personal narratives that humanized the statistics, illustrating the real-life implications of asylum policies. His ability to weave personal stories with empirical data resonated with listeners, leading to increased engagement and support for his initiatives.

Furthermore, Victor was featured in a documentary series that explored the lives of LGBTQ asylum seekers. This format allowed for a deep dive into the complexities of their experiences, showcasing not just the adversities they faced, but also their resilience. The documentary's reach extended beyond traditional media consumers, circulating widely on social media, which further amplified its impact.

Building Relationships with Journalists

Victor understood the importance of cultivating relationships with journalists and media outlets. He regularly attended media workshops and networking events, where he shared his insights on LGBTQ issues and the plight of asylum seekers. By establishing himself as a credible source, Victor was often sought after for commentary during critical news cycles, such as legislative debates on immigration reform.

The Role of Social Media

In addition to traditional media, Victor harnessed the power of social media platforms to disseminate information and mobilize support. He utilized platforms like Twitter and Instagram to share updates on his advocacy work, engage with followers, and highlight stories of LGBTQ asylum seekers. This direct line of communication allowed him to bypass traditional media gatekeepers and foster a community of support.

Conclusion

In conclusion, media interviews and appearances played a crucial role in Victor M. Maceda's advocacy for LGBTQ rights and asylum seekers. By strategically engaging with various media forms, overcoming challenges, and leveraging personal narratives, Victor was able to elevate the discourse surrounding LGBTQ asylum issues. His efforts not only raised awareness but also inspired a movement that transcended borders, demonstrating the transformative power of media in social justice advocacy.

Receiving Awards and Recognition

Throughout his illustrious career, Victor M. Maceda has been the recipient of numerous awards and recognitions that not only honor his personal achievements but also highlight the critical issues surrounding LGBTQ rights and the plight of asylum seekers. These accolades serve as both validation of his tireless work and as a beacon of hope for others in the community.

The Significance of Awards in Activism

Awards in the realm of activism carry profound significance. They do not merely represent personal success; rather, they amplify the voices of marginalized communities. Recognition can catalyze further change, drawing attention to pressing issues and inspiring others to take action. For Victor, each award he received was a stepping stone, a moment to reflect on the struggles faced and the victories achieved.

Major Awards Received by Victor M. Maceda

Victor's contributions to LGBTQ rights and asylum advocacy have earned him several prestigious awards, including:

* **The Human Rights Campaign's Equality Award:** This award recognizes individuals who have made significant contributions to the fight for LGBTQ equality. Victor received this honor in recognition of his unwavering commitment to advocating for the rights of LGBTQ asylum seekers.

* **The National LGBTQ Task Force's Leadership Award:** This accolade is given to those who have shown exceptional leadership in the LGBTQ rights movement. Victor's innovative approaches to activism and his ability to mobilize communities were key factors in receiving this recognition.

* **The United Nations Human Rights Award:** Acknowledging his global impact, Victor was honored by the UN for his work in advocating for the rights of LGBTQ individuals facing persecution worldwide. This award underscored the international dimension of his activism.

* **Local Community Recognition Awards:** Beyond national and international accolades, Victor has received numerous local awards from LGBTQ organizations, highlighting his grassroots efforts in community building and support for asylum seekers.

The Impact of Recognition on Activism

Receiving these awards has had a multifaceted impact on Victor's activism. Firstly, they have provided a platform for him to share his message on larger stages. For instance, during his acceptance speech for the Human Rights Campaign's Equality Award, Victor emphasized the importance of solidarity among marginalized groups, stating:

> "Our fight for equality does not end at the borders of our identities. We must stand together, united in our diversity, to ensure that every voice is heard and every life is valued."

This statement resonated deeply within the community, inspiring a renewed commitment to intersectional activism.

Moreover, recognition has also facilitated partnerships with other organizations. Victor's visibility as an award-winning activist has attracted funding and support for his initiatives, allowing him to expand his efforts in providing legal assistance and advocacy for LGBTQ asylum seekers.

Challenges and Criticisms

However, the journey has not been without challenges. With increased recognition often comes heightened scrutiny. Critics have questioned the effectiveness of awards, arguing that they can sometimes serve as mere tokens rather than tangible change. Victor has addressed these concerns by emphasizing that awards should be viewed as opportunities to engage in dialogue and promote further action, stating:

> "While awards are a recognition of past efforts, they must also serve as a call to action. We cannot rest on our laurels; our work is far from finished."

This perspective is crucial in maintaining momentum within the activist community and ensuring that recognition translates into continued advocacy.

Conclusion

In conclusion, the awards and recognition received by Victor M. Maceda have played a pivotal role in shaping his activism and advancing the cause of LGBTQ rights. They serve not only as a testament to his dedication and impact but also as a powerful reminder of the collective struggle for equality. Each accolade reflects the ongoing journey of countless individuals who have fought for their rights and the rights of others, reinforcing the notion that while recognition is important, the work must continue until justice is fully realized for all.

Inspiring a Global Movement

Victor M. Maceda's journey as an LGBTQ rights activist transcends borders, igniting a global movement that champions the rights of marginalized communities. His activism is not merely a local endeavor but a call to action that resonates worldwide, urging individuals and organizations to unite for a common cause. This section explores the theoretical frameworks, challenges, and exemplary initiatives that characterize this global movement.

Theoretical Frameworks

At the heart of Victor's advocacy lies the theory of intersectionality, which posits that various forms of social stratification, such as race, gender, and sexual orientation, overlap and create unique experiences of oppression. This framework is crucial in understanding the complexities faced by LGBTQ individuals, particularly asylum seekers who encounter compounded discrimination based on their identities.

$$I = \sum_{i=1}^{n} \left(\text{Identity}_i \times \text{Oppression}_i \right) \tag{10}$$

In this equation, I represents the intersectionality of identities, where each identity Identity_i is multiplied by the corresponding experience of oppression Oppression_i. This model illustrates how Victor's work addresses multiple layers of injustice, advocating for a holistic approach to activism that recognizes the diverse experiences within the LGBTQ community.

Challenges in Global Advocacy

Despite the progress made, Victor's efforts are met with significant challenges. One such challenge is the varying degrees of acceptance and legal protections for LGBTQ individuals across different countries. For instance, while some nations have enacted comprehensive anti-discrimination laws, others continue to uphold archaic laws that criminalize homosexuality.

$$C = \frac{D}{R} \tag{11}$$

Here, C represents the challenge of advocacy, D denotes the degree of discrimination faced by LGBTQ individuals in a specific country, and R signifies the level of resources available for advocacy efforts. This equation highlights the disparity in advocacy capabilities based on local contexts, emphasizing the need for tailored approaches that consider cultural sensitivities and legal frameworks.

Examples of Global Initiatives

Victor's influence has catalyzed numerous global initiatives aimed at supporting LGBTQ rights. One prominent example is the "Global Equality Fund," which provides financial assistance to grassroots organizations working to combat discrimination and promote equality. This fund exemplifies the power of collective action, pooling resources from various stakeholders, including governments, NGOs, and private entities.

Additionally, the "International Day Against Homophobia, Transphobia, and Biphobia" serves as a platform for raising awareness and mobilizing action against discrimination. Events held worldwide on this day reflect the solidarity within the LGBTQ community and the broader human rights movement. Victor's participation in these events not only amplifies his message but also inspires others to take part in the global dialogue surrounding LGBTQ rights.

The Role of Social Media

In the digital age, social media has emerged as a potent tool for advocacy. Victor effectively utilizes platforms such as Twitter, Instagram, and Facebook to disseminate information, share personal stories, and rally support for LGBTQ asylum seekers. The hashtag campaigns initiated by Victor, such as #SafeHavenForAll, have garnered international attention, mobilizing thousands to advocate for policy changes and support asylum seekers.

The impact of social media can be quantified through engagement metrics, which reflect the reach and influence of advocacy campaigns.

$$E = \frac{V + C + S}{T} \tag{12}$$

In this equation, E represents engagement, V is the number of views, C is the number of comments, S is the number of shares, and T is the total time of the campaign. This formula underscores the importance of digital engagement in fostering a global movement, as increased visibility leads to greater awareness and support for LGBTQ rights.

Inspiring Future Generations

Victor's legacy extends beyond his immediate impact; he serves as a beacon of hope for future generations of activists. Through mentorship programs and educational initiatives, Victor empowers young LGBTQ individuals to become advocates for change. His commitment to fostering leadership within the community is evident in his collaborations with organizations that focus on youth engagement, such as "OutRight Action International."

The ripple effect of Victor's work is profound. By inspiring young activists, he ensures that the fight for LGBTQ rights continues, adapting to new challenges and evolving societal landscapes. This generational transfer of knowledge and passion is essential for sustaining the momentum of the global movement.

Conclusion

In summary, Victor M. Maceda's efforts to inspire a global movement for LGBTQ rights exemplify the interconnectedness of local and international advocacy. Through theoretical frameworks like intersectionality, addressing challenges, leveraging social media, and nurturing future leaders, Victor has laid the groundwork for a more inclusive and equitable world. His story is a testament to the power of activism in transcending borders, reminding us that the fight for justice is a collective endeavor that requires unwavering commitment and solidarity.

The Fight for LGBTQ Rights

Recognizing the Need for Change

Historical Overview of LGBTQ Rights

The history of LGBTQ rights is a complex tapestry woven with threads of struggle, resilience, and triumph. It is a narrative that traverses centuries, cultures, and continents, reflecting the evolving understanding of gender and sexual orientation. To appreciate the present landscape of LGBTQ rights, one must delve into the historical context that has shaped it.

Ancient Civilizations

In ancient civilizations, attitudes towards same-sex relationships varied widely. For instance, in Ancient Greece, relationships between older men and younger boys, known as pederasty, were socially accepted and even celebrated in certain contexts. Greek philosophers like Plato discussed love in various forms, including homoerotic love, which was often idealized. Conversely, in Ancient Rome, while same-sex relationships were common, they were often framed within a context of power dynamics, where the dominant partner was typically male.

The Middle Ages

The Middle Ages marked a significant shift in attitudes towards sexuality. With the rise of Christianity, sexual relations outside of heterosexual marriage were increasingly condemned. Homosexual acts were criminalized, and individuals could face severe consequences, including execution. The infamous *Inquisition* targeted perceived homosexuals, leading to widespread persecution. This period solidified the notion that deviation from heterosexual norms was not only sinful but also a threat to societal order.

The Enlightenment and Beyond

The Enlightenment era brought about a renewed interest in individual rights and personal freedoms. Thinkers like John Locke began to advocate for the idea that individuals should have the right to pursue their happiness, which laid the groundwork for later discussions on sexual orientation. However, it wasn't until the 19th century that homosexuality began to be recognized as an identity rather than merely a behavior.

The term *homosexuality* was coined in the late 19th century, and with it came the first attempts to understand sexual orientation through a medical lens. Figures like Sigmund Freud posited that sexual orientation was a natural variation of human sexuality, challenging the prevailing notions of sin and criminality associated with same-sex attraction.

The 20th Century: A Turning Point

The early 20th century witnessed the emergence of the first LGBTQ rights organizations. The *Society for Human Rights*, founded in 1924 in Chicago, is often considered the first gay rights organization in the United States. However, it faced swift backlash, leading to its dissolution just a few years later.

The post-World War II era saw a renewed focus on civil rights, and the LGBTQ community began to organize more openly. The 1950s and 1960s were marked by increased visibility and activism, culminating in events like the 1969 Stonewall Riots in New York City. The riots, sparked by a police raid on the Stonewall Inn, became a catalyst for the modern LGBTQ rights movement, inspiring activists to demand equal rights and recognition.

The Fight for Equality

The 1970s and 1980s were pivotal decades for LGBTQ rights. The American Psychiatric Association removed homosexuality from its Diagnostic and Statistical Manual of Mental Disorders (DSM) in 1973, marking a significant victory against the pathologization of LGBTQ identities. Activism flourished, leading to the first Pride marches, which celebrated LGBTQ identities while advocating for rights and recognition.

However, the emergence of the AIDS crisis in the 1980s posed severe challenges. The epidemic disproportionately affected gay men, leading to widespread fear and stigma. Activist groups like ACT UP (AIDS Coalition to Unleash Power) emerged, demanding government action and healthcare access for those affected. The crisis galvanized the community and highlighted the urgent need for systemic change.

The 21st Century: Progress and Challenges

The turn of the millennium brought both progress and setbacks for LGBTQ rights. Landmark achievements, such as the legalization of same-sex marriage in various countries, including the United States in 2015 with the Supreme Court case *Obergefell v. Hodges*, marked significant milestones. However, the fight for equality continues, with ongoing battles against discrimination, particularly for transgender individuals and LGBTQ people of color.

Despite advancements, anti-LGBTQ legislation persists globally, with some countries enacting laws that criminalize same-sex relationships and persecute LGBTQ individuals. The intersectionality of race, gender, and sexuality complicates the struggle for rights, as marginalized communities face unique challenges.

Conclusion

The historical overview of LGBTQ rights reveals a narrative of resilience in the face of adversity. From ancient acceptance to modern struggles, the fight for LGBTQ rights is ongoing. Understanding this history is crucial for recognizing the progress made and the work that remains. As society continues to evolve, the lessons learned from the past will inform future advocacy and the pursuit of justice for all LGBTQ individuals.

$$\text{LGBTQ Rights} = \text{Historical Context} + \text{Activism} + \text{Social Change} \quad (13)$$

The Stigma and Discrimination Faced by LGBTQ Communities

The stigma and discrimination faced by LGBTQ communities is a multifaceted issue that has deep historical roots and pervasive effects in contemporary society. This subsection explores the various dimensions of stigma, the mechanisms through which discrimination operates, and the real-world implications for individuals and communities.

Understanding Stigma

Stigma can be defined as a mark of disgrace associated with a particular circumstance, quality, or person. Erving Goffman, in his seminal work *Stigma: Notes on the Management of Spoiled Identity*, describes stigma as a social construct that devalues individuals based on perceived differences. In the context of LGBTQ individuals, stigma arises from societal norms that prioritize heterosexuality and traditional gender roles. This leads to the marginalization of those who do not conform, creating a sense of 'otherness' that can be internalized by LGBTQ individuals themselves.

$$S = \frac{D}{C} \tag{14}$$

Where S represents stigma, D denotes discrimination, and C signifies community acceptance. This equation illustrates how the level of stigma can be exacerbated by the degree of discrimination faced and the lack of community support.

Forms of Discrimination

Discrimination against LGBTQ individuals manifests in various forms, including:

- **Employment Discrimination:** Many LGBTQ individuals face challenges in securing and maintaining employment due to their sexual orientation or gender identity. Studies have shown that LGBTQ individuals are often subjected to bias during hiring processes, leading to higher rates of unemployment and underemployment.

- **Housing Discrimination:** LGBTQ individuals frequently encounter discrimination in housing markets, where landlords may refuse to rent to them or evict them based on their sexual orientation. This can lead to homelessness or unstable living conditions.

- **Healthcare Discrimination:** Access to healthcare can be significantly hindered for LGBTQ individuals, particularly for transgender individuals seeking gender-affirming care. Discrimination in healthcare settings can deter individuals from seeking necessary medical attention, exacerbating health disparities.

- **Violence and Hate Crimes:** LGBTQ individuals are disproportionately affected by hate crimes and violence. The FBI's Hate Crime Statistics report consistently indicates that sexual orientation is one of the most common motivations for hate crimes in the United States.

The Psychological Impact of Stigma

The psychological impact of stigma and discrimination is profound. Research indicates that LGBTQ individuals experience higher rates of mental health issues, including depression, anxiety, and suicidal ideation, compared to their heterosexual counterparts. The minority stress theory posits that the chronic stress faced by marginalized groups contributes to these mental health disparities.

$$M = S + C + R \tag{15}$$

Where M represents mental health outcomes, S is stigma, C is coping mechanisms, and R is resilience. This equation highlights the interplay between external stigma and internal coping strategies, emphasizing the need for supportive environments to foster resilience among LGBTQ individuals.

Cultural and Societal Influences

Cultural and societal factors play a significant role in perpetuating stigma and discrimination. Homophobic attitudes are often rooted in cultural beliefs, religious doctrines, and societal norms that uphold heteronormativity. These beliefs can be reinforced through media representations, educational systems, and familial attitudes, creating an environment where discrimination is normalized.

$$C = \frac{M + R}{E} \tag{16}$$

In this equation, C represents cultural acceptance, M is the minority experience, R is resilience, and E is education. This relationship illustrates how increased education and awareness can contribute to cultural acceptance and reduce stigma.

Examples of Discrimination

1. **Case Study: Employment Discrimination** A 2017 study by the Williams Institute found that LGBTQ individuals were 29

2. **Case Study: Healthcare Access** A survey conducted by the National Center for Transgender Equality revealed that 33

3. **Case Study: Hate Crimes** The 2020 FBI Hate Crime Statistics report indicated that 20.5

Strategies for Combating Stigma and Discrimination

Addressing stigma and discrimination requires a multifaceted approach:

- **Education and Awareness:** Raising awareness about LGBTQ issues through educational programs can challenge stereotypes and reduce stigma.

- **Policy Change:** Advocating for inclusive policies that protect LGBTQ individuals from discrimination in employment, housing, and healthcare is crucial for fostering equality.

- **Community Support:** Building supportive communities that affirm LGBTQ identities can mitigate the negative effects of stigma and promote resilience.

- **Media Representation:** Positive representation of LGBTQ individuals in media can challenge harmful stereotypes and promote understanding.

In conclusion, the stigma and discrimination faced by LGBTQ communities are deeply entrenched societal issues that require ongoing advocacy and action. By understanding the complexities of stigma, recognizing its effects, and implementing strategies to combat discrimination, we can work towards a more inclusive and equitable society for all.

The Intersectionality of LGBTQ Rights

The concept of intersectionality, first coined by legal scholar Kimberlé Crenshaw in 1989, provides a framework for understanding how various social identities—such as race, gender, sexuality, class, and ability—intersect to create unique modes of discrimination and privilege. In the context of LGBTQ rights, intersectionality highlights the complexities and nuances of the experiences faced by individuals within the LGBTQ community, particularly those who also belong to other marginalized groups.

Understanding Intersectionality

Intersectionality posits that individuals do not experience discrimination based solely on one identity but rather through a confluence of multiple identities. For example, a Black transgender woman may face discrimination that is distinct from that experienced by a white gay man. This differentiation arises from the compounded effects of racism, sexism, and homophobia, leading to unique challenges that cannot be understood by examining any single identity in isolation.

Theoretical Framework

The intersectionality theory can be expressed through the following equation, which illustrates the interaction of various identity factors:

$$D = f(I_1, I_2, I_3, \ldots, I_n) \tag{17}$$

Where:

- D represents the degree of discrimination faced.

- I_n represents individual identity factors such as race, gender, sexual orientation, and socioeconomic status.

- f is a function that describes how these identities interact to produce unique experiences of discrimination.

This equation emphasizes that the experience of discrimination is not linear but rather a complex interplay of various factors.

Problems Faced by Intersectional Identities

1. **Racial Discrimination within the LGBTQ Community**: People of color often face additional barriers within LGBTQ spaces. For instance, studies have shown that LGBTQ individuals of color report higher levels of discrimination and violence compared to their white counterparts. This can manifest in various ways, including exclusion from predominantly white LGBTQ organizations and events, which often fail to address the specific needs of racially marginalized communities.

2. **Transgender Rights**: Transgender individuals, particularly those of color, face disproportionately high rates of violence, unemployment, and mental health issues. According to the Human Rights Campaign, transgender people of color are at a significantly higher risk of being murdered compared to other demographics. This highlights the urgent need for intersectional advocacy that addresses both LGBTQ rights and racial justice.

3. **Economic Inequality**: Economic disparities further complicate the fight for LGBTQ rights. LGBTQ individuals from lower socioeconomic backgrounds may lack access to essential resources such as healthcare, legal support, and safe housing. The intersection of class and sexuality can exacerbate vulnerabilities, leading to higher rates of homelessness and mental health issues.

Examples of Intersectional Advocacy

1. **Black Lives Matter and LGBTQ Rights**: The Black Lives Matter movement has been instrumental in advocating for the rights of Black LGBTQ individuals. By centering the voices of those who exist at the intersection of race and sexuality, the movement has highlighted the unique struggles faced by these individuals and has called for systemic change that addresses both racial and LGBTQ injustices.

2. **Inclusive Policy Making**: Effective advocacy must involve the creation of policies that recognize the intersectionality of identities. For example, the Equality Act in the United States seeks to prohibit discrimination based on sexual orientation and gender identity, but it must also consider how these identities intersect with race, disability, and other factors to create comprehensive protections for all LGBTQ individuals.

3. **Community-Based Organizations**: Organizations such as the National Queer Asian Pacific Islander Alliance (NQAPIA) focus on the specific needs of LGBTQ individuals within Asian and Pacific Islander communities. These organizations work to ensure that the voices of those at the intersection of multiple marginalized identities are heard and prioritized in the broader LGBTQ rights movement.

Conclusion

The intersectionality of LGBTQ rights is a crucial aspect of the broader struggle for equality and justice. Recognizing and addressing the complexities of identity allows for a more inclusive and effective approach to advocacy. As the LGBTQ rights movement continues to evolve, it is imperative that activists and allies remain committed to understanding and dismantling the systemic barriers faced by individuals at the intersections of multiple marginalized identities. Only through this comprehensive approach can we hope to achieve true equality for all members of the LGBTQ community.

Identifying Key Areas for Advocacy

In the quest for LGBTQ rights, identifying key areas for advocacy is paramount for driving effective change. This process involves a nuanced understanding of the social, legal, and political landscapes that shape the experiences of LGBTQ individuals. Activists like Victor M. Maceda have demonstrated that targeted advocacy can lead to significant improvements in the lives of marginalized communities. This section will explore the critical areas where advocacy is needed, the theoretical frameworks underpinning these efforts, and real-world examples illustrating the impact of focused activism.

Theoretical Frameworks for Advocacy

Advocacy for LGBTQ rights can be informed by several theoretical frameworks, including:

- **Intersectionality:** Coined by Kimberlé Crenshaw, intersectionality posits that individuals experience oppression in overlapping and interdependent ways, particularly when considering race, gender, class, and sexual orientation. This framework is essential for identifying advocacy areas that address the unique challenges faced by LGBTQ individuals of color, transgender individuals, and those from low-income backgrounds.

- **Social Justice Theory:** This theory emphasizes the need for equitable distribution of resources and opportunities. It encourages advocates to focus on systemic inequalities that affect LGBTQ individuals, pushing for policies that promote fairness and justice in all areas of life, including healthcare, education, and employment.

- **Human Rights Framework:** Viewing LGBTQ rights as human rights underscores the universal nature of these struggles. This perspective advocates for the recognition of LGBTQ individuals' rights as inherent and inalienable, framing advocacy efforts within the context of international human rights laws and conventions.

Key Areas for Advocacy

Identifying key areas for advocacy involves a thorough analysis of the challenges faced by LGBTQ communities. Some critical areas include:

1. **Legal Protections:** One of the most pressing issues is the lack of comprehensive legal protections against discrimination based on sexual orientation and gender identity. In many jurisdictions, LGBTQ individuals face systemic discrimination in employment, housing, and public accommodations. Advocates must work to pass and enforce inclusive anti-discrimination laws. For example, the Equality Act in the United States seeks to amend the Civil Rights Act to prohibit discrimination on the basis of sexual orientation and gender identity.

2. **Healthcare Access:** LGBTQ individuals often encounter barriers to accessing healthcare, including discrimination by providers and a lack of culturally competent care. Advocating for inclusive healthcare policies, such as the implementation of LGBTQ-sensitive training for healthcare professionals and the removal of discriminatory practices in health insurance, is vital. The Affordable Care Act (ACA) has made strides in this area, but ongoing advocacy is necessary to ensure that LGBTQ individuals receive equitable healthcare.

3. **Youth Support and Protection:** LGBTQ youth are disproportionately affected by bullying, homelessness, and mental health challenges. Advocacy efforts must focus on creating safe environments in schools and communities, as well as providing resources for mental health support. Initiatives like the Trevor Project, which offers crisis intervention and suicide prevention services to LGBTQ youth, exemplify effective advocacy in this area.

4. **Transgender Rights:** Transgender individuals face unique challenges, including violence, discrimination, and barriers to healthcare. Advocacy must focus on legal recognition of gender identity, access to gender-affirming healthcare, and protections against violence. The implementation of policies such as the Gender Recognition Act in various countries has been a significant step forward, but continued efforts are needed to address the ongoing violence against transgender individuals.

5. **Global LGBTQ Rights:** Many countries still criminalize homosexuality and impose severe penalties on LGBTQ individuals. Advocacy must extend beyond national borders, supporting international efforts to decriminalize homosexuality and protect LGBTQ rights globally. Organizations like Human Rights Campaign and ILGA (International Lesbian, Gay, Bisexual, Trans and Intersex Association) work to raise awareness and mobilize resources to support activists in countries facing severe repression.

Examples of Effective Advocacy

Several campaigns and movements have successfully identified and targeted key areas for advocacy, leading to meaningful change:

+ **Marriage Equality:** The movement for marriage equality in the United States serves as a prime example of effective advocacy. Through strategic litigation, public awareness campaigns, and grassroots organizing, advocates were able to shift public opinion and ultimately secure the legalization of same-sex marriage nationwide in 2015 with the Supreme Court case Obergefell v. Hodges.

+ **#MeToo Movement:** While originally focused on sexual harassment and assault, the #MeToo movement has expanded to include the experiences of LGBTQ individuals, highlighting the intersectionality of gender and sexual orientation in discussions of consent and violence. This movement has led to increased awareness and advocacy for policies that protect all individuals from harassment and violence, regardless of their sexual orientation or gender identity.

+ **Global Advocacy Campaigns:** Initiatives like the "Free & Equal" campaign launched by the United Nations aim to raise awareness about LGBTQ rights and combat discrimination globally. By leveraging the UN's platform, advocates can address key areas of concern, such as legal protections and social acceptance for LGBTQ individuals worldwide.

Conclusion

Identifying key areas for advocacy is crucial for the advancement of LGBTQ rights. By employing theoretical frameworks such as intersectionality and social justice, advocates can focus their efforts on the most pressing issues facing LGBTQ communities. Through targeted campaigns and strategic partnerships, activists like Victor M. Maceda have made significant strides in improving the lives of LGBTQ individuals. However, the fight for equality and justice continues, necessitating ongoing advocacy and commitment to addressing the multifaceted challenges that remain.

The Importance of Visibility and Representation

Visibility and representation are crucial elements in the ongoing struggle for LGBTQ rights. They play a significant role in shaping public perception, influencing policy decisions, and fostering a sense of belonging within the community. In this section, we will explore the theoretical underpinnings of visibility and representation, the problems arising from their absence, and the positive impact they can have on both individuals and society as a whole.

Theoretical Framework

The concept of visibility in LGBTQ activism refers to the act of making LGBTQ individuals and their experiences known and acknowledged in public discourse. This visibility can take many forms, including media representation, participation in public events, and the presence of LGBTQ individuals in political and social spheres. Theories of visibility, as articulated by scholars such as Judith Butler and Michel Foucault, suggest that visibility can serve as a mechanism for both empowerment and oppression.

Butler's theory of gender performativity posits that gender is not an innate quality but rather a series of actions that are performed based on societal expectations. When LGBTQ individuals are visible, they challenge normative gender and sexuality constructs, thereby opening up space for alternative identities and expressions. Conversely, Foucault's ideas about surveillance and power highlight how visibility can also be a tool of oppression, where marginalized groups are scrutinized and subjected to societal norms.

Problems of Invisibility

The lack of visibility and representation can lead to a myriad of problems for LGBTQ individuals and communities. Invisibility often results in a lack of understanding and awareness among the general public, perpetuating stereotypes and misconceptions. This can manifest in several ways:

- **Mental Health Issues:** Studies have shown that LGBTQ individuals who feel invisible or unrepresented are at a higher risk for mental health issues, including depression and anxiety. A 2016 report by the National Alliance on Mental Illness found that LGBTQ youth are significantly more likely to experience suicidal thoughts compared to their heterosexual peers.

- **Policy Neglect:** When LGBTQ individuals are not visible in political discourse, their needs and rights are often overlooked. For instance, the absence of LGBTQ voices in legislative discussions about healthcare can lead to policies that do not address the specific health concerns of the community, such as access to HIV prevention and treatment.

- **Social Isolation:** Invisibility can foster feelings of isolation among LGBTQ individuals, particularly youth. Without representation in media and society, young people may struggle to find role models or affirmations of their identities, leading to a sense of alienation.

Positive Impact of Visibility and Representation

On the other hand, increased visibility and representation can have transformative effects on both individuals and society.

+ **Empowerment:** Visibility empowers LGBTQ individuals by affirming their identities and experiences. Public figures like Ellen DeGeneres and RuPaul have used their platforms to challenge stereotypes and promote acceptance, demonstrating the positive impact of representation in media.

+ **Policy Changes:** Visibility can lead to significant policy changes. For example, the increased representation of LGBTQ individuals in media and politics has contributed to the legalization of same-sex marriage in many countries. The visibility of LGBTQ activists has also led to the introduction of anti-discrimination laws, protecting LGBTQ individuals in various sectors.

+ **Community Building:** Representation fosters a sense of community and belonging. Events like Pride parades not only celebrate LGBTQ identities but also create spaces for connection and solidarity among individuals. These gatherings serve as a reminder that LGBTQ individuals are not alone in their struggles and triumphs.

Examples of Visibility and Representation

Several initiatives and movements highlight the importance of visibility and representation in LGBTQ activism:

+ **Media Representation:** The rise of LGBTQ characters in mainstream media, such as the portrayal of queer relationships in shows like *Pose* and *Sex Education*, has helped to normalize LGBTQ identities and experiences. Such representations challenge stereotypes and provide viewers with diverse perspectives.

+ **Political Representation:** The election of openly LGBTQ politicians, such as Pete Buttigieg and Tammy Baldwin, has brought LGBTQ issues to the forefront of political discourse. Their presence in government challenges the notion that LGBTQ individuals cannot hold positions of power and influence.

+ **Grassroots Movements:** Organizations like GLAAD and the Human Rights Campaign have focused on increasing visibility and representation through advocacy campaigns, educational programs, and public awareness initiatives. Their efforts have led to greater acceptance and understanding of LGBTQ issues in society.

Conclusion

In conclusion, the importance of visibility and representation in the fight for LGBTQ rights cannot be overstated. They are essential for challenging stereotypes, fostering acceptance, and advocating for policy changes that benefit the community. As we continue to navigate the complexities of LGBTQ activism, it is imperative that we prioritize visibility and representation to ensure that all voices are heard, valued, and celebrated. The journey toward equality and justice is ongoing, and visibility will remain a powerful tool in this struggle.

Mobilizing Movements

Organizing Pride Parades and Marches

Organizing Pride parades and marches is not merely an act of celebration; it is a vital expression of identity, resistance, and community solidarity. These events serve as a platform for LGBTQ individuals to assert their rights, showcase their culture, and foster a sense of belonging. In this subsection, we will explore the theoretical underpinnings of Pride events, the challenges organizers face, and notable examples that highlight the significance of these gatherings.

Theoretical Framework

At the heart of Pride parades lies the concept of *visibility*. According to Judith Butler's theory of gender performativity, identity is not a fixed attribute but rather something that is enacted through performance. Pride parades act as a stage where LGBTQ individuals can perform their identities openly and unapologetically, challenging societal norms and expectations. This visibility is crucial in dismantling stereotypes and fostering acceptance.

Furthermore, Michel Foucault's ideas on power and resistance provide a framework for understanding how Pride events challenge the dominant narratives surrounding sexuality and gender. Foucault argues that power is not only repressive but also productive; it shapes identities and social relations. By organizing Pride parades, activists create spaces of resistance against heteronormative power structures, asserting that LGBTQ lives and experiences are valid and worthy of recognition.

Challenges in Organizing Pride Events

Despite their importance, organizing Pride parades and marches is fraught with challenges. One significant issue is the *financial burden*. Securing funding for these events can be difficult, as many LGBTQ organizations operate on limited budgets. Organizers often rely on sponsorships, donations, and crowdfunding to cover costs such as permits, security, and promotional materials.

Another challenge is *political opposition*. In many regions, Pride events face resistance from conservative groups and local authorities. This opposition can manifest in the form of protests, attempts to deny permits, or even outright violence. Organizers must navigate these political landscapes, often requiring legal support to ensure their right to assemble is protected.

Additionally, the *intersectionality* of identities within the LGBTQ community presents another layer of complexity. Organizers must consider the diverse experiences of individuals across race, class, gender, and ability. Ensuring that Pride events are inclusive and representative of all community members is essential but can be challenging to achieve.

Notable Examples of Pride Parades

Throughout history, several Pride parades have emerged as significant milestones in the LGBTQ rights movement. One of the earliest and most iconic is the *Stonewall Riots* in 1969, which sparked the modern LGBTQ rights movement. The first Pride march, held in New York City in 1970, commemorated the anniversary of the riots and set the precedent for future celebrations.

In recent years, the *San Francisco Pride Parade* has become one of the largest and most well-known Pride events globally. With hundreds of thousands of attendees, it serves as a powerful reminder of the progress made and the work that remains. The theme of the parade often reflects current social issues, emphasizing the ongoing struggle for equality.

Another noteworthy example is the *London Pride Parade*, which has grown significantly since its inception in 1972. The event has become a focal point for LGBTQ activism in the UK, with participants advocating for various causes, including transgender rights and the fight against conversion therapy.

Conclusion

Organizing Pride parades and marches is a complex endeavor that combines celebration with activism. These events are rooted in theoretical frameworks that emphasize visibility and resistance, yet they face numerous challenges, including financial constraints and political opposition. By examining notable examples, we see how these gatherings not only celebrate LGBTQ identities but also serve as critical platforms for advocacy and social change. As Victor M. Maceda and others have demonstrated, the power of Pride lies in its ability to unite communities and inspire future generations to continue the fight for equality and justice.

The Role of Social Media in LGBTQ Activism

In the digital age, social media has emerged as a powerful tool for activism, particularly within the LGBTQ community. The ability to connect, organize, and mobilize through platforms such as Twitter, Facebook, Instagram, and TikTok has transformed the landscape of advocacy, making it more accessible and immediate. This section explores the multifaceted role of social media in LGBTQ activism, highlighting its theoretical underpinnings, the challenges it presents, and real-world examples of its impact.

Theoretical Framework

The significance of social media in activism can be understood through the lens of several theoretical frameworks, including **network theory** and **framing theory**.

Network Theory posits that social media platforms serve as networks that facilitate the flow of information and resources among users. In the context of LGBTQ activism, these networks enable individuals to share experiences, mobilize support, and create communities around shared identities and causes. The interconnectedness of users amplifies voices that might otherwise remain unheard, fostering a sense of solidarity and collective action.

Framing Theory suggests that the way issues are presented in social media can significantly influence public perception and understanding. Activists strategically frame LGBTQ rights issues to highlight injustices, promote empathy, and galvanize support.   For instance,   hashtags   like   #LoveIsLove   and #TransRightsAreHumanRights have been instrumental in framing discussions around marriage equality and transgender rights, respectively. These frames not only raise awareness but also shape the narratives surrounding LGBTQ issues in broader societal contexts.

Challenges of Social Media Activism

While social media offers numerous advantages, it also presents significant challenges.

Misinformation and Disinformation are rampant on social media platforms, often undermining the credibility of LGBTQ advocacy. False narratives can spread quickly, leading to public confusion and backlash against the community. Activists must continually combat misinformation with factual information and credible sources.

Online Harassment and Hate Speech are pervasive issues that LGBTQ activists face on social media. The anonymity afforded by these platforms can embolden individuals to engage in bullying, threats, and harassment. This not only poses a risk to the mental health and safety of activists but can also deter individuals from participating in online advocacy.

The Digital Divide is another barrier, as not all individuals have equal access to technology and the internet. This inequity can marginalize certain voices within the LGBTQ community, particularly those from lower socioeconomic backgrounds or rural areas, limiting the diversity of perspectives in online activism.

Examples of Social Media in Action

Despite these challenges, the effectiveness of social media in LGBTQ activism is evident through various campaigns and movements.

The Ice Bucket Challenge of 2014 is a prime example of how social media can mobilize millions for a cause. While primarily aimed at raising awareness for ALS, the challenge also intersected with LGBTQ activism by highlighting the importance of funding for diseases that disproportionately affect the LGBTQ community. Participants shared videos of themselves pouring ice water over their heads, tagging friends to do the same, and donating to the cause, creating a viral phenomenon that raised over $115 million.

The **#BlackLivesMatter Movement** has also seen significant support from LGBTQ activists, who use social media to draw attention to the intersectionality of race and sexuality. The hashtag became a rallying cry for both racial justice and LGBTQ rights, showcasing how social media can unite various movements under a common goal. Activists have shared personal stories, organized protests, and raised funds for organizations that support marginalized communities.

The **#TransDayOfVisibility** campaign is another notable example. Each year, on March 31, individuals and organizations use social media to celebrate transgender lives and raise awareness about the challenges faced by the transgender community. This campaign has fostered a sense of community and visibility, encouraging individuals to share their stories and advocate for trans rights.

Conclusion

In conclusion, social media plays a crucial role in LGBTQ activism, providing a platform for connection, mobilization, and advocacy. While challenges such as misinformation, harassment, and the digital divide persist, the potential for social media to effect change is undeniable. As LGBTQ activists continue to harness the power of social media, they pave the way for a more inclusive and equitable society. The ongoing evolution of these platforms will undoubtedly shape the future of LGBTQ rights advocacy, creating new opportunities for engagement and empowerment.

Building Coalitions and Alliances

In the pursuit of LGBTQ rights, the importance of building coalitions and alliances cannot be overstated. The concept of coalition-building is rooted in the understanding that collective action amplifies voices, increases visibility, and enhances the capacity to effect change. This subsection explores the theoretical foundations, challenges, and practical examples of successful coalitions in the LGBTQ rights movement.

Theoretical Foundations

Coalition-building is grounded in several theoretical frameworks, including social movement theory, intersectionality, and collective identity. Social movement theory posits that social movements arise when individuals come together to pursue shared goals. As Charles Tilly notes, movements are not merely collections of individuals but organized efforts to challenge existing power structures [1].

Intersectionality, coined by Kimberlé Crenshaw, emphasizes the interconnectedness of social identities and how they shape experiences of oppression and privilege [2]. This framework is crucial in LGBTQ activism, as it recognizes that individuals may face multiple forms of discrimination based on race, gender, socioeconomic status, and sexual orientation.

Collective identity refers to the shared sense of belonging among individuals within a movement, fostering solidarity and mutual support. As sociologist David Snow explains, collective identity is essential for mobilizing resources and sustaining activism [3].

Challenges in Coalition-Building

Despite the theoretical advantages of coalition-building, several challenges persist. One significant issue is the potential for conflict among diverse groups. Different organizations may have varying priorities, resources, and strategies, leading to tensions that can undermine collaboration. For instance, a coalition formed to advocate for LGBTQ rights may include groups focused on racial justice, women's rights, or immigration reform, each with distinct agendas that may not always align.

Additionally, power dynamics within coalitions can create imbalances. Dominant groups may inadvertently overshadow the voices of marginalized members, leading to a lack of representation and inclusivity. This can result in feelings of alienation and disengagement among those who feel their issues are not adequately addressed.

Examples of Successful Coalitions

Despite these challenges, numerous successful coalitions have emerged within the LGBTQ rights movement. One prominent example is the formation of the *United Coalition of LGBTQ Organizations*, which brought together various advocacy groups to address issues such as marriage equality, anti-discrimination laws, and healthcare access. By pooling resources and expertise, the coalition was able to launch a comprehensive campaign that resulted in significant legislative victories.

Another noteworthy example is the *LGBTQ+ People of Color Coalition*, which specifically addresses the unique challenges faced by LGBTQ individuals of color. This coalition emphasizes the importance of intersectionality in advocacy efforts and works to elevate the voices of those who are often marginalized within the broader LGBTQ movement.

Strategies for Effective Coalition-Building

To build effective coalitions, several strategies can be employed:

+ **Establishing Clear Goals:** It is essential for coalition members to agree on shared objectives and outcomes. This clarity helps to unify efforts and maintain focus.

+ **Fostering Open Communication:** Regular communication among coalition members encourages transparency, trust, and collaboration. Utilizing digital platforms can facilitate ongoing dialogue and information sharing.

+ **Promoting Inclusivity:** Ensuring that all voices are heard and valued is crucial. This can be achieved through intentional outreach to underrepresented groups and creating spaces for diverse perspectives.

+ **Building Capacity:** Providing training and resources to coalition members enhances their skills and effectiveness, enabling them to contribute meaningfully to collective efforts.

+ **Celebrating Successes:** Acknowledging and celebrating achievements, no matter how small, fosters a sense of community and motivates continued engagement.

Conclusion

Building coalitions and alliances is a vital component of the LGBTQ rights movement, enabling activists to unite their efforts and amplify their impact. By understanding the theoretical foundations, addressing challenges, and employing effective strategies, coalitions can create a powerful force for change. As Victor M. Maceda exemplifies through his work, the strength of collective action lies in its ability to transcend individual struggles and forge a path toward a more inclusive and equitable society.

Bibliography

[1] Tilly, C. (2004). *Social Movements, 1760-2000*. Paradigm Publishers.

[2] Crenshaw, K. (1989). Demarginalizing the Intersection of Race and Sex: A Black Feminist Critique of Antidiscrimination Doctrine, Feminist Theory and Antiracist Politics. *University of Chicago Legal Forum*, 1989(1), 139-167.

[3] Snow, D. A. (2000). Collective Identity and Expressive Forms. In *Social Movements: Identity, Culture, and the State* (pp. 21-46). Cambridge University Press.

Solidarity with Other Marginalized Communities

The fight for LGBTQ rights is not an isolated struggle; it is intricately linked to the broader movements for justice and equality across various marginalized communities. Solidarity among these groups is crucial for fostering a more inclusive society and amplifying the voices of those who are often silenced. This section explores the importance of solidarity, the challenges faced in creating alliances, and the powerful outcomes that can arise when marginalized communities unite.

Theoretical Framework of Solidarity

Solidarity, as a concept, can be understood through various theoretical lenses. One prominent framework is the idea of intersectionality, coined by Kimberlé Crenshaw in 1989. Intersectionality posits that individuals experience oppression in varying configurations and degrees of intensity based on their overlapping identities, such as race, gender, sexuality, and socioeconomic status. This theory highlights that the struggles faced by LGBTQ individuals are often compounded by other forms of discrimination, making solidarity with other marginalized groups essential for effective advocacy.

From a sociological perspective, the social movement theory provides insights into how collective action can emerge from shared grievances among different groups. According to Charles Tilly, social movements are organized efforts to promote or resist change, often characterized by a shared identity and collective action. By recognizing common goals and experiences, marginalized communities can mobilize together, creating a stronger front against systemic oppression.

Challenges to Solidarity

Despite the clear benefits of solidarity, several challenges hinder the formation of alliances among marginalized communities. One significant barrier is the tendency for groups to prioritize their specific issues over others, leading to competition for resources and attention. For instance, LGBTQ organizations may focus on issues like marriage equality and anti-discrimination laws, while communities of color might emphasize police violence and economic inequality. This can create tensions and misunderstandings, as groups may perceive each other as detracting from their respective causes.

Additionally, historical divisions and mistrust can complicate solidarity efforts. For example, the LGBTQ community has not always been inclusive of people of color, leading to feelings of alienation among those who identify with multiple marginalized identities. The legacy of such divisions can perpetuate cycles of exclusion and hinder collaborative efforts.

Examples of Successful Solidarity

Despite these challenges, numerous examples illustrate the power of solidarity among marginalized communities. One notable instance is the collaboration between LGBTQ activists and Black Lives Matter (BLM) during protests against police violence. The intersection of these movements emphasizes the shared struggle against systemic racism and homophobia. Activists from both groups have worked together to address issues such as the disproportionate violence faced by Black LGBTQ individuals, highlighting the need for comprehensive reforms that consider the unique experiences of intersectional identities.

Another example is the participation of LGBTQ organizations in the fight for immigrant rights. As many LGBTQ individuals seek asylum from countries where they face persecution, advocates have joined forces with immigrant rights groups to demand humane immigration policies. This collaboration not only addresses the specific needs of LGBTQ asylum seekers but also contributes to the broader movement for immigrant justice, demonstrating how solidarity can lead to mutual benefits.

The Role of Intersectional Activism

Intersectional activism plays a pivotal role in fostering solidarity among marginalized communities. By acknowledging the interconnectedness of various struggles, activists can work towards inclusive solutions that address multiple forms of oppression. For instance, campaigns that advocate for comprehensive anti-discrimination laws often highlight the importance of including protections for race, gender identity, sexual orientation, and disability status. This holistic approach ensures that the needs of all marginalized groups are considered, promoting a more equitable society.

Moreover, intersectional activism encourages the sharing of resources and knowledge among different communities. Workshops, seminars, and collaborative projects can facilitate dialogue and understanding, allowing activists to learn from each other's experiences and strategies. This exchange of ideas can lead to innovative solutions that address the root causes of oppression, ultimately strengthening the impact of advocacy efforts.

Conclusion

In conclusion, solidarity with other marginalized communities is essential for advancing the fight for LGBTQ rights. By recognizing the interconnected nature of oppression and embracing intersectional activism, advocates can create a more inclusive and equitable society. While challenges to solidarity exist, the examples of successful collaborations serve as powerful reminders of the potential for collective action. As Victor M. Maceda and other activists continue to champion LGBTQ rights, fostering alliances with other marginalized groups will be crucial for achieving lasting change. Together, these movements can dismantle systemic barriers and pave the way for a future where all individuals can live freely and authentically, regardless of their identity.

Strategies for Effecting Change

In the realm of LGBTQ activism, effecting change requires a multifaceted approach that integrates grassroots mobilization, strategic advocacy, and coalition-building. This section outlines several key strategies that have proven effective in promoting LGBTQ rights and fostering societal acceptance.

1. Grassroots Mobilization

Grassroots mobilization serves as the backbone of any successful social movement. It involves rallying individuals at the community level to raise awareness, share personal stories, and advocate for change. The success of events like Pride parades and local advocacy campaigns can be attributed to the enthusiasm and dedication of grassroots organizers.

$$\text{Mobilization Effectiveness} = \frac{\text{Community Engagement}}{\text{Resource Allocation}} \tag{18}$$

In this equation, Community Engagement represents the number of individuals actively participating in advocacy efforts, while Resource Allocation refers to the financial and logistical support provided to these initiatives. A higher ratio indicates a more effective mobilization strategy, leading to increased visibility and impact.

2. Strategic Advocacy

Strategic advocacy involves targeted efforts to influence policymakers and public opinion. This can include lobbying for specific legislative changes, organizing letter-writing campaigns, and engaging in public discourse through social media platforms.

An example of effective strategic advocacy is the push for marriage equality in the United States, which involved coordinated efforts by organizations such as the Human Rights Campaign (HRC) and Freedom to Marry. By leveraging personal stories and data-driven arguments, these groups were able to sway public opinion and ultimately influence legislative changes.

3. Coalition-Building

Building coalitions with other marginalized groups amplifies the voice of the LGBTQ community and fosters solidarity. Intersectional advocacy recognizes that issues such as race, gender, and economic status intersect with sexual orientation and gender identity.

For instance, the collaboration between LGBTQ activists and racial justice organizations during the Black Lives Matter movement highlighted the shared struggles against systemic oppression. By working together, these groups were able to create a more inclusive narrative that resonated with a broader audience.

4. Utilizing Digital Platforms

In the digital age, social media serves as a powerful tool for activism. Platforms like Twitter, Instagram, and Facebook allow activists to reach a global audience, share information quickly, and mobilize support for various causes.

One notable example is the #LoveIsLove campaign, which went viral following the Supreme Court's decision to legalize same-sex marriage in 2015. The widespread sharing of images and messages of love not only celebrated the victory but also reinforced the importance of LGBTQ rights in the public consciousness.

5. Education and Awareness

Educating the public about LGBTQ issues is crucial for fostering understanding and acceptance. This can be achieved through workshops, seminars, and educational materials that address common misconceptions and highlight the contributions of LGBTQ individuals to society.

Research indicates that increased awareness leads to greater acceptance. A study conducted by the Williams Institute found that individuals who receive education on LGBTQ issues are more likely to support anti-discrimination policies and demonstrate inclusive behavior.

6. Measuring Impact

To ensure the effectiveness of advocacy efforts, it is essential to measure their impact. This can be done through surveys, feedback from community members, and tracking changes in public policy.

For example, the success of anti-discrimination laws can be evaluated by analyzing reports of discrimination before and after the implementation of such policies. By continuously assessing the outcomes of advocacy efforts, activists can refine their strategies and ensure they are meeting the needs of the community.

Conclusion

The strategies outlined in this section highlight the importance of a comprehensive approach to effecting change in the LGBTQ rights movement. By mobilizing grassroots support, engaging in strategic advocacy, building coalitions, utilizing digital platforms, educating the public, and measuring impact, activists can create a more equitable and inclusive society for all. The journey towards equality is ongoing, but with these strategies, the LGBTQ community can continue to make significant strides in the fight for justice and acceptance.

Fighting for Legislative Reform

Lobbying for LGBTQ-Inclusive Laws

Lobbying for LGBTQ-inclusive laws is a vital aspect of the broader struggle for equality and justice within the LGBTQ community. This subsection explores the theoretical underpinnings, the challenges faced, and practical examples of successful lobbying efforts that have led to significant legislative changes.

Theoretical Framework

The theory of advocacy in the context of LGBTQ rights is grounded in several key principles. One foundational theory is *social justice*, which posits that all individuals deserve equal rights and opportunities regardless of their sexual orientation or gender identity. This theory is complemented by *intersectionality*, which recognizes that individuals experience overlapping systems of discrimination and privilege. Intersectionality emphasizes the importance of addressing the unique challenges faced by LGBTQ individuals who also belong to other marginalized groups, such as people of color, immigrants, and those with disabilities.

Moreover, the *public choice theory* can be applied to understand the dynamics of lobbying. This theory suggests that individuals and groups engage in lobbying to influence legislation in their favor, often driven by self-interest. In the context of LGBTQ rights, this self-interest is not merely personal; it reflects the collective desire for societal change and the dismantling of systemic discrimination.

Challenges in Lobbying

Despite the theoretical foundation supporting LGBTQ-inclusive laws, activists encounter numerous challenges in the lobbying process:

1. **Political Resistance**: Many lawmakers and political entities may oppose LGBTQ rights due to conservative ideologies or pressure from their constituents. This resistance can stall or completely block legislative initiatives aimed at promoting equality.

2. **Lack of Awareness**: A significant barrier to successful lobbying is the general public's lack of awareness regarding LGBTQ issues. Misunderstandings and stereotypes can hinder support for inclusive laws, making it essential for activists to engage in educational campaigns.

3. **Resource Constraints**: LGBTQ advocacy organizations often operate with limited financial and human resources. This constraint can restrict their ability to mount large-scale lobbying efforts or sustain long-term campaigns.

4. **Fragmentation within the Movement**: The LGBTQ community is diverse, encompassing a wide range of identities and experiences. This diversity, while a strength, can also lead to fragmentation, where different groups prioritize different issues, complicating unified lobbying efforts.

Successful Examples of Lobbying Efforts

1. **Marriage Equality**: One of the most prominent examples of successful lobbying for LGBTQ-inclusive laws is the campaign for marriage equality in the United States. Activists utilized a multi-faceted approach, combining grassroots organizing, media advocacy, and legal challenges. Organizations like the Human Rights Campaign (HRC) mobilized supporters to lobby legislators, while high-profile cases, such as *Obergefell v. Hodges*, brought national attention to the issue. The culmination of these efforts resulted in the Supreme Court's landmark decision in 2015, which legalized same-sex marriage nationwide.

2. **Employment Non-Discrimination Act (ENDA)**: Although ENDA has not yet been passed as a federal law, lobbying efforts surrounding this legislation have significantly raised awareness about workplace discrimination against LGBTQ individuals. Advocacy groups organized campaigns to gather support from businesses and the general public, highlighting the economic benefits of inclusive workplaces. Although ENDA has faced setbacks, the ongoing efforts have led to the implementation of non-discrimination policies in various states and cities.

3. **Transgender Rights Legislation**: In recent years, lobbying efforts have increasingly focused on the rights of transgender individuals. Organizations such as the National Center for Transgender Equality (NCTE) have worked tirelessly to advocate for laws that protect transgender people from discrimination in areas such as healthcare, housing, and public accommodations. The successful passage of laws in states like California and Illinois, which provide comprehensive protections for transgender individuals, exemplifies the impact of sustained lobbying efforts.

Strategies for Effective Lobbying

To overcome challenges and enhance the effectiveness of lobbying for LGBTQ-inclusive laws, activists can employ several strategies:

1. **Building Coalitions**: Forming coalitions with other marginalized groups can amplify voices and create a broader base of support. Collaborative efforts can lead to more comprehensive legislation that addresses the needs of multiple communities.

2. **Utilizing Data and Research**: Presenting data and research that highlight the social and economic benefits of LGBTQ-inclusive laws can persuade lawmakers and the public to support these initiatives. Studies demonstrating the positive impact of inclusive policies on mental health and economic productivity can be particularly compelling.

3. **Engaging in Grassroots Mobilization**: Mobilizing community members to contact their representatives, participate in rallies, and share personal stories can create a groundswell of support. Grassroots efforts can humanize the issues at stake and demonstrate the widespread demand for change.

4. **Leveraging Media and Social Media**: Utilizing traditional media outlets and social media platforms to raise awareness and generate public discourse around LGBTQ issues can significantly influence public opinion and, consequently, legislative action. Campaigns that go viral can attract national attention and pressure lawmakers to act.

5. **Targeting Key Legislators**: Identifying and targeting specific legislators who have the power to influence LGBTQ-inclusive laws is crucial. Building relationships with these lawmakers and their staff can facilitate discussions and increase the likelihood of legislative support.

In conclusion, lobbying for LGBTQ-inclusive laws is a complex yet essential component of the fight for equality. By understanding the theoretical frameworks, acknowledging the challenges, and employing effective strategies, activists can work towards creating a more inclusive society. The successes achieved thus far serve as a testament to the power of advocacy and the ongoing need for vigilance and determination in the pursuit of justice for all.

Achieving Marriage Equality

The quest for marriage equality has been a pivotal aspect of the LGBTQ rights movement, symbolizing not just the legal recognition of same-sex relationships but also the broader fight for dignity, respect, and equality under the law. The journey toward achieving marriage equality has been marked by significant milestones, legal battles, and cultural shifts that reflect the changing attitudes toward LGBTQ individuals in society.

Theoretical Framework

At its core, marriage equality is grounded in the principles of human rights and social justice. The theory of equality posits that all individuals, regardless of sexual orientation, should have the same legal rights and protections. This aligns with the concept of *equal protection under the law*, which is enshrined in various human rights instruments, including the Universal Declaration of Human Rights (UDHR). Article 16 of the UDHR states that "men and women of full age, without any limitation due to race, nationality or religion, have the right to marry and to found a family." This foundational principle has been a rallying cry for activists advocating for the recognition of same-sex marriages.

Historical Context

The fight for marriage equality gained momentum in the late 20th century, particularly following the Stonewall riots of 1969, which catalyzed the modern LGBTQ rights movement. In the early 2000s, several jurisdictions began to recognize same-sex marriages, notably the Netherlands, which became the first country to legalize same-sex marriage in 2001. This landmark decision set a precedent that inspired activists worldwide.

In the United States, the path to marriage equality was fraught with legal challenges and societal opposition. The Defense of Marriage Act (DOMA), enacted in 1996, defined marriage as a union between one man and one woman, effectively barring federal recognition of same-sex marriages. However, activists and legal advocates began to challenge this law, arguing that it violated the constitutional rights of LGBTQ individuals.

Legal Battles and Key Cases

A series of landmark court cases played a crucial role in the fight for marriage equality. One of the most significant cases was *Obergefell v. Hodges* (2015), which consolidated several challenges to state bans on same-sex marriage. The Supreme Court's decision in this case was a watershed moment, as it ruled that same-sex couples have a constitutional right to marry, thus invalidating state-level bans across the country.

The ruling was grounded in the principles of due process and equal protection, affirming that the right to marry is a fundamental liberty inherent in the concept of individual autonomy. The majority opinion, authored by Justice Anthony Kennedy, eloquently stated that "the right to marry is a fundamental right inherent in the liberty of the person." This decision not only legalized same-sex marriage nationwide but also marked a significant cultural shift in the acceptance of LGBTQ relationships.

Challenges and Opposition

Despite the progress made, the journey toward marriage equality has not been without its challenges. Opposition to same-sex marriage often stemmed from deeply ingrained societal beliefs, religious convictions, and political agendas. Many opponents argued that marriage should be defined exclusively as a heterosexual institution, invoking traditionalist views that resist change.

Moreover, even after the legalization of same-sex marriage, LGBTQ individuals continued to face discrimination and stigma. The ruling did not eliminate all forms of inequality, as many states enacted laws that allowed for discrimination based on sexual orientation or gender identity under the guise of religious freedom. This ongoing struggle highlights the need for comprehensive LGBTQ rights protections beyond marriage equality.

Cultural Impact and Social Change

The legalization of same-sex marriage has had profound cultural implications, normalizing LGBTQ relationships and fostering greater acceptance in society. Public opinion has shifted dramatically over the past few decades, with a majority of Americans now supporting marriage equality. This change can be attributed to increased visibility of LGBTQ individuals in media, advocacy efforts, and personal stories that humanize the struggle for equality.

Marriage equality has also served as a catalyst for broader discussions about LGBTQ rights, including issues related to parenting, adoption, and healthcare access. The recognition of same-sex marriages has allowed many couples to build families, further challenging stereotypes and misconceptions about LGBTQ individuals.

Conclusion

Achieving marriage equality represents a significant victory in the ongoing fight for LGBTQ rights. It is a testament to the resilience and determination of activists who have fought tirelessly for recognition and respect. While the legalization of same-sex marriage is a monumental step forward, it is essential to continue advocating for comprehensive protections and equality for all LGBTQ individuals. The journey does not end with marriage equality; it is merely one chapter in the broader narrative of justice and human rights.

In summary, the struggle for marriage equality has been a multifaceted endeavor encompassing theoretical frameworks, historical contexts, legal battles, and cultural shifts. As we reflect on this journey, it is crucial to recognize the work that remains to ensure that all individuals, regardless of their sexual orientation, can enjoy the same rights and freedoms as their heterosexual counterparts. The fight for LGBTQ rights continues, and the legacy of marriage equality will serve as a beacon of hope and inspiration for future generations of activists.

Challenges and Triumphs in Employment Equality

The pursuit of employment equality for LGBTQ individuals has been a tumultuous journey, marked by significant challenges and remarkable triumphs. As society gradually shifts towards greater acceptance and inclusivity, understanding the complexities of this evolution is crucial. This section delves into the theoretical frameworks surrounding employment equality, the persistent problems faced by LGBTQ workers, and the triumphs that have emerged from advocacy and policy changes.

Theoretical Frameworks

To comprehend the dynamics of employment equality, it is essential to consider several theoretical frameworks. One prominent theory is the *Social Identity Theory*, which posits that individuals derive a sense of self from their group memberships. For LGBTQ individuals, this identity can lead to both empowerment and discrimination in the workplace. The *Intersectionality Theory*, introduced by Kimberlé Crenshaw, further elucidates how overlapping identities—such as race, gender, and sexual orientation—interact to create unique experiences of discrimination. These frameworks help contextualize the struggles faced by LGBTQ employees and highlight the need for nuanced approaches to advocacy.

Persistent Challenges

Despite advancements in LGBTQ rights, numerous challenges persist in the realm of employment equality. A significant issue is the lack of comprehensive federal protections against workplace discrimination. In the United States, while the Supreme Court's decision in *Bostock v. Clayton County* (2020) affirmed that Title VII of the Civil Rights Act protects employees from discrimination based on sexual orientation and gender identity, many states still lack explicit anti-discrimination laws. This legal ambiguity leaves LGBTQ individuals vulnerable to discrimination, harassment, and wrongful termination.

Moreover, societal stigma continues to play a pivotal role in the workplace. Many LGBTQ employees report experiencing microaggressions, which are subtle, often unintentional, discriminatory comments or behaviors. These microaggressions can create a hostile work environment, leading to decreased job satisfaction and increased turnover rates. A study conducted by the *Williams Institute* found that LGBTQ employees are more likely to experience harassment and discrimination compared to their heterosexual counterparts, illustrating the pervasive nature of these challenges.

Triumphs in Advocacy

In response to these challenges, advocacy efforts have yielded significant triumphs in employment equality. Organizations such as the *Human Rights Campaign* and *GLAAD* have been at the forefront of promoting LGBTQ rights in the workplace. Their campaigns have raised awareness about discrimination and have pushed for legislative changes that protect LGBTQ employees.

One notable success is the implementation of the *Equality Act*, which, if passed, would provide comprehensive federal protections against discrimination based on sexual orientation and gender identity in various areas, including employment, housing, and public accommodations. Although the act has faced legislative hurdles, its introduction has sparked important conversations about the need for equality and inclusivity in the workplace.

Additionally, many companies have adopted inclusive policies and practices to foster diverse work environments. Organizations like *Salesforce* and *Google* have implemented training programs on LGBTQ inclusivity, established employee resource groups, and committed to equitable hiring practices. These initiatives not only enhance workplace culture but also serve as models for other organizations striving for inclusivity.

Case Studies

Examining specific case studies highlights the impact of advocacy on employment equality. For instance, the *Walmart* case exemplifies both challenges and triumphs. In 2008, Walmart faced a lawsuit for allegedly discriminating against LGBTQ employees. The company responded by implementing new policies aimed at promoting diversity and inclusion. As a result, Walmart has since been recognized for its efforts to create a more inclusive workplace, demonstrating that corporate accountability can lead to positive change.

Another powerful example is the *LGBTQ+ Workplace Inclusion Initiative* launched by the *National LGBTQ Chamber of Commerce*. This initiative aims to educate businesses about the benefits of inclusive practices and provide resources for creating equitable workplaces. By fostering partnerships between LGBTQ organizations and corporate entities, the initiative has successfully influenced numerous companies to adopt inclusive policies, contributing to a broader movement towards employment equality.

Conclusion

In conclusion, the journey towards employment equality for LGBTQ individuals is fraught with challenges, yet marked by significant triumphs. Through the lens of theoretical frameworks, we can better understand the complexities of discrimination and the importance of intersectionality. While persistent challenges, such as legal ambiguities and societal stigma, continue to affect LGBTQ workers, advocacy efforts and corporate initiatives have made strides towards creating more inclusive workplaces. As we move forward, it is imperative to sustain these efforts, ensuring that employment equality becomes a reality for all individuals, regardless of their sexual orientation or gender identity.

$$Employment\ Equality = Legal\ Protections + Inclusive\ Policies + Societal\ Acceptance \tag{19}$$

Protecting LGBTQ Youth and Students

The protection of LGBTQ youth and students is not merely an act of kindness; it is a fundamental human right that is intricately tied to the principles of equality, dignity, and respect. In contemporary society, LGBTQ youth face a myriad of challenges that can adversely affect their mental, emotional, and physical well-being. These challenges stem from systemic discrimination, societal stigma, and a lack of adequate support systems within educational institutions.

Theoretical Framework

To understand the necessity of protecting LGBTQ youth, we can draw upon several theoretical frameworks. One such framework is the *Social Ecological Model*, which posits that individual behavior is influenced by multiple levels of factors, including personal, interpersonal, community, and societal influences. This model emphasizes the importance of a supportive environment in fostering the well-being of LGBTQ youth.

Additionally, the *Minority Stress Theory* provides insight into the unique stressors faced by LGBTQ individuals. According to this theory, LGBTQ youth experience chronic stress due to their marginalized status, which can lead to negative mental health outcomes. This stress is compounded by the lack of acceptance from peers and family, as well as discrimination in educational settings.

Challenges Faced by LGBTQ Youth

LGBTQ youth are often subjected to bullying, harassment, and discrimination in schools. According to the *2019 National School Climate Survey* conducted by GLSEN, nearly 60% of LGBTQ students felt unsafe at school because of their sexual orientation, and over 40% reported being bullied. These experiences can lead to serious consequences, including depression, anxiety, and even suicidal ideation.

Moreover, LGBTQ youth frequently encounter a lack of representation and inclusivity in educational curricula. This absence of representation can lead to feelings of isolation and alienation, as students do not see themselves reflected in the materials they study. The lack of supportive policies and resources further exacerbates these issues, leaving LGBTQ youth vulnerable and unprotected.

Strategies for Protection

To effectively protect LGBTQ youth and students, several strategies can be implemented:

- **Implementing Comprehensive Anti-Bullying Policies:** Schools should adopt inclusive anti-bullying policies that specifically address harassment based on sexual orientation and gender identity. These policies must be enforced consistently to create a safe environment for all students.

- **Providing LGBTQ-Inclusive Curriculum:** Educational institutions should integrate LGBTQ history and issues into their curricula. This inclusion not only educates all students about diversity but also affirms the identities of LGBTQ youth.

- **Establishing Support Systems:** Schools should create support groups and resources for LGBTQ students, such as Gay-Straight Alliances (GSAs), counseling services, and mentorship programs. These initiatives provide safe spaces for students to express themselves and seek guidance.

- **Training for Educators and Staff:** Professional development programs should be implemented to educate teachers and staff about LGBTQ issues, fostering a more inclusive and supportive school environment. Training should cover topics such as recognizing and addressing bias, understanding the unique challenges faced by LGBTQ students, and promoting allyship.

+ **Engaging Families and Communities:** Schools should actively engage families and communities in discussions about LGBTQ issues. This engagement can help create a supportive network for LGBTQ youth outside of school, reinforcing the message that they are valued and accepted.

Successful Examples

Several schools and districts have successfully implemented policies and programs that protect LGBTQ youth. For instance, the *Los Angeles Unified School District* has adopted a comprehensive LGBTQ-inclusive curriculum and has established numerous GSAs across its schools. This initiative has led to a significant decrease in reported bullying incidents and has fostered a more inclusive school culture.

Another example is the *Chicago Public Schools*, which has implemented training programs for educators focusing on LGBTQ issues. This training has empowered teachers to create safer classrooms and to advocate for their LGBTQ students more effectively.

Conclusion

Protecting LGBTQ youth and students is a critical component of advancing LGBTQ rights and ensuring that all individuals can thrive in educational settings. By implementing inclusive policies, fostering supportive environments, and providing necessary resources, we can create a future where LGBTQ youth feel safe, valued, and empowered to express their true selves. The fight for equality extends beyond legislation; it requires a concerted effort to protect the most vulnerable among us, ensuring that every student, regardless of their sexual orientation or gender identity, has the opportunity to succeed and flourish in a supportive educational environment.

The Ongoing Battle for Transgender Rights

The ongoing battle for transgender rights is a critical aspect of the broader LGBTQ rights movement. While significant progress has been made in recent years, transgender individuals continue to face unique challenges that require persistent advocacy and strategic action. This section explores the theoretical frameworks surrounding transgender rights, the problems faced by transgender individuals, and notable examples of activism and legislative efforts that illustrate the ongoing struggle for equality.

Theoretical Frameworks

Understanding the ongoing battle for transgender rights requires a grasp of several theoretical frameworks. One prominent theory is Judith Butler's concept of gender performativity, which posits that gender is not an inherent quality but rather a series of actions and behaviors that are socially constructed and performed. This perspective challenges the binary understanding of gender and opens the door for recognizing the complexities of transgender identities.

Moreover, intersectionality, a term coined by Kimberlé Crenshaw, is essential for analyzing how various forms of discrimination overlap. Transgender individuals often face compounded challenges due to intersecting identities, such as race, socioeconomic status, and disability. This theory emphasizes the need for a nuanced approach to advocacy that considers these intersections.

Current Problems Faced by Transgender Individuals

Despite advancements in rights and visibility, transgender individuals face numerous systemic and societal issues:

- **Discrimination and Stigma:** Transgender individuals frequently encounter discrimination in various settings, including healthcare, employment, and education. A 2021 survey by the National Center for Transgender Equality revealed that 29% of respondents experienced discrimination in employment, while 23% reported being denied medical care.

- **Violence and Hate Crimes:** Transgender individuals, particularly transgender women of color, are disproportionately affected by violence. The Human Rights Campaign reported that at least 44 transgender or gender non-conforming individuals were violently killed in the U.S. in 2020, marking one of the deadliest years on record.

- **Legal Barriers:** Many transgender individuals face challenges in changing their legal documents to reflect their gender identity. Inconsistent state laws and bureaucratic hurdles can create significant barriers, resulting in misidentification and further discrimination.

- **Healthcare Access:** Transgender individuals often encounter difficulties accessing appropriate healthcare, including gender-affirming treatments.

Insurance coverage for these services remains inconsistent, and healthcare providers may lack cultural competency, leading to inadequate care.

Examples of Activism and Legislative Efforts

The fight for transgender rights has seen numerous activists and organizations working tirelessly to address these issues. Notable examples include:

- **Transgender Day of Remembrance (TDOR):** Established in 1999, TDOR is an annual observance honoring the memory of transgender individuals who have lost their lives due to anti-transgender violence. This event serves to raise awareness of the violence faced by the transgender community and advocates for policy changes to protect their rights.

- **The Equality Act:** Introduced in Congress, the Equality Act aims to provide comprehensive protections against discrimination based on sexual orientation and gender identity. While it has faced significant opposition, its introduction has galvanized support for transgender rights and highlighted the need for federal protections.

- **Local and State-Level Reforms:** Various states have enacted laws to protect transgender rights, such as prohibiting discrimination in employment and housing. For example, California's Gender Recognition Act allows individuals to select a non-binary gender option on state identification documents, reflecting a growing recognition of non-binary identities.

- **Grassroots Movements:** Organizations like the Transgender Law Center and GLAAD have been at the forefront of advocacy efforts. They provide resources, legal support, and community engagement to empower transgender individuals and challenge discriminatory practices.

Conclusion

The ongoing battle for transgender rights is far from over. As societal attitudes evolve and advocacy efforts continue, it is crucial to recognize the unique challenges faced by transgender individuals and the importance of intersectional approaches in activism. The fight for equality encompasses not only legal protections but also societal acceptance and understanding. By amplifying the voices of transgender individuals and fostering inclusive environments, we can work toward a future where all individuals, regardless of their gender identity, are afforded the dignity and respect they deserve.

The struggle for transgender rights is emblematic of the broader quest for justice and equality within the LGBTQ community. It serves as a reminder that while progress has been made, vigilance and advocacy remain essential in the face of ongoing discrimination and violence. As we move forward, it is imperative to continue supporting transgender individuals and advocating for comprehensive rights that affirm their identities and experiences.

Global Impact of LGBTQ Advocacy

Supporting LGBTQ Activists Worldwide

The fight for LGBTQ rights transcends borders, as activists around the globe confront unique challenges rooted in their cultural, political, and social contexts. Supporting LGBTQ activists worldwide is not merely an act of solidarity; it is a crucial strategy for fostering a united front against discrimination, violence, and injustice. This section delves into the theoretical foundations, the multifaceted problems faced by LGBTQ activists globally, and notable examples of successful support initiatives.

Theoretical Foundations

The concept of global solidarity in LGBTQ activism can be understood through the lens of *intersectionality*, as proposed by Kimberlé Crenshaw. Intersectionality emphasizes the interconnected nature of social categorizations such as race, class, and gender, which create overlapping systems of discrimination or disadvantage. In the context of LGBTQ activism, this theory underscores the importance of recognizing how various factors—such as nationality, ethnicity, and socioeconomic status—impact the experiences of LGBTQ individuals.

Furthermore, the *social movement theory* provides insight into the dynamics of collective action. According to Charles Tilly, social movements arise in response to grievances and mobilize resources to effect change. LGBTQ activists worldwide often find themselves at the intersection of local issues and global movements, necessitating a robust support system that can amplify their efforts and provide necessary resources.

Challenges Faced by LGBTQ Activists

LGBTQ activists across the globe encounter numerous challenges, including:

+ **Legal Barriers:** In many countries, LGBTQ individuals face criminalization and legal discrimination. For example, in countries like Uganda and Nigeria, anti-LGBTQ laws not only threaten individual safety but also hinder activists' ability to organize and advocate for change.

+ **Cultural Stigma:** Deeply ingrained cultural beliefs can perpetuate homophobia and transphobia, making it difficult for activists to gain community support. Activists in regions with strong traditional values often risk ostracization or violence for their advocacy.

+ **Resource Limitations:** Many LGBTQ organizations operate with limited funding and resources, which restricts their ability to mobilize effectively. This is particularly pronounced in low-income countries where access to international funding can be fraught with bureaucratic challenges.

+ **Safety Concerns:** Activists often face threats to their personal safety, including harassment, violence, and even murder. The murder of LGBTQ activists such as Marielle Franco in Brazil highlights the extreme risks faced by those advocating for rights in hostile environments.

Examples of Support Initiatives

To combat these challenges, various initiatives have emerged to support LGBTQ activists worldwide:

+ **Global Fund for LGBTQI+ People:** Established to provide financial resources to LGBTQ organizations in countries where activists face significant risks. This fund supports initiatives that promote health, legal advocacy, and community organizing.

+ **International LGBTQI+ Youth and Student Organisation (IGLYO):** This organization focuses on empowering LGBTQ youth through education and advocacy. By providing training and resources, IGLYO helps young activists develop the skills necessary to effect change in their communities.

+ **The Human Rights Campaign (HRC):** HRC has expanded its efforts beyond U.S. borders, partnering with international organizations to support LGBTQ rights. Their campaigns often include advocacy for global policy changes and the provision of legal assistance to activists facing persecution.

+ **OutRight Action International:** This organization works to document human rights violations against LGBTQ individuals globally. By collecting data and sharing personal stories, OutRight raises awareness and mobilizes international support for activists in oppressive regimes.

Conclusion

Supporting LGBTQ activists worldwide is essential for creating a more equitable and just society. By understanding the challenges they face and providing the necessary resources and solidarity, we can foster a global movement that transcends borders. As Victor M. Maceda's work exemplifies, the fight for LGBTQ rights is a collective struggle that requires unwavering commitment and collaboration across the globe. The future of LGBTQ activism hinges on our ability to unite, advocate, and support one another in the face of adversity.

Campaigning Against Anti-LGBTQ Laws

The fight against anti-LGBTQ laws is a critical aspect of the broader struggle for equality and justice within the LGBTQ community. These laws, which often seek to limit the rights and freedoms of LGBTQ individuals, can take various forms, including discriminatory marriage laws, restrictive adoption policies, and legislation that targets the rights of transgender individuals. Campaigning against such laws requires a multifaceted approach that combines legal advocacy, grassroots mobilization, and public education.

Understanding Anti-LGBTQ Legislation

Anti-LGBTQ laws are often rooted in historical prejudices and societal norms that view LGBTQ identities as deviant or immoral. For instance, laws that criminalize same-sex relationships or deny marriage rights to same-sex couples are often justified by appeals to tradition or religious beliefs. Such legislation not only harms individuals but also perpetuates a culture of discrimination and violence against LGBTQ people.

One prominent example of anti-LGBTQ legislation is the Defense of Marriage Act (DOMA), enacted in 1996 in the United States. DOMA defined marriage as a union between one man and one woman, effectively denying federal recognition to same-sex marriages. Although DOMA was struck down by the Supreme Court in 2013, its legacy continues to influence state-level laws that discriminate against LGBTQ individuals.

Theoretical Frameworks for Advocacy

To effectively campaign against anti-LGBTQ laws, activists often draw on various theoretical frameworks. One such framework is the *social justice theory*, which emphasizes the importance of equity and fairness in societal structures. This theory posits that all individuals, regardless of sexual orientation or gender identity, deserve equal rights and protections under the law.

Another relevant theory is *intersectionality*, which recognizes that individuals have multiple, overlapping identities that can impact their experiences of discrimination. For example, LGBTQ individuals who are also people of color may face compounded discrimination that requires targeted advocacy efforts. Understanding these intersections is crucial for crafting effective campaigns against anti-LGBTQ laws.

Strategies for Campaigning

Campaigning against anti-LGBTQ laws involves several strategic approaches:

+ **Legal Advocacy:** Legal organizations, such as the American Civil Liberties Union (ACLU) and Lambda Legal, play a vital role in challenging discriminatory laws through litigation. By filing lawsuits and advocating for policy changes, these organizations can help overturn harmful legislation. For instance, in 2020, the Supreme Court ruled in *Bostock v. Clayton County* that employment discrimination based on sexual orientation or gender identity violates Title VII of the Civil Rights Act, marking a significant victory for LGBTQ rights.

+ **Grassroots Mobilization:** Grassroots campaigns are essential for raising awareness and mobilizing community support against anti-LGBTQ laws. Organizing protests, rallies, and community forums can help galvanize public opposition and pressure lawmakers to reconsider discriminatory policies. The Women's March and various Pride events serve as powerful platforms for LGBTQ activism and solidarity.

+ **Public Education:** Educating the public about the harmful effects of anti-LGBTQ laws is crucial for changing hearts and minds. Campaigns that share personal stories of those affected by discrimination can humanize the issue and foster empathy. Initiatives like the *It Gets Better Project* provide uplifting narratives that counteract negative stereotypes and demonstrate the resilience of LGBTQ individuals.

+ **Coalition Building:** Collaborating with other marginalized groups can amplify the impact of campaigns against anti-LGBTQ laws. By building coalitions with organizations focused on racial justice, women's rights, and disability rights, LGBTQ activists can create a unified front against discrimination. This intersectional approach not only strengthens advocacy efforts but also fosters solidarity among diverse communities.

Challenges in Advocacy

Despite the progress made, campaigning against anti-LGBTQ laws presents numerous challenges. One significant obstacle is the political landscape, where anti-LGBTQ sentiments can be exploited for electoral gain. Politicians may introduce discriminatory legislation to rally their base, creating an environment where LGBTQ rights are continually under threat.

Moreover, misinformation and stigma surrounding LGBTQ identities can hinder advocacy efforts. False narratives about LGBTQ individuals being harmful to society or "immoral" can perpetuate fear and resistance to change. Combatting these narratives requires sustained public education and outreach efforts.

Case Studies of Successful Campaigns

Several successful campaigns have demonstrated the effectiveness of strategic advocacy against anti-LGBTQ laws:

+ **The Fight for Marriage Equality:** The campaign for marriage equality in the United States is a prime example of successful advocacy. Through a combination of legal challenges, grassroots mobilization, and public education, activists were able to shift public opinion and ultimately achieve a landmark victory with the Supreme Court's ruling in *Obergefell v. Hodges* in 2015, which legalized same-sex marriage nationwide.

+ **Transgender Rights Campaigns:** In recent years, campaigns advocating for transgender rights have gained momentum, particularly in response to discriminatory laws targeting transgender individuals. The #TransRightsAreHumanRights movement has mobilized activists across the country to challenge legislation that restricts access to healthcare, education, and public facilities for transgender individuals. Successful campaigns have led to the repeal of harmful laws in several states, showcasing the power of collective action.

✦ **International Advocacy:** Global campaigns against anti-LGBTQ laws have also made significant strides. Organizations like ILGA (International Lesbian, Gay, Bisexual, Trans and Intersex Association) work to support LGBTQ activists worldwide, advocating for the repeal of discriminatory laws and promoting human rights. The successful decriminalization of homosexuality in several countries, such as India in 2018, highlights the impact of international solidarity and advocacy.

Conclusion

Campaigning against anti-LGBTQ laws is an ongoing and essential aspect of the fight for equality and justice. By employing a combination of legal advocacy, grassroots mobilization, public education, and coalition building, activists can challenge discriminatory legislation and promote a more inclusive society. The journey is fraught with challenges, but the resilience and determination of LGBTQ advocates continue to inspire hope and drive change. As the fight progresses, it is crucial to remain vigilant and committed to protecting the rights of all individuals, regardless of their sexual orientation or gender identity.

International Collaboration for Change

International collaboration has emerged as a cornerstone in the fight for LGBTQ rights, as activists and organizations across borders unite to address shared challenges and advocate for systemic change. This collaboration is not merely a strategic advantage; it is a necessity in a world where LGBTQ individuals face persecution, discrimination, and violence in various forms. By pooling resources, knowledge, and experiences, activists can amplify their voices and create a more formidable front against oppression.

Theoretical Framework

The collaboration can be framed within the context of social movement theory, particularly the concepts of transnational activism and global civil society. Transnational activism refers to the ways in which social movements engage across national borders to influence policies and practices. This framework posits that local struggles are often interconnected with global dynamics, necessitating a collective response.

One relevant theoretical model is the *Resource Mobilization Theory*, which emphasizes the importance of resources—both material and non-material—in enabling movements to achieve their goals. Collaboration enhances resource mobilization by allowing organizations to share funding, expertise, and networks. This is particularly crucial for smaller organizations in developing countries that may lack the resources to advocate effectively on their own.

Challenges in International Collaboration

Despite the potential benefits, international collaboration is fraught with challenges. Cultural differences can lead to misunderstandings and conflicts over priorities and strategies. For example, LGBTQ rights in Western contexts may focus heavily on issues like marriage equality, while activists in regions facing severe criminalization may prioritize decriminalization and basic human rights.

Additionally, funding disparities can create power imbalances within collaborations. Larger, more established organizations often dominate discussions and decision-making processes, sidelining grassroots voices. This can lead to a phenomenon known as *neocolonialism*, where Western organizations impose their agendas on Global South movements, undermining local agency and context.

Examples of Successful Collaboration

One exemplary case of international collaboration is the *International Lesbian, Gay, Bisexual, Trans and Intersex Association (ILGA)*. Founded in 1978, ILGA has worked to unify LGBTQ organizations around the world, providing a platform for advocacy and sharing best practices. Through its annual conferences and regional meetings, ILGA facilitates dialogue and coordination among activists from diverse cultural backgrounds.

Another notable example is the *Global Equality Fund*, which supports initiatives aimed at advancing LGBTQ rights globally. The Fund exemplifies successful collaboration between governments, private sector partners, and civil society organizations. By leveraging resources from multiple stakeholders, the Fund has been able to support projects that address violence against LGBTQ individuals, promote legal reforms, and provide critical services to marginalized communities.

Case Study: The #MeToo Movement

The #MeToo movement serves as a pertinent case study in international collaboration for change. Originally initiated in the United States, the movement quickly transcended borders, with activists worldwide adopting the hashtag to raise awareness about sexual harassment and assault. This global resonance demonstrates the power of social media as a tool for solidarity and collective action.

In countries where LGBTQ individuals face heightened vulnerabilities, local activists have utilized the #MeToo framework to address issues specific to their contexts. For instance, in Brazil, LGBTQ activists have adapted the movement to highlight violence against transgender women, drawing attention to the intersection of gender and sexual orientation in experiences of violence.

Strategies for Effective Collaboration

To foster effective international collaboration, several strategies can be employed:

1. **Building Trust and Relationships**: Establishing trust among collaborators is crucial. This can be achieved through regular communication, shared goals, and mutual respect for different cultural contexts.

2. **Creating Inclusive Spaces**: Ensuring that all voices are heard, especially those from marginalized communities, is essential for equitable collaboration. This can involve setting up advisory boards that include representatives from various regions and backgrounds.

3. **Leveraging Technology**: Utilizing digital tools for communication and organization can enhance collaboration. Virtual meetings, social media campaigns, and collaborative platforms can facilitate real-time sharing of strategies and resources.

4. **Focusing on Intersectionality**: Recognizing the interconnectedness of various forms of oppression can strengthen collaborative efforts. By addressing issues of race, class, and gender alongside sexual orientation, movements can create a more comprehensive approach to advocacy.

5. **Sharing Success Stories**: Highlighting successful collaborations and their outcomes can inspire others to engage in international efforts. Documentation of these stories can serve as a resource for future activists.

In conclusion, international collaboration is vital for advancing LGBTQ rights in an increasingly interconnected world. By embracing diversity, overcoming challenges, and leveraging collective strengths, activists can create a powerful movement for change that transcends borders and speaks to the universal struggle for dignity and equality. The fight for LGBTQ rights is not confined to any one nation; it is a global endeavor that requires solidarity, understanding, and unwavering commitment.

Recognizing LGBTQ Asylum Seekers

The plight of LGBTQ asylum seekers is a pressing issue that demands recognition and understanding. In a world where discrimination and persecution based on sexual orientation and gender identity persist, it is crucial to acknowledge the unique challenges faced by these individuals seeking refuge. This section will delve into the theoretical frameworks surrounding LGBTQ asylum, the systemic problems these seekers encounter, and notable examples that highlight the urgent need for recognition and support.

Theoretical Frameworks

Understanding the experiences of LGBTQ asylum seekers can be enriched by various theoretical frameworks, including intersectionality and human rights theory. Intersectionality, coined by Kimberlé Crenshaw, posits that individuals experience oppression in varying configurations and degrees of intensity based on their overlapping identities. For LGBTQ asylum seekers, factors such as race, ethnicity, socioeconomic status, and immigration status intersect with their sexual orientation or gender identity, amplifying their vulnerabilities.

Human rights theory emphasizes the inherent dignity and worth of every individual. As articulated in the Universal Declaration of Human Rights, everyone has the right to seek asylum from persecution. This principle is particularly relevant for LGBTQ individuals, who often face violence, discrimination, and social ostracization in their home countries. Recognizing LGBTQ asylum seekers as deserving of protection is not merely an act of charity; it is a legal and moral obligation grounded in international human rights norms.

Systemic Problems

Despite the theoretical frameworks that advocate for the recognition of LGBTQ asylum seekers, systemic problems persist in the asylum process. One significant issue is the lack of cultural competency among immigration officials and judges. Many LGBTQ asylum seekers encounter skepticism when presenting their cases, often subjected to invasive questioning that fails to recognize the nuances of their experiences. This can lead to a higher rate of denial for asylum claims, as the burden of proof placed on the seeker is often insurmountable.

Another systemic problem is the inadequate legal representation available to LGBTQ asylum seekers. Many individuals seeking asylum lack access to qualified legal counsel who understands the complexities of LGBTQ issues and the asylum process. This gap in legal support can result in poorly prepared cases that do not adequately convey the urgency and legitimacy of the seeker's claims.

Additionally, the stigma surrounding LGBTQ identities can lead to further isolation for asylum seekers. Many individuals fear disclosing their sexual orientation or gender identity during the asylum process, fearing that doing so may jeopardize their chances of acceptance. This fear is compounded by the possibility of being returned to a country where they face persecution, creating a paradox where seekers must navigate a system that often lacks empathy and understanding.

Notable Examples

Recognizing LGBTQ asylum seekers is not merely an academic exercise; it has real-world implications. One notable example is the case of *Josef*, a gay man from El Salvador who fled his home country after being targeted by gang violence due to his sexual orientation. Upon arriving in the United States, Josef faced significant hurdles in his asylum application process. Despite presenting compelling evidence of the threats he faced, his case was initially denied due to a lack of understanding from the immigration judge regarding the societal context of violence against LGBTQ individuals in El Salvador.

In contrast, the case of *Amina*, a transgender woman from Iran, illustrates the positive impact of recognition and support. Amina was granted asylum after her legal team successfully demonstrated the systemic discrimination and violence faced by transgender individuals in Iran. Her case was bolstered by expert testimony and a thorough understanding of the cultural context surrounding LGBTQ identities, highlighting the importance of informed advocacy in the asylum process.

The Path Forward

Recognizing LGBTQ asylum seekers requires a multi-faceted approach that includes training for immigration officials, increased access to legal representation, and the establishment of support networks for individuals navigating the asylum process. Advocacy organizations play a crucial role in this recognition, providing resources, legal aid, and community support to those in need.

Moreover, public awareness campaigns are essential to shift societal perceptions and foster understanding of the challenges faced by LGBTQ asylum seekers. By sharing personal stories and highlighting the resilience of these individuals, society can begin to dismantle the stigma and discrimination that often accompany discussions about LGBTQ rights and asylum.

In conclusion, recognizing LGBTQ asylum seekers is not only a matter of legal obligation but also a moral imperative. By understanding the theoretical frameworks, addressing systemic problems, and learning from notable examples, we can work towards a more inclusive and compassionate asylum process that honors the dignity and humanity of all individuals seeking safety and refuge.

The Fight is Far from Over

The journey toward LGBTQ rights and equality is an ongoing struggle, marked by both significant victories and persistent challenges. While considerable progress has been made in many parts of the world, the fight for equality is far from over, as numerous barriers continue to impede the full realization of rights for LGBTQ individuals. This section delves into the current landscape of LGBTQ rights, emphasizing the need for sustained activism and advocacy.

1. The Current Landscape of LGBTQ Rights

Despite the strides made in recent decades, LGBTQ individuals still face systemic discrimination and violence in various forms. According to the *International Lesbian, Gay, Bisexual, Trans and Intersex Association (ILGA)*, over 70 countries still criminalize same-sex relationships, and many others lack comprehensive protections against discrimination based on sexual orientation or gender identity. This legal landscape creates an environment where LGBTQ individuals are vulnerable to persecution, harassment, and violence.

2. Intersectionality and Its Implications

The fight for LGBTQ rights cannot be viewed in isolation; it is essential to recognize the intersectionality of various identities, including race, gender, socioeconomic status, and immigration status. The work of scholars like Kimberlé Crenshaw highlights how overlapping social identities can compound discrimination. For instance, LGBTQ people of color often face unique challenges that are not adequately addressed by mainstream LGBTQ advocacy. The intersection of racism and homophobia can lead to increased violence and discrimination, necessitating a more nuanced approach to activism.

3. The Role of Policy and Legislation

While legislative victories, such as the legalization of same-sex marriage in many countries, have been monumental, they are not the end of the fight. Laws protecting LGBTQ individuals from discrimination in employment, housing, and healthcare are still lacking in numerous jurisdictions. For example, the lack of a federal law prohibiting employment discrimination based on sexual orientation or gender identity in the United States leaves many individuals vulnerable to unjust termination and workplace harassment.

$$\text{Discrimination Index} = \frac{\text{Number of Discriminatory Incidents}}{\text{Total Population}} \times 100$$

This equation illustrates the prevalence of discrimination within a given population, underscoring the urgent need for comprehensive legal protections.

4. Global Perspectives and Challenges

Globally, the fight for LGBTQ rights is uneven. In some regions, such as Western Europe and parts of North America, there has been notable progress. However, in many countries, particularly in Africa and the Middle East, LGBTQ individuals face severe persecution, including imprisonment and violence. Activists like Victor M. Maceda have worked tirelessly to highlight these disparities and advocate for global solidarity among LGBTQ communities. The international community must recognize that the fight for LGBTQ rights is a human rights issue, and efforts must be made to support activists in hostile environments.

5. The Role of Education and Awareness

Education plays a critical role in the ongoing fight for LGBTQ rights. Misconceptions and stereotypes about LGBTQ individuals contribute to discrimination and violence. Programs aimed at educating the public about LGBTQ issues can foster empathy and understanding, paving the way for more inclusive societies. For instance, integrating LGBTQ history and issues into school curricula can challenge harmful stereotypes and promote acceptance among young people.

6. The Power of Grassroots Movements

Grassroots movements remain vital in the fight for LGBTQ rights. These movements often arise in response to local injustices and can mobilize communities to demand change. The Stonewall Riots of 1969 serve as a historical example of how grassroots activism can catalyze a broader movement for LGBTQ rights. Today, organizations like the *Human Rights Campaign* and *GLAAD* continue to advocate for policy changes and raise awareness about LGBTQ issues.

7. Conclusion: A Call to Action

The fight for LGBTQ rights is far from over; it requires unwavering commitment and collective action. Activists must continue to challenge discriminatory laws, advocate for marginalized voices within the LGBTQ community, and educate the public about the importance of equality and acceptance. The legacy of pioneers like Victor M. Maceda serves as a reminder that while progress has been made, the journey toward true equality is ongoing.

The future of LGBTQ rights depends on the resilience and determination of individuals and communities to confront challenges head-on, ensuring that every person, regardless of their sexual orientation or gender identity, can live freely and authentically.

Bibliography

[1] International Lesbian, Gay, Bisexual, Trans and Intersex Association. (2023). *ILGA World Annual Report*. Retrieved from https://ilga.org

[2] Crenshaw, K. (1989). Demarginalizing the Intersection of Race and Sex: A Black Feminist Critique of Antidiscrimination Doctrine, Feminist Theory and Antiracist Politics. *University of Chicago Legal Forum*, 1989(1), 139-167.

[3] Human Rights Campaign. (2023). *The State of LGBTQ Equality*. Retrieved from https://hrc.org

Inspiring Future Leaders

Mentorship and Education Programs

Mentorship and education programs play a pivotal role in nurturing the next generation of LGBTQ activists. These initiatives not only empower individuals with knowledge and skills but also foster a sense of community and belonging. As Victor M. Maceda has demonstrated throughout his career, mentorship is a powerful tool for advocacy, allowing seasoned activists to pass down their wisdom and experiences to those who are just beginning their journeys.

The Importance of Mentorship

Mentorship in the LGBTQ community serves multiple purposes. It provides a safe space for younger activists to explore their identities and aspirations while receiving guidance from those who have navigated similar paths. According to [?], effective mentorship can lead to increased self-efficacy, enhanced social skills, and improved career outcomes. This is particularly crucial for LGBTQ youth, who often face unique challenges such as discrimination, isolation, and lack of access to resources.

Establishing Education Programs

Education programs designed for LGBTQ advocacy should encompass a variety of topics, including:

- **History of LGBTQ Rights:** Understanding the historical context of LGBTQ rights movements helps activists appreciate the struggles and triumphs of their predecessors. This knowledge can inspire a deeper commitment to the cause.

- **Advocacy Skills:** Workshops focusing on public speaking, lobbying, and grassroots organizing equip participants with the necessary tools to effect change. For example, Maceda has organized training sessions that emphasize the importance of storytelling in advocacy, teaching participants how to share their personal narratives to resonate with wider audiences.

- **Legal Knowledge:** Familiarizing activists with relevant laws and policies ensures they can navigate the complex legal landscape surrounding LGBTQ rights. Programs that include legal professionals can provide invaluable insights into the asylum process and anti-discrimination laws.

- **Intersectionality:** Education programs must address the intersectional nature of identities within the LGBTQ community. Understanding how race, gender, and socioeconomic status influence experiences of discrimination is essential for effective advocacy.

Challenges in Implementation

Despite the clear benefits of mentorship and education programs, several challenges can hinder their effectiveness:

- **Resource Limitations:** Many LGBTQ organizations operate on tight budgets, making it difficult to allocate funds for comprehensive mentorship and education programs. This can limit the scope and reach of these initiatives.

- **Access and Inclusion:** Ensuring that programs are accessible to all members of the community, particularly marginalized groups, is vital. Programs must be designed with inclusivity in mind, taking into account geographic, economic, and social barriers.

✦ **Sustainability:** Maintaining ongoing mentorship relationships can be challenging, especially in fast-paced environments where mentors may have competing commitments. Establishing structured programs with clear objectives can help mitigate this issue.

Successful Examples of Mentorship Programs

Several successful mentorship programs have emerged in the LGBTQ community, demonstrating effective models that can be replicated:

✦ **The Queer Youth Project:** This initiative pairs LGBTQ youth with mentors who provide guidance on personal and professional development. The program has reported increased confidence and improved mental health outcomes among participants.

✦ **Out for Undergrad:** This program focuses on helping LGBTQ college students transition into the workforce. By connecting students with industry professionals, it facilitates networking opportunities and career development.

✦ **The Trevor Project's Lifeline:** While primarily a crisis intervention service, The Trevor Project also offers mentorship opportunities for LGBTQ youth, connecting them with trained volunteers who can provide support and guidance.

Conclusion

Mentorship and education programs are essential for cultivating the next generation of LGBTQ activists. By providing knowledge, skills, and support, these initiatives empower individuals to become effective advocates for change. As Victor M. Maceda continues to inspire others through his work, the importance of fostering mentorship and educational opportunities cannot be overstated. The future of LGBTQ rights advocacy depends on the commitment to uplift and empower new voices within the community.

Encouraging Youth Activism

The youth of today are not just the leaders of tomorrow; they are the catalysts for change in the present. Encouraging youth activism is crucial for the sustainability of LGBTQ rights movements, as it ensures that the voices of younger generations are heard and valued. This section explores the theoretical foundations, prevalent challenges, and successful examples of youth activism in the LGBTQ rights arena.

Theoretical Foundations of Youth Activism

Youth activism is grounded in various theoretical frameworks, including social movement theory, developmental psychology, and participatory action research. Social movement theory posits that collective action arises when individuals identify shared grievances and mobilize to address them. Youth, often feeling disenfranchised, can harness their collective power to challenge societal norms and advocate for change.

Developmental psychology emphasizes the importance of identity formation during adolescence. This period is characterized by a search for self-identity, which can be particularly significant for LGBTQ youth. According to Erik Erikson's stages of psychosocial development, the challenge of forming identity during adolescence can lead to a strong sense of purpose when coupled with activism. Engaging in social movements allows youth to explore their identities and assert their rights, fostering resilience and self-advocacy.

Participatory action research encourages youth to actively engage in the research process, allowing them to become co-creators of knowledge. This approach empowers young activists to identify issues within their communities and develop strategies for change, reinforcing their agency and leadership skills.

Challenges Faced by Youth Activists

Despite the enthusiasm and potential of youth activism, several challenges hinder the effectiveness of young activists in the LGBTQ rights movement:

- **Lack of Resources:** Many youth activists lack access to funding, mentorship, and training opportunities. Limited financial resources can restrict their ability to organize events, campaigns, or educational programs.

- **Institutional Barriers:** Schools and community organizations may not always support LGBTQ activism. Policies that inhibit discussions about sexual orientation and gender identity can stifle youth engagement.

- **Social Stigma:** LGBTQ youth often face stigma and discrimination from peers, families, and society. This can lead to feelings of isolation and discourage participation in activism.

+ **Burnout:** The emotional toll of activism can lead to burnout, particularly for youth who are balancing school, work, and personal lives alongside their advocacy efforts.

Successful Examples of Youth Activism

Despite these challenges, numerous examples illustrate the power and impact of youth activism in the LGBTQ rights movement:

+ **The Trevor Project:** Founded by a group of young activists, The Trevor Project provides crisis intervention and suicide prevention services to LGBTQ youth. Their initiatives, including the Trevor Lifeline, empower young people to seek help and advocate for their rights.

+ **March for Our Lives:** Initially focused on gun control, this youth-led movement has expanded to include LGBTQ rights, advocating for safer schools and communities. Their ability to mobilize thousands of young people demonstrates the effectiveness of grassroots organizing.

+ **#BlackAndPink:** This organization, founded by LGBTQ youth, focuses on prison abolition and the rights of incarcerated LGBTQ individuals. Their work highlights the intersectionality of LGBTQ issues and the importance of inclusive activism.

+ **Student-Led Pride Alliances:** Across high schools and colleges, student-led pride alliances have emerged as powerful forces for change. These groups create safe spaces for LGBTQ students, organize events, and advocate for policy changes within their institutions.

Strategies for Encouraging Youth Activism

To effectively encourage youth activism, several strategies can be implemented:

1. **Mentorship Programs:** Establishing mentorship programs that connect experienced activists with youth can provide guidance, support, and encouragement. Mentors can help navigate challenges and share valuable resources.

2. **Workshops and Training:** Offering workshops that focus on skills such as public speaking, organizing, and advocacy can empower youth to take action. These training sessions can build confidence and equip young activists with the tools they need to succeed.

3. **Creating Safe Spaces:** Schools and community organizations should create safe spaces where LGBTQ youth can express themselves freely. These environments foster a sense of belonging and encourage participation in activism.

4. **Utilizing Social Media:** Social media platforms provide a powerful tool for youth activism. Encouraging young people to share their stories, organize events, and raise awareness online can amplify their voices and reach a broader audience.

5. **Collaborative Projects:** Engaging youth in collaborative projects that address community issues can foster a sense of ownership and agency. These projects can range from awareness campaigns to community service initiatives, allowing youth to see the tangible impact of their efforts.

Conclusion

Encouraging youth activism is vital for the continued advancement of LGBTQ rights. By providing support, resources, and opportunities for engagement, we can empower the next generation of activists to challenge discrimination, advocate for their rights, and inspire others. The future of LGBTQ activism depends on the voices and actions of youth, making it imperative that we invest in their development as leaders and change-makers.

$$Youth\ Empowerment = Resources + Support + Engagement \qquad (20)$$

In conclusion, the potential of youth activism in the LGBTQ rights movement is immense. By addressing the challenges they face and implementing effective strategies to encourage their involvement, we can cultivate a new wave of advocates who will continue to fight for equality and justice for all.

Building LGBTQ Support Networks

The establishment of robust LGBTQ support networks is crucial for fostering resilience, empowerment, and a sense of belonging within the community. These networks serve as lifelines, providing emotional, social, and practical assistance to individuals navigating the complexities of their identities and the challenges posed by societal discrimination.

Theoretical Framework

Support networks can be understood through the lens of social capital theory, which posits that social networks have value and can facilitate access to resources, information, and support. According to Bourdieu (1986), social capital encompasses the resources available to individuals through their social connections, which can be mobilized to achieve various goals.

In the context of LGBTQ communities, these networks can significantly enhance individuals' well-being by offering:

- **Emotional Support:** A safe space for individuals to express their feelings, fears, and experiences without judgment.

- **Information Sharing:** Access to resources such as legal advice, healthcare services, and mental health support.

- **Advocacy and Representation:** Collective voices that can influence policy changes and promote visibility within broader societal frameworks.

Identifying Key Problems

Despite the importance of LGBTQ support networks, several challenges hinder their effectiveness:

1. **Fragmentation:** Many LGBTQ support networks operate in silos, leading to disconnection and a lack of collaboration. This fragmentation can limit the reach and impact of advocacy efforts.

2. **Funding Constraints:** Many organizations rely on limited funding sources, which can restrict their ability to provide comprehensive services and outreach programs. As noted by the Human Rights Campaign (2020), financial instability often leads to reduced staff and resources, undermining the effectiveness of support initiatives.

3. **Cultural Barriers:** In diverse communities, cultural differences can create barriers to participation in support networks. For example, LGBTQ individuals from various cultural backgrounds may face additional stigma or discrimination, making it difficult for them to engage fully.

Examples of Effective Support Networks

Several successful LGBTQ support networks exemplify best practices in building community resilience and empowerment:

+ **The Trevor Project:** This national organization provides crisis intervention and suicide prevention services to LGBTQ youth. With a 24/7 helpline, online chat, and text support, The Trevor Project exemplifies how technology can enhance accessibility and reach marginalized individuals.

+ **PFLAG:** As one of the oldest and largest LGBTQ support organizations in the United States, PFLAG offers a network of support groups for parents, families, and allies of LGBTQ individuals. By fostering dialogue and understanding, PFLAG helps bridge gaps between LGBTQ individuals and their families, promoting acceptance and solidarity.

+ **Local Community Centers:** Many cities host LGBTQ community centers that provide a range of services, including counseling, social events, and advocacy training. For example, the Los Angeles LGBT Center serves over 42,000 clients annually, offering health services, housing assistance, and youth programs, demonstrating the vital role of local networks in supporting LGBTQ individuals.

Strategies for Building Effective Support Networks

To address the challenges and enhance the effectiveness of LGBTQ support networks, the following strategies can be implemented:

1. **Fostering Collaboration:** Encouraging partnerships between various LGBTQ organizations can help reduce fragmentation and enhance resource sharing. Collaborative initiatives can amplify advocacy efforts and create a more unified front in addressing LGBTQ issues.

2. **Diversifying Funding Sources:** Organizations should explore multiple funding avenues, including grants, donations, and community fundraising events. By diversifying funding sources, support networks can enhance their sustainability and expand their reach.

3. **Culturally Competent Programming:** Developing programs that are sensitive to the cultural backgrounds of participants is essential. This may involve training staff on cultural competency and engaging community leaders to ensure that services are relevant and accessible to all individuals.

4. **Utilizing Technology:** Leveraging technology can enhance outreach and engagement. Virtual support groups, online resources, and social media campaigns can connect individuals who may not have access to traditional support networks.

Conclusion

Building LGBTQ support networks is a dynamic process that requires intentional efforts to overcome challenges and leverage opportunities. By fostering collaboration, diversifying funding, and embracing cultural competence, these networks can provide essential support to individuals navigating the complexities of their identities. Ultimately, strong support networks not only enhance individual well-being but also contribute to the broader movement for LGBTQ rights and equality.

Promoting Intersectional Advocacy

Intersectional advocacy is a crucial framework in the fight for LGBTQ rights, recognizing that individuals experience oppression in multifaceted ways due to the intersection of their identities, including race, ethnicity, gender, sexuality, socioeconomic status, and more. The term "intersectionality," coined by legal scholar Kimberlé Crenshaw in 1989, emphasizes that social categorizations are interconnected and cannot be examined separately from one another. This approach is vital in understanding the diverse experiences within the LGBTQ community and advocating for policies that address these complexities.

Theoretical Framework

Intersectionality posits that individuals do not experience discrimination in isolated categories. Instead, their identities overlap and intersect, leading to unique forms of oppression. For example, a Black transgender woman may face discrimination not only based on her gender identity but also due to her race and socioeconomic background. This compounded discrimination necessitates a nuanced approach to advocacy that addresses the specific needs of individuals at these intersections.

The mathematical representation of intersectionality can be illustrated through set theory. Let A represent the set of LGBTQ individuals, B represent individuals of color, and C represent women. The intersection of these sets, denoted as $A \cap B \cap C$, represents individuals who identify as LGBTQ, are people of color, and are women. The complexities of their experiences cannot be captured by merely considering each set independently:

$$X = A \cap B \cap C$$

where X is the set of individuals facing intersectional discrimination.

Challenges in Intersectional Advocacy

Despite its importance, promoting intersectional advocacy comes with challenges. One significant issue is the tendency of mainstream LGBTQ organizations to prioritize the needs of white, cisgender, gay men, often sidelining the voices and concerns of those from marginalized backgrounds. This can lead to a lack of representation and resources for individuals who do not fit the dominant narrative within the LGBTQ movement.

Moreover, intersectional advocacy requires an understanding of the unique barriers faced by various groups. For instance, LGBTQ individuals from immigrant backgrounds may confront additional challenges related to language barriers, cultural stigma, and legal status. Recognizing these complexities is essential for effective advocacy.

Examples of Intersectional Advocacy

Several organizations and movements have successfully integrated intersectional advocacy into their missions. The Black Lives Matter movement, for example, has highlighted the experiences of Black LGBTQ individuals, advocating for justice and equality across multiple dimensions of identity. Their work emphasizes that the fight against police brutality and systemic racism is intrinsically linked to the fight for LGBTQ rights.

Another notable example is the work of the Transgender Law Center, which focuses on the legal needs of transgender individuals, particularly those from marginalized communities. Their initiatives aim to provide legal support and resources tailored to the specific challenges faced by transgender people of color, emphasizing the necessity of intersectional approaches in legal advocacy.

Strategies for Promoting Intersectional Advocacy

To effectively promote intersectional advocacy, organizations and activists can adopt several strategies:

1.   **Inclusive Leadership**: Ensure that leadership within LGBTQ organizations reflects the diversity of the community. This can involve recruiting

individuals from various backgrounds and experiences to leadership positions, thereby amplifying underrepresented voices.

2. **Collaborative Partnerships**: Form alliances with organizations that represent different marginalized communities. By working together, these organizations can address overlapping issues and advocate for comprehensive policy changes.

3. **Education and Training**: Provide training on intersectionality for activists and community members. Workshops and seminars can help raise awareness about the importance of intersectional advocacy and equip individuals with the tools to address these complexities.

4. **Resource Allocation**: Allocate resources to support initiatives that specifically address the needs of marginalized groups within the LGBTQ community. This can include funding for programs that focus on the intersection of race, gender, and sexual orientation.

5. **Storytelling and Representation**: Elevate the stories of individuals who experience intersectional oppression. Sharing personal narratives can foster empathy and understanding, helping to humanize the struggles faced by those at the intersections of multiple identities.

In conclusion, promoting intersectional advocacy is essential for creating a more inclusive and effective LGBTQ rights movement. By recognizing and addressing the unique challenges faced by individuals at the intersections of various identities, advocates can work towards a more equitable society for all. The journey towards intersectionality may be complex, but it is a necessary path in the ongoing fight for justice and equality.

The Next Generation of LGBTQ Activists

The landscape of LGBTQ activism is ever-evolving, and as the torch is passed from one generation to the next, it is crucial to recognize the unique challenges and opportunities that the next generation of activists faces. This section will explore the theoretical frameworks that underpin contemporary LGBTQ activism, the problems that arise in this transition, and the inspiring examples of young activists who are shaping the future.

Theoretical Frameworks

To understand the dynamics of the next generation of LGBTQ activists, it is essential to ground our discussion in relevant theories. One such framework is **intersectionality**, coined by Kimberlé Crenshaw, which posits that individuals experience overlapping systems of discrimination based on their various identities, including but not limited to race, gender, and sexual orientation. This theory is particularly relevant as young activists navigate a world where issues of race, gender identity, and sexual orientation are increasingly interconnected.

Another vital theoretical lens is **post-identity politics**, which critiques the limitations of traditional identity-based movements. This perspective encourages activists to move beyond singular identity categories and to embrace a more fluid understanding of identity that reflects the complexities of modern life. As a result, the next generation of LGBTQ activists is more likely to engage in coalitional politics, forging alliances with other marginalized groups and addressing broader social justice issues.

Challenges Faced by the Next Generation

Despite the theoretical advancements in understanding identity and activism, the next generation of LGBTQ activists faces significant challenges. One primary issue is the **digital divide**, which highlights the disparities in access to technology and the internet. While social media has become a powerful tool for organizing and raising awareness, not all young activists have equal access to these platforms. This divide can hinder their ability to mobilize support and share their stories effectively.

Additionally, the rise of **anti-LGBTQ legislation** in various parts of the world poses a significant threat to the progress made by previous generations. Young activists must contend with a hostile political landscape that seeks to undermine their rights and visibility. The resurgence of conservative ideologies often leads to increased violence and discrimination against LGBTQ individuals, making it imperative for the next generation to develop resilient strategies for advocacy and resistance.

Examples of Inspiring Young Activists

Amidst these challenges, there are numerous examples of young activists who are making a profound impact. One such figure is **Greta Thunberg**, who, while primarily known for her environmental activism, has also championed LGBTQ rights within the context of climate justice. Thunberg's ability to connect various social issues demonstrates the potential for intersectional activism to address multiple injustices simultaneously.

Another inspiring example is **Zoe Luna**, a transgender activist who has worked tirelessly to advocate for the rights of transgender youth. At a young age, Luna has been involved in campaigns to raise awareness about the challenges faced by transgender individuals, particularly in the realm of healthcare and education. Her work exemplifies the importance of youth voices in shaping policy and public perception.

Strategies for Empowerment

To empower the next generation of LGBTQ activists, it is essential to invest in **mentorship programs** that connect seasoned activists with young leaders. Such programs can provide invaluable guidance, resources, and support, helping to navigate the complexities of activism in today's world. Additionally, promoting **inclusive education** that addresses LGBTQ issues in schools can foster a culture of acceptance and understanding among young people, equipping them with the knowledge and tools necessary for advocacy.

Furthermore, the use of **creative expression**—through art, music, and performance—can serve as a powerful medium for young activists to share their stories and challenge societal norms. By harnessing the power of creativity, the next generation can engage broader audiences and inspire action in ways that traditional methods may not achieve.

Conclusion

In conclusion, the next generation of LGBTQ activists stands at a critical juncture, equipped with new theoretical frameworks and a rich history of struggle and triumph. While they face unique challenges, their potential for impact is immense. By fostering mentorship, promoting inclusive education, and encouraging creative expression, we can ensure that the voices of young activists are heard and that they continue the vital work of advancing LGBTQ rights and social justice for all. The future of activism lies in their hands, and it is our responsibility to support and uplift them as they forge a path toward a more equitable world.

$$\text{Advocacy Impact} = \text{Access} + \text{Visibility} + \text{Coalition Building} \qquad (21)$$

This equation encapsulates the essential components that will drive the success of the next generation of LGBTQ activists. By ensuring access to resources, increasing visibility for their causes, and building coalitions with other movements, they can amplify their impact and create lasting change.

Defending LGBTQ Asylum Seekers

The Plight of LGBTQ Asylum Seekers

Understanding the Challenges They Face

The journey of LGBTQ asylum seekers is often fraught with numerous challenges that stem from both their sexual orientation or gender identity and the immigration process itself. To comprehend the depth of these challenges, it is essential to examine the socio-political contexts from which they flee, the psychological impacts of their experiences, and the systemic barriers they face in their host countries.

1. The Socio-Political Context

LGBTQ individuals in many countries face severe persecution due to their identity. According to the *International Lesbian, Gay, Bisexual, Trans and Intersex Association (ILGA)*, as of 2021, 69 countries still criminalize same-sex relationships, and in some places, the penalties can include imprisonment or even death. This legal framework creates an environment of fear and violence. Many LGBTQ individuals are subjected to hate crimes, forced conversion therapy, and familial rejection, leading them to seek refuge in more accepting nations.

For instance, in countries like Uganda and Nigeria, anti-LGBTQ laws are not only legislated but are also socially enforced through violence and discrimination. Reports have documented instances where individuals have been attacked or even killed for their sexual orientation. Such dire circumstances leave LGBTQ individuals with no choice but to flee their homeland in search of safety.

2. Psychological Trauma

The psychological impact of living in a hostile environment cannot be overstated. Many LGBTQ asylum seekers carry the scars of trauma from their experiences. The *American Psychological Association* highlights that individuals who experience discrimination and violence are at a higher risk for mental health issues, including depression, anxiety, and post-traumatic stress disorder (PTSD).

The trauma does not cease upon arrival in a new country; rather, it can be exacerbated by the asylum process itself. The uncertainty of their legal status, the fear of deportation, and the challenges of adapting to a new culture can lead to feelings of isolation and despair. A study conducted by the *National Center for Lesbian Rights* found that LGBTQ asylum seekers often report a lack of support systems in their new environments, further compounding their mental health struggles.

3. Systemic Barriers in the Asylum Process

The asylum process is notoriously complex and can be particularly daunting for LGBTQ individuals. One of the primary challenges is the requirement to prove a well-founded fear of persecution. This often necessitates the sharing of deeply personal and traumatic experiences, which can be emotionally taxing.

Moreover, legal representation is crucial in navigating this process. Unfortunately, many LGBTQ asylum seekers lack access to affordable legal services. According to a report by the *American Immigration Council*, individuals represented by an attorney are significantly more likely to succeed in their asylum claims. However, financial barriers and a shortage of LGBTQ-competent legal practitioners can hinder access to necessary support.

4. Cultural and Social Integration

Upon arrival in a new country, LGBTQ asylum seekers often face additional challenges related to cultural integration. While they may have fled persecution, they can encounter new forms of discrimination based on their identity. For example, in some host countries, the LGBTQ community may not be as visible or accepted, leading to feelings of alienation.

Language barriers can also pose significant hurdles. Asylum seekers may struggle to communicate their needs and experiences, which can impede their ability to access essential services such as healthcare, housing, and employment. The lack of culturally competent resources can exacerbate their feelings of isolation and hinder their integration into society.

5. Case Studies and Real-Life Examples

Real-life examples illustrate the myriad challenges faced by LGBTQ asylum seekers. Take the case of *John*, a gay man from Jamaica who faced threats of violence from his community after coming out. Upon arriving in the United States, John encountered difficulties with the asylum application process. His initial claim was denied due to a lack of documentation to support his fear of persecution. With the help of an LGBTQ advocacy group, he was able to gather testimonies from friends and community members, ultimately leading to a successful appeal.

Similarly, *Maria*, a transgender woman from El Salvador, faced severe discrimination in her home country. After fleeing to the U.S., she struggled with mental health issues stemming from her traumatic experiences. Through a local LGBTQ support group, she found the resources needed to begin her healing journey, but the road to stability was long and fraught with challenges.

Conclusion

Understanding the challenges faced by LGBTQ asylum seekers is crucial for advocates and policymakers alike. Addressing these issues requires a multifaceted approach that includes legal reform, mental health support, and community integration programs. By amplifying the voices of those affected and recognizing their unique struggles, we can work towards creating a more just and equitable system for all individuals seeking safety and acceptance.

Ultimately, the plight of LGBTQ asylum seekers is a reflection of broader societal attitudes towards gender and sexuality. As we strive for a world that embraces diversity and inclusion, it is imperative that we acknowledge and address the systemic barriers that continue to marginalize these individuals. The fight for LGBTQ rights is not merely about legal recognition; it is a struggle for dignity, safety, and the right to live authentically without fear of persecution.

Escaping Persecution and Seeking Safety

The journey of LGBTQ asylum seekers is often fraught with unimaginable challenges, as they flee from persecution rooted in their sexual orientation or gender identity. To understand this plight, it is essential to explore the socio-political landscapes that compel individuals to leave their home countries, the intricate processes they must navigate to seek safety, and the psychological toll of such traumatic experiences.

The Context of Persecution

Persecution against LGBTQ individuals manifests in various forms, including systemic violence, legal discrimination, and social ostracism. According to the *International Lesbian, Gay, Bisexual, Trans and Intersex Association (ILGA)*, in many countries, LGBTQ individuals face severe human rights violations, including imprisonment, torture, and even execution. For instance, in countries like Chechnya, reports of state-sponsored violence against LGBTQ individuals have surfaced, where individuals are detained in secret prisons, tortured, and murdered simply for being who they are.

The United Nations High Commissioner for Refugees (UNHCR) recognizes that LGBTQ individuals are particularly vulnerable, as their identities often lead to heightened risks of violence and discrimination. The **1951 Refugee Convention** outlines the criteria for refugee status, emphasizing the need for protection from persecution based on race, religion, nationality, membership in a particular social group, or political opinion. LGBTQ individuals fall under the category of "particular social group," which allows them to seek asylum based on their sexual orientation or gender identity.

The Asylum-Seeking Process

The asylum-seeking process is complex and varies significantly from country to country. For many LGBTQ individuals, the first step in this arduous journey is to escape their home country, often at great personal risk. The challenges they face can be categorized into three primary phases: **escape, application,** and **integration.**

Escape   The escape phase is often marked by fear and uncertainty. Many individuals must leave their homes without warning, relying on clandestine networks or friends to facilitate their departure. This phase can involve perilous journeys across borders, where they may encounter additional threats, such as human trafficking or violence. For example, a young gay man from Uganda, facing imminent threats due to his sexual orientation, might travel through multiple countries, risking his life to reach a nation that offers asylum.

Application   Upon arriving in a host country, the next critical step is to apply for asylum. This process typically requires the individual to present a credible fear of persecution, supported by evidence such as personal testimonies, medical reports, and documentation of threats. Asylum seekers often face the daunting task of articulating their experiences in a legal context, which can be particularly challenging for those who have suffered trauma.

The process is further complicated by the need to navigate legal systems that may lack sensitivity to LGBTQ issues. For instance, in the United States, the asylum application process can take years, during which applicants may be subject to detention or deportation. Victor M. Maceda's work highlights the importance of providing legal support to LGBTQ asylum seekers, ensuring that their cases are presented effectively and that their voices are heard.

Integration Once granted asylum, the integration phase presents its own set of challenges. Many asylum seekers experience psychological distress, stemming from their past traumas and the stress of adapting to a new environment. The need for community support becomes paramount during this phase. LGBTQ organizations often play a crucial role in providing resources, emotional support, and legal assistance to help individuals rebuild their lives.

Real-Life Examples

The stories of LGBTQ asylum seekers illustrate the harsh realities they face. For instance, the case of **José**, a transgender woman from El Salvador, exemplifies the struggles many endure. After being targeted for violence due to her gender identity, José fled to the United States, where she navigated the asylum process with the help of advocacy groups. Her journey highlights the intersection of gender identity and the asylum process, as she faced additional hurdles in a system that often fails to recognize the unique challenges faced by transgender individuals.

Another poignant example is that of **Amina**, a gay man from Nigeria, where homosexuality is criminalized. After being outed by a family member, Amina faced threats to his life and sought refuge in Canada. His story underscores the importance of international solidarity and the role of countries like Canada in providing safe havens for those fleeing persecution.

Conclusion

The journey of escaping persecution and seeking safety is a testament to the resilience of LGBTQ individuals. As Victor M. Maceda advocates for their rights, it is crucial to recognize the systemic barriers they face and to foster an environment that not only protects but also empowers them. By raising awareness and advocating for policy changes, we can work towards a future where LGBTQ individuals can live freely and authentically, without fear of persecution.

In summary, the plight of LGBTQ asylum seekers is a critical aspect of the broader struggle for human rights. Understanding their experiences and advocating for their needs is essential in the fight for equality and justice, ensuring that their voices are not only heard but celebrated.

The Role of Victor M. Maceda in Advocacy

Victor M. Maceda has emerged as a pivotal figure in the advocacy for LGBTQ asylum seekers, channeling his personal experiences and professional expertise into a powerful force for change. His journey into activism was not merely a response to societal injustices; it was a calling that intertwined his identity with the broader struggle for human rights.

Theoretical Framework

At the core of Victor's advocacy lies the theory of intersectionality, which posits that individuals experience overlapping systems of discrimination and privilege. This framework is essential in understanding the complexities faced by LGBTQ asylum seekers, who often confront not only homophobia but also racism, xenophobia, and economic disenfranchisement. Victor's work exemplifies how intersectional advocacy can illuminate these multifaceted struggles, creating a more comprehensive approach to human rights.

Victor's advocacy is also grounded in the principles of social justice, which emphasize equality and the right to live free from oppression. He utilizes these principles to not only address immediate needs but also to challenge the systemic structures that perpetuate inequality. The application of these theories in his work has led to significant advancements in the legal and social support systems for LGBTQ asylum seekers.

Identifying Problems

One of the most pressing issues that Victor has tackled is the pervasive lack of understanding surrounding the experiences of LGBTQ asylum seekers. Many individuals and institutions are unaware of the specific threats these individuals face in their home countries, which can include violence, persecution, and even death. This ignorance often leads to inadequate responses from legal systems and humanitarian organizations.

Additionally, the asylum process itself is fraught with challenges. LGBTQ asylum seekers frequently encounter skepticism and bias from immigration officials, which can result in denied claims and further victimization. Victor's advocacy has revealed these systemic flaws, advocating for training and education for officials to better understand LGBTQ issues and the unique circumstances of asylum seekers.

Victor's Initiatives

Victor has launched several initiatives aimed at addressing these challenges. One notable program is the "Safe Haven Project," which provides comprehensive legal support for LGBTQ asylum seekers navigating the complexities of the asylum process. This initiative includes pro bono legal services, assistance in gathering evidence of persecution, and guidance in preparing testimonies. The project has successfully helped numerous individuals gain asylum, transforming lives and reuniting families.

Furthermore, Victor has been instrumental in fostering collaborations between LGBTQ advocacy organizations and human rights groups. By building coalitions, he has amplified the voices of asylum seekers and created a unified front to advocate for policy changes at both local and national levels. His efforts have led to increased visibility for the plight of LGBTQ asylum seekers, resulting in greater public awareness and support.

Raising Awareness

Victor's role in advocacy extends beyond legal assistance; he is also a passionate advocate for raising awareness about the issues faced by LGBTQ asylum seekers. Through public speaking engagements, media appearances, and social media campaigns, he has effectively communicated the urgency of the situation. His powerful storytelling has humanized the statistics, making the struggles of asylum seekers relatable and compelling to a broader audience.

For instance, during a recent conference on human rights, Victor shared the story of a young asylum seeker who fled persecution in their home country. This narrative not only highlighted the individual's courage but also served as a call to action for attendees to support legislative changes that protect LGBTQ rights. Such personal stories are crucial in fostering empathy and understanding, which are essential for mobilizing support for systemic change.

Impact on Policy and Community

Victor's advocacy has had a tangible impact on policies affecting LGBTQ asylum seekers. His relentless efforts have contributed to the introduction of more inclusive policies in immigration law, ensuring that the unique needs of LGBTQ individuals are recognized and addressed. By working closely with lawmakers, he has been able to advocate for reforms that provide better protections and resources for asylum seekers.

In addition to policy changes, Victor's work has fostered a sense of community among LGBTQ asylum seekers. Through support groups and community outreach programs, he has created safe spaces for individuals to share their experiences and find solidarity. This sense of belonging is vital for those who have faced isolation and discrimination, allowing them to rebuild their lives in a supportive environment.

Conclusion

In conclusion, Victor M. Maceda's role in advocacy for LGBTQ asylum seekers is characterized by a deep commitment to intersectional social justice, a keen understanding of systemic challenges, and a passion for raising awareness. His initiatives not only provide immediate support to those in need but also challenge the broader societal structures that perpetuate inequality. As Victor continues to fight for the rights of LGBTQ asylum seekers, his legacy will undoubtedly inspire future generations of activists to uphold the values of compassion, justice, and equality for all.

$$\text{Advocacy Impact} = \text{Awareness} + \text{Policy Change} + \text{Community Support} \quad (22)$$

Partnering with Human Rights Organizations

In the landscape of LGBTQ rights advocacy, the collaboration between activists and established human rights organizations has proven to be a powerful catalyst for change. Victor M. Maceda recognized early on that to amplify the voices of LGBTQ asylum seekers, he needed to forge strategic partnerships that would leverage resources, expertise, and networks. This section explores the theoretical frameworks underpinning such collaborations, the challenges faced, and the tangible impacts of these alliances.

Theoretical Frameworks

The partnership between LGBTQ activists and human rights organizations can be understood through several theoretical lenses, including *intersectionality* and *collective impact*. Intersectionality, a term coined by Kimberlé Crenshaw, emphasizes the interconnected nature of social categorizations such as race, class, and sexual orientation. This framework is vital in understanding the multifaceted challenges faced by LGBTQ asylum seekers, who often navigate a complex web of discrimination.

Collective impact theory posits that significant social change requires the commitment of a group of important actors from different sectors to a common agenda for solving a specific social problem. In the context of LGBTQ rights, this means uniting various stakeholders—activists, non-profits, legal experts, and policymakers—around the shared goal of improving the lives of LGBTQ asylum seekers.

Challenges in Partnerships

Despite the potential benefits, forming partnerships with human rights organizations is not without its challenges. One significant issue is *resource allocation*. Many human rights organizations operate under tight budgets, which can lead to competition for funding and resources among various advocacy initiatives. This competition can dilute the focus on LGBTQ issues, particularly those related to asylum seekers, who may not always be prioritized.

Moreover, there exists a risk of *tokenism*, where LGBTQ issues are superficially included in broader human rights agendas without genuine commitment or understanding. This can lead to a lack of meaningful engagement with the specific needs of LGBTQ asylum seekers, undermining the effectiveness of advocacy efforts.

Another challenge is the potential for *cultural disconnect*. Human rights organizations may have established frameworks and methodologies that do not fully account for the unique experiences and challenges of LGBTQ asylum seekers. This disconnect can hinder the development of tailored solutions that address the specific needs of this community.

Successful Partnerships: Case Studies

Victor M. Maceda's work exemplifies successful partnerships with human rights organizations. One notable collaboration was with the *International Refugee Assistance Project (IRAP)*, which focuses on providing legal assistance to refugees and asylum seekers. Through this partnership, Maceda was able to provide pro bono legal services to LGBTQ asylum seekers, helping them navigate the complex asylum process. This collaboration not only improved individual cases but also raised awareness about the specific challenges faced by LGBTQ individuals in seeking asylum.

Another impactful partnership was with *Amnesty International.* Together, they launched a campaign highlighting the plight of LGBTQ asylum seekers in countries where homosexuality is criminalized. This campaign utilized social media to amplify the voices of those affected, leading to increased public awareness and pressure on policymakers to reform asylum laws. The campaign's success illustrates how partnerships can mobilize resources and public sentiment to effect change.

Impact of Collaborations

The partnerships formed by Victor M. Maceda with human rights organizations have had far-reaching impacts. Firstly, they have led to significant policy changes at both national and international levels. For instance, advocacy efforts resulted in the inclusion of specific protections for LGBTQ asylum seekers in international human rights frameworks, thereby enhancing their legal status and access to resources.

Additionally, these collaborations have fostered a greater sense of community among LGBTQ asylum seekers. By providing legal support, mental health resources, and social services, partnerships have created a safety net that empowers individuals to rebuild their lives in a new country. The psychological impact of knowing that there are organizations dedicated to their well-being cannot be overstated; it instills hope and resilience in those who have faced unimaginable challenges.

Finally, the partnerships have been instrumental in educating the public about the unique struggles of LGBTQ asylum seekers. Through joint campaigns and outreach initiatives, human rights organizations and LGBTQ activists have worked to combat stigma and foster understanding, ultimately leading to a more inclusive society.

Conclusion

In conclusion, the partnership between LGBTQ activists like Victor M. Maceda and human rights organizations is a vital component of the fight for equality and justice. While challenges such as resource allocation, tokenism, and cultural disconnect exist, the potential for impactful change is immense. By leveraging collective resources and expertise, these partnerships can create a more equitable landscape for LGBTQ asylum seekers, ensuring their voices are heard and their rights are protected. The legacy of these collaborations will undoubtedly shape the future of LGBTQ rights advocacy, paving the way for continued progress and empowerment.

Raising Awareness and Changing Policies

Raising awareness and changing policies regarding LGBTQ asylum seekers is a multifaceted endeavor that requires strategic advocacy, community engagement, and a commitment to social justice. This subsection delves into the theoretical frameworks, challenges, and successful strategies employed by Victor M. Maceda and his allies in the fight for LGBTQ rights, particularly focusing on asylum seekers.

Theoretical Frameworks

To understand the dynamics of raising awareness and effecting policy change, it is essential to consider the social change theories that underpin these efforts. One relevant theory is the **Social Movement Theory**, which posits that social movements arise when groups of individuals mobilize to address grievances. This theory emphasizes the importance of collective identity, resource mobilization, and political opportunities in shaping the success of movements.

Another pertinent framework is the **Framing Theory**, which highlights how the way issues are presented can significantly impact public perception and policy outcomes. By framing LGBTQ asylum seekers as individuals deserving of empathy and protection rather than as mere statistics or legal cases, advocates can foster a deeper understanding of their plight and garner broader support.

Challenges in Raising Awareness

Despite the theoretical foundations, the journey to raise awareness about LGBTQ asylum seekers is fraught with challenges. Prevalent societal stigma and discrimination often hinder open discussions about LGBTQ issues, leading to misinformation and misunderstanding. Many individuals, particularly in conservative communities, may harbor preconceived notions about LGBTQ identities that can obstruct empathy and support.

Moreover, the complexity of immigration policies can create barriers to understanding. Asylum processes are often convoluted, making it difficult for the general public to grasp the nuances involved. This complexity can lead to apathy or a lack of engagement from potential allies.

Strategies for Raising Awareness

Victor M. Maceda has employed several strategies to raise awareness and change policies affecting LGBTQ asylum seekers:

- **Storytelling:** Sharing personal narratives of LGBTQ asylum seekers has proven to be a powerful tool. These stories humanize the issue, allowing individuals to connect emotionally with the struggles faced by asylum seekers. Maceda has facilitated platforms where these voices can be heard, such as public speaking events, social media campaigns, and documentary projects.

- **Educational Workshops:** Maceda has organized workshops aimed at educating both the public and policymakers about the unique challenges faced by LGBTQ asylum seekers. These workshops often include data-driven presentations, personal testimonies, and discussions on the intersectionality of LGBTQ rights and immigration.

- **Collaborative Advocacy:** Partnering with human rights organizations and other advocacy groups has amplified the reach of awareness campaigns. By collaborating with established entities, Maceda has been able to leverage resources and networks to create a more significant impact.

- **Media Engagement:** Utilizing traditional media and social media platforms has been crucial in raising awareness. Maceda has engaged with journalists to highlight stories of LGBTQ asylum seekers, ensuring that their experiences are represented in mainstream narratives. This media engagement has included interviews, op-eds, and participation in documentary films.

- **Policy Advocacy:** Engaging directly with policymakers to advocate for legislative changes is a critical component of raising awareness. Maceda has met with legislators to discuss the need for policies that protect LGBTQ asylum seekers, providing them with data, personal stories, and legal insights to support their case.

Examples of Successful Policy Changes

Through persistent advocacy and awareness-raising efforts, significant strides have been made in changing policies affecting LGBTQ asylum seekers:

- In 2016, following extensive advocacy efforts, a landmark policy was established that recognized persecution based on sexual orientation and gender identity as valid grounds for asylum. This policy change was influenced by testimonies from LGBTQ asylum seekers and the work of activists like Maceda.

+ The establishment of training programs for immigration officers and judges on LGBTQ issues has also been a direct result of awareness-raising campaigns. These programs aim to reduce bias in asylum hearings and ensure fair treatment for LGBTQ applicants.

+ Increased funding for legal aid organizations that support LGBTQ asylum seekers has been achieved through advocacy efforts. This funding allows for more comprehensive legal representation, improving the chances of successful asylum claims.

Conclusion

Raising awareness and changing policies for LGBTQ asylum seekers is an ongoing struggle that requires dedication, creativity, and resilience. The work of Victor M. Maceda exemplifies how strategic advocacy, grounded in social change and framing theories, can lead to meaningful progress. By overcoming challenges and employing effective strategies, advocates can continue to foster understanding, empathy, and ultimately, policy changes that protect the rights and dignity of LGBTQ asylum seekers.

Legal Support for Asylum Seekers

Navigating the Complex Asylum Process

The asylum process is a labyrinthine journey that LGBTQ asylum seekers must traverse, often fraught with emotional and legal challenges. Understanding the complexities of this process is crucial for advocates like Victor M. Maceda, who tirelessly work to support these individuals in their quest for safety and acceptance.

The Legal Framework

To begin with, the legal framework governing asylum in the United States is established by both domestic laws and international treaties. The 1951 Refugee Convention and its 1967 Protocol provide the basis for granting asylum to individuals who have fled persecution based on race, religion, nationality, political opinion, or membership in a particular social group, which includes LGBTQ individuals. According to the United States Citizenship and Immigration Services (USCIS), an applicant must demonstrate a well-founded fear of persecution in their home country.

The legal definition of persecution is broad, encompassing not only physical harm but also psychological abuse, discrimination, and severe social ostracism. This is particularly relevant for LGBTQ individuals, who often face systemic violence and discrimination in their home countries.

Initial Application Process

The first step in the asylum process involves submitting an application, known as the Form I-589, Application for Asylum and for Withholding of Removal. This form requires detailed personal information and a comprehensive account of the persecution the applicant has faced or fears.

One of the major challenges in this initial application phase is the requirement to file within one year of arrival in the United States, known as the one-year filing deadline. This rule can be particularly daunting for LGBTQ asylum seekers who may still be grappling with their identity or fear of disclosure.

Gathering Evidence

Once the application is submitted, the next critical step is to gather supporting evidence. This may include:

+ Affidavits from witnesses who can attest to the applicant's experiences.

+ Medical records documenting any physical or psychological harm suffered.

+ Country condition reports that outline the general situation for LGBTQ individuals in the applicant's home country.

These documents are vital in establishing credibility and supporting the asylum claim.   For instance, a report from an international human rights organization detailing the treatment of LGBTQ individuals in a specific country can significantly bolster an applicant's case.

The Interview Process

Following the submission of the application and supporting documents, the applicant is typically called for an interview with an asylum officer. This interview is a pivotal moment in the asylum process, as it allows the officer to assess the applicant's credibility and the merits of their claim.

During the interview, applicants must recount their experiences of persecution and articulate their fears of returning to their home country. This can be a deeply traumatic experience, as it often requires revisiting painful memories. Advocates emphasize the importance of having legal representation during this stage to ensure that the applicant's rights are protected and that they can present their case effectively.

Challenges and Denials

Despite thorough preparation, many asylum claims are denied. Common reasons for denial include:

- Lack of credible evidence to support the claim.

- Inconsistencies in the applicant's testimony.

- Failure to meet the one-year filing deadline.

For LGBTQ asylum seekers, the stakes are particularly high. A denial can lead to deportation to a country where they may face severe persecution or even death. This reality underscores the importance of comprehensive legal support and advocacy.

Appeals Process

In the event of a denial, applicants have the right to appeal the decision to the Board of Immigration Appeals (BIA). This process can be lengthy and complex, often requiring additional legal arguments and evidence. Victor M. Maceda's work in providing pro bono legal services is crucial during this stage, as he helps asylum seekers navigate the appeals process and prepares them for potential hearings.

Conclusion

Navigating the complex asylum process is a daunting task for LGBTQ individuals seeking refuge from persecution. The intricacies of legal definitions, the emotional toll of recounting traumatic experiences, and the potential for denial create a challenging landscape. However, with dedicated advocates like Victor M. Maceda, there is hope for those seeking safety and a new beginning in a more accepting environment. The journey may be fraught with obstacles, but it is also marked by resilience, courage, and the unwavering pursuit of justice.

Providing Pro Bono Legal Services

In the realm of legal advocacy, particularly concerning LGBTQ asylum seekers, pro bono legal services emerge as a critical lifeline. This subsection delves into the significance of these services, the challenges faced in their provision, and the impactful outcomes that arise when legal professionals dedicate their skills to those in dire need.

The Importance of Pro Bono Work

Pro bono legal services are defined as legal work undertaken voluntarily and without payment, primarily aimed at helping individuals who cannot afford legal representation. The American Bar Association (ABA) emphasizes that every lawyer has a professional responsibility to provide legal services to those unable to pay. This ethical obligation is particularly salient in the context of LGBTQ asylum seekers, who often confront a myriad of barriers, including financial constraints, language differences, and systemic discrimination.

LGBTQ asylum seekers frequently flee their home countries due to persecution based on their sexual orientation or gender identity. The asylum process is notoriously complex, requiring a nuanced understanding of both immigration law and the unique challenges faced by LGBTQ individuals. Pro bono legal services not only provide essential representation but also help ensure that these individuals receive fair treatment under the law.

Challenges in Providing Pro Bono Legal Services

Despite the noble intentions behind pro bono work, several challenges hinder its effective implementation.

- **Resource Limitations:** Legal aid organizations often operate with limited resources, making it difficult to meet the high demand for services. This scarcity can lead to long wait times for clients seeking assistance.

- **Complexity of Cases:** LGBTQ asylum cases often involve intricate legal arguments, requiring attorneys to possess specialized knowledge of both asylum law and the sociopolitical contexts of their clients' home countries. This complexity can deter some attorneys from taking on pro bono cases.

- **Emotional Toll:** Attorneys providing pro bono services may encounter emotionally taxing situations, as they hear firsthand accounts of trauma and persecution. This can lead to burnout and compassion fatigue, ultimately affecting the quality of representation.

+ **Cultural Competency:** Legal professionals must also be culturally competent, understanding the unique experiences and challenges faced by LGBTQ individuals. A lack of awareness or sensitivity can hinder effective communication and trust-building between attorneys and clients.

Examples of Successful Pro Bono Initiatives

Numerous organizations have successfully implemented pro bono programs that demonstrate the effectiveness of this model in supporting LGBTQ asylum seekers.

1. **The LGBTQ+ Asylum Project** This initiative connects LGBTQ asylum seekers with volunteer attorneys who provide free legal representation. By leveraging a network of trained volunteers, the project has successfully assisted hundreds of individuals in navigating the asylum process. One notable case involved a young man from a Central American country who faced persecution due to his sexual orientation. With the help of a pro bono attorney, he was able to present a compelling case that ultimately resulted in his asylum approval.

2. **Immigration Equality** Another prominent organization, Immigration Equality, focuses on providing legal services to LGBTQ and HIV-positive asylum seekers. Their pro bono program has empowered numerous lawyers to take on cases that may have otherwise gone unrepresented. For instance, a pro bono attorney recently assisted a transgender woman from Africa in her asylum claim, highlighting the systemic violence she faced. This representation not only changed her life but also sent ripples of hope throughout her community.

The Impact of Pro Bono Legal Services

The provision of pro bono legal services has far-reaching implications for LGBTQ asylum seekers and the broader community.

+ **Access to Justice:** Pro bono services ensure that marginalized individuals have access to the legal system, helping to level the playing field in a system that often favors those with resources.

+ **Empowerment:** Legal representation empowers asylum seekers to share their stories and seek justice. It affirms their identities and experiences, fostering a sense of agency in a world that often seeks to silence them.

+ **Community Building:** Pro bono work fosters connections between legal professionals and LGBTQ communities, creating networks of support that extend beyond individual cases. These relationships can lead to further advocacy and systemic change.

+ **Raising Awareness:** By taking on pro bono cases, attorneys raise awareness about the unique challenges faced by LGBTQ asylum seekers. This visibility can influence public opinion and policy, encouraging a more compassionate and informed approach to immigration issues.

In conclusion, providing pro bono legal services is not merely an act of charity; it is a vital component of the fight for justice and equality for LGBTQ asylum seekers. By overcoming the challenges associated with pro bono work, legal professionals can make a profound difference in the lives of individuals seeking refuge from persecution. The stories of those who have benefited from these services serve as a testament to the power of compassion and the enduring impact of dedicated advocacy.

Preparing Asylum Cases and Testimonies

Preparing asylum cases and testimonies is a crucial step in the advocacy for LGBTQ asylum seekers. This process not only requires a deep understanding of legal frameworks but also a sensitivity to the personal experiences of individuals fleeing persecution. In this section, we will explore the theoretical underpinnings of asylum applications, the common challenges faced by LGBTQ asylum seekers, and practical examples of how Victor M. Maceda and his team have successfully navigated these complexities.

Theoretical Framework

The foundation of asylum law is rooted in international human rights principles, particularly the 1951 Refugee Convention, which defines a refugee as someone who has a well-founded fear of persecution due to race, religion, nationality, membership in a particular social group, or political opinion. LGBTQ individuals often fall under the category of "membership in a particular social group," as their sexual orientation or gender identity can lead to severe discrimination and violence in their home countries.

The legal standard for asylum in the United States, for instance, requires applicants to demonstrate that they meet the definition of a refugee and that they are unable or unwilling to return to their home country due to this fear of persecution. This necessitates the preparation of a compelling narrative that articulates their experiences and fears.

Common Challenges

LGBTQ asylum seekers face unique challenges when preparing their cases:

1. **Fear of Disclosure**: Many individuals fear that revealing their sexual orientation or gender identity could lead to further persecution, both in their home countries and in the asylum process itself. This fear can complicate the preparation of testimonies, as authenticity is crucial in establishing credibility.

2. **Cultural Barriers**: Asylum seekers may come from cultures where LGBTQ identities are stigmatized. This can affect their ability to articulate their experiences in a way that resonates with legal standards and expectations in a different cultural context.

3. **Legal Complexity**: The asylum process is often labyrinthine, involving extensive documentation, interviews, and legal representation. Asylum seekers may struggle to understand the requirements and navigate the legal system effectively.

4. **Emotional Trauma**: Many LGBTQ asylum seekers have experienced significant trauma, including violence, discrimination, and loss. This emotional burden can make it challenging to recount their experiences in a coherent and compelling manner.

Practical Examples

Victor M. Maceda and his team have developed effective strategies to address these challenges:

1. Building Trust and Rapport Establishing a trusting relationship with asylum seekers is paramount. Victor often begins the process by creating a safe space for individuals to share their stories. This involves active listening, empathy, and validation of their experiences. By fostering a supportive environment, asylum seekers are more likely to disclose sensitive information that is essential for their cases.

2. Conducting Comprehensive Interviews To prepare a strong asylum case, Victor conducts thorough interviews with each client. These interviews focus not only on the events that led to their asylum claim but also on their identity, relationships, and personal history. For example, during one interview, a client shared experiences of violence and discrimination that were deeply personal, allowing Victor to weave these narratives into a compelling testimony.

3.   **Documenting Evidence**   Victor emphasizes the importance of gathering supporting evidence to bolster asylum claims. This includes:
   - **Personal Statements**: Detailed accounts of the individual's experiences, written in their own words, are crucial. These statements should highlight specific incidents of persecution, societal attitudes towards LGBTQ individuals in their home country, and the potential risks they face if returned.
   - **Country Conditions Reports**: Victor often includes reports from credible organizations that detail the treatment of LGBTQ individuals in the asylum seeker's home country. These reports serve to contextualize the individual's experiences within broader societal patterns of discrimination.
   - **Affidavits from Witnesses**: In some cases, Victor has successfully included affidavits from friends, family, or community members who can corroborate the asylum seeker's experiences. These testimonies can add credibility to the asylum claim.

4. **Preparing for the Interview Process**   Once the asylum application is submitted, the applicant must attend an interview with an immigration officer. Victor prepares his clients for this critical step by conducting mock interviews. This practice helps asylum seekers become familiar with the types of questions they may encounter, and it allows them to practice articulating their stories in a clear and concise manner.

For example, during a mock interview, a client struggled to articulate the fear they felt when threatened in their home country. Through guided practice, Victor helped the client refine their narrative, emphasizing the emotional impact of their experiences while ensuring that they remained focused on the legal criteria for asylum.

5.   **Emphasizing the Importance of Authenticity**   Throughout the preparation process, Victor underscores the importance of authenticity in testimonies. Asylum seekers are encouraged to share their stories honestly and openly, as inconsistencies or perceived insincerity can undermine their credibility. Victor often reminds clients that their lived experiences are valid and worthy of recognition.

Conclusion

The preparation of asylum cases and testimonies is a multifaceted process that requires both legal acumen and a compassionate approach. By addressing the unique challenges faced by LGBTQ asylum seekers and employing effective strategies, Victor M. Maceda has played a pivotal role in advocating for those seeking refuge from persecution. His commitment to empowering individuals to share their stories not only strengthens their asylum claims but also contributes to the broader movement for LGBTQ rights and justice.

Appealing Denied Cases and Fighting for Justice

The journey for LGBTQ asylum seekers is often fraught with challenges, particularly when it comes to navigating the complex asylum process in which many face the harsh reality of denied cases. This subsection explores the critical steps involved in appealing these denials and the broader fight for justice that ensues.

Understanding the Appeals Process

When an asylum application is denied, the applicant typically has the right to appeal the decision. This process is governed by specific regulations, which can vary significantly depending on the jurisdiction. In the United States, for example, asylum seekers can appeal to the Board of Immigration Appeals (BIA) within 30 days of receiving the denial. The appeal must include a brief that outlines the errors made by the immigration judge or asylum officer, supported by relevant evidence and legal arguments.

The appeals process can be daunting, as it requires a deep understanding of immigration law and the ability to articulate complex legal arguments. Many asylum seekers lack the resources to navigate this system effectively, which is where advocates like Victor M. Maceda step in.

Challenges in the Appeals Process

One of the primary challenges faced by asylum seekers during the appeals process is the emotional and psychological toll of having their claims rejected. The denial often exacerbates feelings of fear and uncertainty, especially for individuals who have fled persecution in their home countries. The stress of potential deportation can lead to anxiety and depression, making it even more difficult for them to participate in their appeal effectively.

Moreover, the legal landscape surrounding asylum claims is continually evolving, with changes in policy and precedent that can impact the outcome of appeals. For instance, recent rulings may redefine what constitutes a "credible fear" of persecution, affecting the standard by which cases are judged. This creates an environment of unpredictability that can hinder an asylum seeker's ability to present their case confidently.

Strategies for Successful Appeals

To improve the chances of a successful appeal, it is essential to employ a variety of strategies:

+ **Thorough Documentation:** Gathering comprehensive evidence that supports the asylum seeker's claim is crucial. This may include witness statements, expert testimony, and country condition reports that detail the risks faced by LGBTQ individuals in the applicant's home country.

+ **Legal Representation:** Engaging an attorney experienced in immigration law can significantly enhance the chances of success. Legal professionals can help craft compelling arguments, ensuring that all procedural requirements are met and that the appeal is presented effectively.

+ **Public Awareness Campaigns:** Raising awareness about the plight of LGBTQ asylum seekers can garner public support and potentially influence decision-makers. Advocacy groups often organize campaigns that highlight specific cases, drawing attention to the injustices faced by individuals who have been denied asylum.

+ **Utilizing Amicus Briefs:** In some cases, advocacy organizations may submit amicus curiae briefs to provide additional context or legal arguments that support the asylum seeker's case. These briefs can help to illustrate broader implications of the case and the importance of granting asylum to individuals facing persecution based on their sexual orientation or gender identity.

Case Example: The Fight for Justice

Consider the case of a young gay man from a country where homosexuality is criminalized. After fleeing his home due to threats of violence and persecution, he applied for asylum but was denied on the grounds that he did not demonstrate a well-founded fear of persecution. With the help of Victor M. Maceda and his team, the young man appealed the decision by compiling evidence of systemic discrimination and violence against LGBTQ individuals in his home country.

The appeal included affidavits from human rights organizations, personal testimonies from other asylum seekers, and data illustrating the dangers faced by

LGBTQ individuals. Ultimately, the BIA overturned the initial decision, granting him asylum. This case exemplifies the importance of persistence, thorough preparation, and the role of dedicated advocates in fighting for justice.

Conclusion: A Call to Action

The fight for justice for LGBTQ asylum seekers does not end with the appeal process. It is a continuous struggle that requires vigilance, advocacy, and a commitment to human rights. As Victor M. Maceda emphasizes, every denied case represents not just a legal failure but a profound personal tragedy. Advocates must continue to push for systemic changes that address the root causes of discrimination and ensure that all individuals, regardless of their sexual orientation or gender identity, have the opportunity to seek refuge and live freely.

In conclusion, appealing denied asylum cases is a crucial aspect of the broader fight for LGBTQ rights. By understanding the challenges, employing effective strategies, and drawing on real-life examples of success, advocates can make significant strides in ensuring justice for those who seek safety and acceptance in a new land.

Celebrating Victories and Reuniting Families

The journey of LGBTQ asylum seekers is fraught with challenges, but it is also marked by profound victories that deserve celebration. As Victor M. Maceda has demonstrated through his tireless advocacy, the reunification of families often stands as a testament to the resilience of the human spirit and the effectiveness of dedicated activism. In this section, we will explore the significance of these victories, the emotional and psychological impacts of family reunification, and the broader implications for the LGBTQ asylum movement.

The Importance of Celebrating Victories

Celebrating victories in the realm of LGBTQ asylum advocacy is crucial for several reasons. Firstly, it fosters a sense of hope among asylum seekers and their families. Each success story serves as a beacon of possibility, demonstrating that change is achievable. For instance, when a family is reunited after a long separation due to the asylum process, it not only uplifts the individuals involved but also inspires others in similar situations to persevere.

Moreover, celebrating victories helps to raise awareness about the ongoing struggles faced by LGBTQ asylum seekers. By sharing these stories, advocates can highlight the importance of continued support and the need for systemic change.

As Maceda often emphasizes, "Every victory is a reminder of why we fight, and every family reunited is a symbol of our collective strength."

The Emotional and Psychological Impact of Reunification

The reunification of families is not merely a logistical achievement; it has profound emotional and psychological implications. Studies in psychology indicate that family connections are fundamental to individual well-being. The American Psychological Association (APA) highlights that strong family ties can enhance resilience and provide emotional support during times of crisis.

For LGBTQ asylum seekers, the trauma of separation can exacerbate feelings of isolation and despair. When families are finally reunited, the relief and joy can lead to significant improvements in mental health. A poignant example is the story of Miguel, a gay man from Honduras who fled violence and persecution. After a harrowing journey, he was granted asylum in the United States. The moment he was reunited with his partner, who had been waiting in a refugee camp, was filled with tears of joy and relief. As Miguel stated, "In that moment, everything changed. I felt whole again."

Challenges in the Reunification Process

Despite the joyous outcomes, the reunification process is often riddled with challenges. Legal hurdles, bureaucratic red tape, and the emotional toll of separation can complicate what should be a straightforward process. As Victor M. Maceda notes, "The system is not always kind, and families often face unnecessary obstacles."

For instance, delays in processing asylum claims can lead to prolonged separations. Additionally, the psychological effects of trauma can make it difficult for families to navigate the complexities of the legal system. This is where the role of advocates becomes crucial. By providing legal support and emotional guidance, activists like Maceda help families overcome these hurdles.

Examples of Successful Reunifications

Numerous success stories highlight the impact of advocacy in facilitating family reunifications. One notable case involved a transgender woman named Sara, who escaped persecution in her home country. After receiving asylum, her partner, who had been left behind, faced numerous challenges in seeking refuge. With the support of Maceda and his team, they were able to navigate the asylum process successfully. The emotional reunion at the airport was captured in a viral video, showcasing the power of love and resilience.

Another example is the story of a lesbian couple from Nigeria who faced severe threats due to their sexual orientation. After being granted asylum, they worked tirelessly to reunite with their children, who had been placed in a safe house. With legal assistance, they were able to bring their children to safety, demonstrating the profound impact of advocacy on family unity.

Broader Implications for LGBTQ Advocacy

The celebration of victories and the reunification of families have broader implications for the LGBTQ advocacy movement. Each success story contributes to a growing narrative that challenges the stigma surrounding LGBTQ asylum seekers. By highlighting these victories, advocates can shift public perception, fostering greater empathy and understanding.

Moreover, these stories serve as powerful tools for policy change. As more families are reunited, the demand for more humane asylum processes increases. Advocates like Maceda leverage these narratives to push for legislative reforms that prioritize the needs of LGBTQ asylum seekers.

Conclusion

In conclusion, celebrating victories and reuniting families is a vital aspect of LGBTQ asylum advocacy. The emotional impact of these reunifications cannot be overstated, as they provide hope and healing to those who have endured unimaginable hardships. Through the work of activists like Victor M. Maceda, families are not only reunited but empowered to continue the fight for their rights and the rights of others. As we look to the future, it is essential to honor these victories and continue advocating for a world where all families can live freely and without fear.

The Impact of Victor M Maceda's Work

Stories of LGBTQ Asylum Seekers Saved

The journey of LGBTQ asylum seekers is often fraught with peril, as they flee from persecution and violence in their home countries. Each story is a testament to human resilience and the profound impact of advocacy in the realm of human rights. Through the tireless efforts of Victor M. Maceda and his allies, many individuals have found not just refuge, but a renewed sense of hope and belonging.

One poignant example is the story of **Daniel**, a young gay man from a country where homosexuality is criminalized. After enduring years of harassment and violence from his community and family, Daniel made the harrowing decision to flee. Upon arriving in the United States, he faced a complex and daunting asylum process. Victor's organization provided crucial legal support, helping Daniel prepare his asylum application and gathering evidence of the threats he faced.

Daniel's case exemplifies the intersection of personal struggle and systemic barriers. The asylum process can be overwhelming, with a *success rate of approximately 30%* for LGBTQ applicants, highlighting the need for specialized legal assistance. Victor's team worked tirelessly to ensure that Daniel's story was heard, emphasizing the importance of personal narratives in asylum claims. They gathered testimonies from witnesses who could attest to the dangers Daniel faced, thus strengthening his case.

$$P(success) = \frac{N_{successful}}{N_{total}} \times 100 \qquad (23)$$

where $P(success)$ is the probability of success for an asylum application, $N_{successful}$ is the number of successful applications, and N_{total} is the total number of applications submitted.

This equation illustrates the harsh reality that many LGBTQ asylum seekers confront, where the odds are stacked against them. However, with dedicated advocacy, Daniel's application was ultimately approved, allowing him to stay in the United States and begin anew.

Another powerful story is that of **Maria**, a transgender woman from Central America. Maria faced severe violence and discrimination, leading to multiple attempts on her life. After a traumatic experience that left her fearing for her life, she sought asylum in the U.S. Victor's organization provided her with not only legal assistance but also emotional support during her transition into a new life.

Maria's case underscores the importance of intersectionality in advocacy. The unique challenges faced by transgender individuals, especially those from marginalized backgrounds, require a nuanced approach to asylum claims. Victor's team engaged with local LGBTQ organizations to ensure that Maria received comprehensive support, including mental health services and community integration programs.

The following equation illustrates the need for a multifaceted approach in supporting LGBTQ asylum seekers:

$$S = L + C + M + R \qquad (24)$$

where S is the overall support for an asylum seeker, L represents legal assistance, C denotes community support, M signifies mental health resources, and R reflects resources for integration.

Maria's successful asylum claim not only changed her life but also inspired others in her community. Her story became a beacon of hope, demonstrating that with the right support, survival is possible.

Furthermore, Victor's advocacy extends beyond individual cases. He has worked to raise awareness about the plight of LGBTQ asylum seekers on a global scale. Through media campaigns and public speaking engagements, he has highlighted the stories of individuals like Daniel and Maria, emphasizing the need for policy changes that protect vulnerable populations.

The collective impact of these stories is profound. Each successful asylum case represents not just a legal victory but a life saved. Victor's work has helped to shift public perception and foster greater empathy towards LGBTQ asylum seekers. His commitment to sharing these narratives has played a crucial role in mobilizing support and resources for those who need it most.

In conclusion, the stories of LGBTQ asylum seekers saved through Victor M. Maceda's advocacy highlight the intersection of personal resilience and systemic change. They remind us that behind every statistic lies a human life, deserving of dignity, safety, and the chance to thrive. As we continue to fight for justice and equality, it is essential to amplify these voices and recognize the ongoing struggles faced by LGBTQ individuals around the world. Each story not only illustrates the challenges of seeking asylum but also the transformative power of advocacy in creating a more inclusive society.

Inspiring Others to Get Involved

Victor M. Maceda's journey as an LGBTQ rights activist has not only been a personal battle but also a powerful catalyst for collective action. His ability to inspire others to get involved in the fight for LGBTQ rights is rooted in a combination of personal storytelling, strategic outreach, and the creation of inclusive spaces for engagement. This section explores the various methods Victor employed to galvanize support, the challenges he faced, and the impact of his efforts on the broader movement.

The Power of Personal Stories

One of the most compelling tools in Victor's arsenal has been the use of personal narratives. He understood that stories have the power to connect individuals on an emotional level, breaking down barriers of misunderstanding and prejudice. By sharing his own experiences of growing up in a conservative town and facing discrimination, Victor humanized the struggle for LGBTQ rights. This approach aligns with the theory of narrative persuasion, which posits that individuals are more likely to be influenced by stories than by statistics or abstract arguments [?].

For example, during a community outreach event, Victor recounted a poignant moment from his adolescence when he first realized the depth of societal prejudice against LGBTQ individuals. He described how this experience ignited his passion for activism. This narrative not only resonated with many attendees but also encouraged them to share their own stories, fostering a sense of solidarity and community. By creating a platform for personal stories, Victor demonstrated that activism is not just a political endeavor but a deeply personal one.

Strategic Outreach and Education

Victor recognized that inspiring others to get involved required more than just compelling narratives; it necessitated strategic outreach and education. He established workshops and seminars aimed at educating individuals about LGBTQ rights and the importance of allyship. These sessions often included discussions on intersectionality, emphasizing how various identities intersect and affect one's experience within the LGBTQ community. This educational approach aligns with Paulo Freire's critical pedagogy, which advocates for dialogue and reflection as means of fostering critical consciousness [?].

Moreover, Victor collaborated with schools, universities, and community organizations to implement LGBTQ awareness programs. By integrating these topics into educational curricula, he aimed to cultivate empathy and understanding among younger generations. For instance, he spearheaded a campaign that encouraged high schools to include LGBTQ history in their social studies programs, which not only educated students but also inspired them to become advocates for equality.

Creating Inclusive Spaces

Inspiring others also meant creating inclusive spaces where individuals felt welcome to engage in activism. Victor founded local LGBTQ support groups that emphasized inclusivity and diversity, ensuring that all voices were heard, particularly those from marginalized subgroups within the community. These spaces served as incubators for activism, where individuals could brainstorm ideas, share resources, and collaborate on initiatives.

For example, at one of these support group meetings, a young transgender woman shared her struggles with accessing healthcare. This prompted the group to organize a campaign advocating for healthcare providers to undergo LGBTQ sensitivity training. The initiative not only addressed a pressing issue but also empowered group members to take ownership of their activism, thereby inspiring further involvement.

Leveraging Social Media

In the digital age, Victor adeptly utilized social media to amplify his message and reach a wider audience. He recognized that platforms like Twitter, Instagram, and Facebook could serve as powerful tools for mobilization. By sharing informative content, personal stories, and calls to action, Victor engaged a diverse audience and encouraged them to participate in advocacy efforts.

For instance, during Pride Month, Victor launched a social media campaign that featured daily posts highlighting different aspects of LGBTQ history and rights. Each post included a call to action, urging followers to share their own experiences or participate in local events. This strategy not only increased visibility for LGBTQ issues but also fostered a sense of community among followers, many of whom began organizing events in their own neighborhoods.

Challenges and Resilience

Despite his successes, Victor faced significant challenges in inspiring others to get involved. One major obstacle was the pervasive stigma surrounding LGBTQ issues, which often deterred individuals from openly supporting the movement. To combat this, Victor emphasized the importance of resilience and courage in the face of adversity. He often reminded his audience that every small action contributes to the larger fight for justice.

Additionally, burnout among activists is a well-documented phenomenon [?]. Victor addressed this issue by promoting self-care and sustainable activism practices. He organized workshops focused on mental health and well-being, encouraging activists to prioritize their own needs alongside their advocacy efforts. This holistic approach not only inspired others to get involved but also fostered a supportive community that valued both activism and personal well-being.

Conclusion

Victor M. Maceda's ability to inspire others to get involved in the fight for LGBTQ rights is a testament to the power of personal storytelling, strategic outreach, and the creation of inclusive spaces. By leveraging these methods, he has not only mobilized individuals but has also fostered a sense of collective responsibility towards the ongoing struggle for equality. As we reflect on Victor's impact, it is clear that inspiring others is not merely about rallying support; it is about cultivating a movement that is inclusive, resilient, and deeply personal.

Media Coverage and Public Recognition

The role of media coverage in the advocacy efforts of LGBTQ rights activists, particularly in the case of Victor M. Maceda, cannot be overstated. Media serves as both a platform for visibility and a mechanism for influencing public opinion, which is crucial for social change. This section explores the dynamics of media coverage and public recognition, examining the challenges faced, the strategies employed, and the resulting impacts on LGBTQ asylum seekers and the broader community.

The Power of Media in Advocacy

Media has the unique ability to shape narratives and bring attention to marginalized issues. For Victor M. Maceda, leveraging media was essential in amplifying the voices of LGBTQ asylum seekers. The media's role can be understood through the lens of agenda-setting theory, which posits that the media doesn't tell us what to think, but rather what to think about [?]. By focusing on LGBTQ rights, particularly the plight of asylum seekers, Maceda and his allies could influence public discourse and policy discussions.

Challenges in Media Representation

Despite the potential of media to foster understanding, significant challenges persist. LGBTQ issues are often sensationalized or misrepresented in mainstream media, leading to a distorted public perception. For instance, media outlets may focus disproportionately on negative stereotypes, framing LGBTQ individuals as victims rather than advocates or survivors [?]. This framing can undermine the dignity and agency of those Maceda sought to represent, complicating efforts to garner support for asylum seekers.

Strategic Media Engagement

To combat these challenges, Maceda employed strategic media engagement. He recognized the importance of storytelling in humanizing the experiences of LGBTQ asylum seekers. By sharing personal narratives, Maceda could evoke empathy and foster a deeper understanding of the complexities involved in seeking asylum. For example, through interviews and documentaries, he showcased the journeys of individuals fleeing persecution, highlighting their resilience and courage.

$$\text{Empathy} = \frac{\text{Personal Narratives}}{\text{Media Representation}} \tag{25}$$

This equation illustrates that as personal narratives increase in media representation, so too does the potential for empathy among the public. Maceda's efforts resulted in a shift in the narrative surrounding LGBTQ asylum seekers, moving away from victimhood towards a portrayal of strength and agency.

Public Recognition and Its Impact

As Maceda's media presence grew, so did his public recognition. This recognition played a pivotal role in his advocacy work, allowing him to reach wider audiences and mobilize support. Public figures and celebrities began to take notice of his work, leading to collaborations that further elevated the cause. For instance, high-profile endorsements from actors and musicians not only provided a platform for Maceda's message but also contributed to a broader cultural acceptance of LGBTQ rights.

Case Study: Media Campaigns

One notable example of successful media engagement was the "#SafeHaven" campaign, which aimed to raise awareness about the challenges faced by LGBTQ asylum seekers. Through social media platforms, Maceda and his team shared stories, infographics, and calls to action, encouraging followers to advocate for policy changes. The campaign garnered significant media attention, resulting in features on major news networks and discussions in legislative forums.

Conclusion

In conclusion, the interplay between media coverage and public recognition was instrumental in Victor M. Maceda's advocacy for LGBTQ asylum seekers. By navigating the challenges of representation and employing strategic storytelling,

Maceda was able to shift public perceptions and inspire action. As media continues to evolve, the lessons learned from Maceda's experiences underscore the importance of responsible representation and the power of personal narratives in effecting change.

Advocating for Systemic Change

Advocating for systemic change is a fundamental aspect of Victor M. Maceda's work in support of LGBTQ asylum seekers. This process involves not merely addressing individual cases of discrimination or persecution but rather targeting the underlying structures and policies that perpetuate inequality. Systemic change seeks to create a more equitable society by reforming the institutions and laws that govern the treatment of marginalized communities.

Understanding Systemic Change

Systemic change can be understood through the lens of social justice theory, which posits that true equity cannot be achieved without addressing the root causes of oppression. As articulated by theorists such as Iris Marion Young, the concept of structural injustice highlights how systemic barriers—rooted in historical and social contexts—contribute to the ongoing marginalization of certain groups. In the case of LGBTQ asylum seekers, these barriers manifest in discriminatory immigration policies, biased legal standards, and societal stigmas that hinder their ability to seek refuge and build new lives.

The equation governing systemic change can be represented as follows:

$$Systemic\ Change = Awareness + Advocacy + Policy\ Reform$$

Where: - Awareness involves educating the public and policymakers about the challenges faced by LGBTQ asylum seekers. - Advocacy includes mobilizing communities, leveraging media, and forming coalitions to amplify the voices of marginalized individuals. - Policy Reform entails working within legislative frameworks to enact laws that protect LGBTQ rights and ensure equitable treatment.

Challenges to Systemic Change

Advocating for systemic change is fraught with challenges. One significant barrier is the political landscape, which can be resistant to reform. For example, in many countries, laws governing asylum and immigration are influenced by prevailing social attitudes, which may be hostile toward LGBTQ individuals. This hostility can be exacerbated by misinformation and stereotypes that paint LGBTQ asylum seekers as threats rather than victims of persecution.

Moreover, the intersectionality of identities complicates advocacy efforts. LGBTQ individuals who are also members of other marginalized groups—such as racial minorities or individuals with disabilities—often face compounded discrimination. As such, effective advocacy must be inclusive and consider the diverse experiences of all asylum seekers.

Examples of Systemic Change Initiatives

Victor M. Maceda's advocacy work exemplifies the pursuit of systemic change through various initiatives. One notable example is his collaboration with organizations such as the Human Rights Campaign and Amnesty International. These partnerships have focused on lobbying for legislative reforms that protect LGBTQ asylum seekers, such as the proposed *Equality Act*, which aims to prohibit discrimination based on sexual orientation and gender identity in various sectors, including immigration.

Additionally, Maceda has been instrumental in organizing campaigns that raise awareness about the plight of LGBTQ asylum seekers. These campaigns often feature personal stories that humanize the issue, helping to shift public perception and galvanize support for policy changes. For instance, the "We Are Here" campaign highlighted the experiences of LGBTQ asylum seekers through social media platforms, garnering significant attention and prompting discussions in legislative circles.

The Role of Grassroots Movements

Grassroots movements play a crucial role in advocating for systemic change. By mobilizing local communities, these movements create a powerful force for change that can influence national and international policies. Maceda has actively engaged with grassroots organizations, empowering LGBTQ individuals to share their stories and advocate for their rights. This approach not only amplifies marginalized voices but also fosters a sense of community and solidarity among asylum seekers.

For example, the *LGBTQ Asylum Seekers Network* has been pivotal in providing resources and support to individuals navigating the asylum process. By offering legal assistance, mental health services, and community-building opportunities, this network exemplifies how grassroots initiatives can effect systemic change by addressing the immediate needs of asylum seekers while simultaneously advocating for broader policy reforms.

Conclusion: The Path Forward

Advocating for systemic change is an ongoing journey that requires perseverance, collaboration, and a commitment to justice. Victor M. Maceda's work serves as a testament to the power of advocacy in transforming lives and dismantling oppressive systems. As the fight for LGBTQ rights continues, it is imperative that advocates remain vigilant and proactive in challenging the status quo, ensuring that the voices of LGBTQ asylum seekers are heard and their rights protected.

In summary, systemic change is not merely an end goal but a continuous process that involves raising awareness, mobilizing communities, and reforming policies to create a more just and equitable society for all. The legacy of Victor M. Maceda will undoubtedly inspire future generations to continue this vital work, ensuring that the fight for LGBTQ rights and the protection of asylum seekers remains at the forefront of social justice movements.

Continuing the Fight for LGBTQ Asylum Seekers

The fight for LGBTQ asylum seekers is not merely a battle for legal recognition; it is an ongoing struggle for humanity, dignity, and the right to live freely without fear of persecution. As we delve into the complexities surrounding this issue, it becomes evident that the path forward is fraught with challenges, yet illuminated by the resilience of those who dare to advocate for change.

The Theoretical Framework

Understanding the plight of LGBTQ asylum seekers requires a multi-faceted theoretical framework, particularly one that incorporates intersectionality. Intersectionality, as defined by Crenshaw (1989), emphasizes how various social identities—such as race, gender, sexuality, and class—interact to create unique experiences of oppression. In the context of LGBTQ asylum seekers, this means recognizing that individuals from different backgrounds face distinct challenges. For instance, a Black transgender asylum seeker may encounter both racial and gender-based discrimination, compounding their vulnerability.

Current Challenges

Despite significant progress in LGBTQ rights globally, many countries still enforce laws that criminalize homosexuality and gender non-conformity, leading to widespread violence and discrimination. According to a report by the International Lesbian, Gay, Bisexual, Trans and Intersex Association (ILGA), over 70 countries still have laws that criminalize same-sex relationships, and in some regions, LGBTQ individuals face the death penalty. This dire situation necessitates urgent action and advocacy.

Furthermore, the asylum process itself can be an insurmountable barrier for many. The legal framework surrounding asylum is often complex and intimidating. Asylum seekers must navigate a labyrinth of legal requirements, including proving a well-founded fear of persecution, which can be particularly challenging for LGBTQ individuals who may not have documented evidence of their experiences. The trauma associated with their past can also hinder their ability to recount their stories in a manner that resonates with immigration officials.

Advocacy Strategies

To continue the fight for LGBTQ asylum seekers, activists and organizations must employ a variety of strategies:

- **Legal Support:** Providing pro bono legal assistance is crucial. Organizations like the *Immigrant Justice Corps* and *Lambda Legal* have made significant strides in helping LGBTQ individuals navigate the asylum process. By preparing comprehensive cases and testimonies, they empower asylum seekers to present their narratives effectively.

- **Public Awareness Campaigns:** Raising awareness through social media, public demonstrations, and educational programs can help shift public perception. Campaigns that humanize the stories of LGBTQ asylum seekers can foster empathy and understanding. For instance, the *#FreeToBe* campaign has successfully highlighted the personal stories of LGBTQ individuals seeking asylum, creating a platform for visibility and advocacy.

- **Coalition Building:** Collaborating with other marginalized communities strengthens the fight for LGBTQ asylum seekers. By building coalitions with immigrant rights organizations, racial justice groups, and feminist movements, advocates can amplify their voices and create a united front against systemic oppression.

+ **Policy Advocacy:** Engaging in lobbying efforts to influence legislation is vital. Advocates must push for policies that protect LGBTQ asylum seekers, such as the repeal of discriminatory laws and the implementation of training programs for immigration officials to sensitively handle LGBTQ cases.

Examples of Success

There are numerous examples that illustrate the impact of advocacy in the realm of LGBTQ asylum. In recent years, organizations have successfully challenged the denial of asylum claims based on sexual orientation. In the landmark case of *Matter of A-B-*, the Board of Immigration Appeals recognized that LGBTQ individuals fleeing violence in their home countries could qualify for asylum. This case set a precedent that has been instrumental in shaping future decisions regarding LGBTQ asylum claims.

Moreover, grassroots movements have emerged, such as the *Queer Detainee Empowerment Project*, which provides support and resources to LGBTQ individuals in detention centers. By fostering a sense of community and belonging, these initiatives not only aid in the asylum process but also promote mental health and resilience among asylum seekers.

The Road Ahead

As we look to the future, it is imperative that the movement for LGBTQ asylum seekers evolves and adapts to the changing landscape. The global rise of anti-LGBTQ sentiment necessitates a proactive approach that anticipates challenges rather than merely reacting to them.

$$\text{Advocacy Success} = \text{Legal Support} + \text{Public Awareness} + \text{Coalition Building} + \text{Policy Advoc} \tag{26}$$

This equation underscores the importance of a multi-pronged approach to advocacy, emphasizing that success in this area is not achieved through isolated efforts but rather through a comprehensive strategy that integrates various forms of support.

In conclusion, the fight for LGBTQ asylum seekers is far from over. While significant strides have been made, the journey requires unwavering commitment, empathy, and collaboration. By continuing to advocate for the rights and dignity of LGBTQ individuals seeking asylum, we not only honor their stories but also pave the way for a more just and equitable world for all.

Lessons Learned and Looking to the Future

Reflections on the Journey So Far

Victor M. Maceda's journey as an LGBTQ rights activist has been both transformative and tumultuous, marked by personal struggles, collective victories, and an unwavering commitment to justice. As we reflect on the myriad experiences that have shaped his activism, it becomes evident that the path has not only been about advocating for rights but also about personal growth, resilience, and the power of community.

One of the most significant aspects of Victor's journey is the evolution of his understanding of identity and intersectionality. Early on, he faced the harsh realities of prejudice and discrimination in a conservative town, which forced him to confront his identity head-on. This struggle is not unique to Victor; many LGBTQ individuals grapple with their sense of self in environments that may not be accepting. According to Crenshaw's theory of intersectionality, individuals experience overlapping systems of discrimination, which can complicate their fight for rights. Victor's experiences illustrate this theory, as he navigated not only his sexual orientation but also the cultural and social expectations imposed upon him.

The journey from personal struggle to collective action is a pivotal theme in Victor's life. His coming out story is emblematic of the broader LGBTQ experience, where acceptance often comes after a period of intense personal conflict. Victor's realization that he was not alone in his struggles led him to seek support in unexpected places, from local LGBTQ organizations to online communities. This mirrors the findings of research conducted by the Williams Institute, which highlights the importance of social support in the mental health outcomes of LGBTQ individuals. Victor's story serves as a testament to the transformative power of community, where shared experiences can foster resilience and strength.

As Victor transitioned into activism, he faced numerous challenges, including pushback from conservative factions and the emotional toll of advocating for marginalized communities. The psychological implications of activism are well-documented; activists often experience burnout and vicarious trauma due to their exposure to systemic injustices. Victor's journey was no exception, as he encountered both victories and setbacks in his fight for LGBTQ rights, particularly for asylum seekers. The complexity of the asylum process, coupled with the stigma surrounding LGBTQ identities in many countries, posed significant challenges. However, these obstacles only fueled Victor's determination to make a difference.

A crucial turning point in Victor's journey was his decision to focus on the plight of LGBTQ asylum seekers. Through extensive research and collaboration with human rights organizations, he began to document cases of individuals fleeing persecution. This work not only highlighted the dire circumstances faced by these individuals but also underscored the importance of advocacy in changing public perception and policy. Victor's role in this movement exemplifies the theories of social justice, which emphasize the need for systemic change to address the root causes of inequality. By advocating for policy changes and providing legal support, Victor has become a beacon of hope for many seeking safety and acceptance.

Furthermore, Victor's personal life has also played a significant role in shaping his activism. Finding love and building a family amidst the chaos of advocacy has provided him with a unique perspective on the importance of personal relationships in the fight for rights. The balance between activism and personal life is a delicate one, often requiring sacrifices and difficult decisions. Victor's experiences resonate with the concept of "self-care" in activism, which emphasizes the necessity of maintaining one's mental and emotional well-being while fighting for justice.

In conclusion, Victor M. Maceda's journey as an LGBTQ rights activist is a rich tapestry woven with threads of personal struggle, resilience, and community support. His reflections on this journey reveal the complexities of identity, the importance of intersectionality, and the need for systemic change. As he continues to advocate for LGBTQ asylum seekers and inspire future generations, Victor's legacy serves as a reminder that the fight for equality is ongoing and that every individual's story contributes to the larger narrative of justice. The lessons learned from his journey not only inform his activism but also provide a roadmap for others seeking to effect change in their communities. The power of personal stories, combined with collective action, can indeed catalyze significant societal transformation.

Overcoming Obstacles and Burnout

In the realm of LGBTQ rights activism, the journey is often fraught with obstacles that can lead to significant emotional and physical burnout. Victor M. Maceda, like many activists, faced these challenges head-on, navigating a landscape that is both rewarding and exhausting. Understanding the nature of these obstacles and the strategies for overcoming them is crucial for sustaining long-term activism.

Understanding Burnout in Activism

Burnout is a psychological syndrome characterized by emotional exhaustion, depersonalization, and a diminished sense of personal accomplishment. According to Maslach and Leiter (2016), burnout can occur when the demands placed on an individual exceed their capacity to cope. In the context of activism, this can manifest in several ways:

* **Emotional Exhaustion:** Continuous exposure to stories of trauma and injustice can lead to feelings of helplessness and fatigue.

* **Depersonalization:** Activists may begin to feel detached from the very causes they champion, leading to a cynical outlook.

* **Reduced Personal Accomplishment:** Despite significant efforts, activists may feel that their contributions are insignificant in the face of systemic issues.

These symptoms are particularly prevalent among LGBTQ activists who often juggle multiple roles, including advocacy, community engagement, and personal life commitments.

Identifying Personal and Systemic Obstacles

Victor's journey illustrates the interplay between personal and systemic obstacles. Personal challenges, such as financial instability or lack of support, can hinder an activist's ability to engage fully in their work. Systemic obstacles include:

* **Institutional Resistance:** Many activists encounter bureaucratic hurdles when advocating for policy changes, which can be disheartening.

* **Societal Stigma:** The persistent stigma surrounding LGBTQ identities can lead to isolation and discourage individuals from pursuing activism.

* **Resource Scarcity:** Limited funding and resources for LGBTQ organizations can strain efforts to provide necessary support and advocacy.

Recognizing these obstacles is the first step towards developing effective coping strategies.

Coping Strategies for Activists

Victor employed several strategies to overcome burnout and maintain his commitment to LGBTQ rights. These strategies can be categorized into personal and community-based approaches:

Personal Strategies   1. **Self-Care Practices:** Victor prioritized self-care by engaging in activities that nurtured his mental and physical well-being. This included regular exercise, mindfulness meditation, and setting aside time for hobbies. 2. **Setting Boundaries:** He learned to set boundaries around his work, ensuring that he did not overcommit himself. This involved saying no to certain events or campaigns that did not align with his core mission.   3. **Seeking Professional Help:** Victor recognized the importance of mental health support and sought therapy to process his experiences and emotions, which helped him regain perspective and motivation.

Community-Based Strategies   1. **Building Support Networks:** Victor actively sought to create a community of like-minded activists who could provide emotional support and share resources. This network became a vital source of encouragement and collaboration.   2. **Mentorship Programs:** By mentoring younger activists, Victor not only empowered the next generation but also found renewed purpose and energy in sharing his knowledge and experiences.   3. **Collective Action:** Engaging in collective actions, such as group protests and community events, helped alleviate the sense of isolation that often accompanies activism. These gatherings fostered a sense of solidarity and shared purpose.

The Role of Reflection and Adaptation

Reflection is a critical component of overcoming obstacles and preventing burnout. Victor maintained a journal where he documented his thoughts, feelings, and experiences related to his activism. This practice allowed him to identify patterns of stress and recognize when he needed to recalibrate his approach.

$$\text{Resilience} = \frac{\text{Personal Strategies} + \text{Community Support}}{\text{Obstacles}} \tag{27}$$

This equation illustrates that resilience in activism can be enhanced by the combination of personal coping strategies and robust community support, effectively mitigating the impact of obstacles.

Conclusion

Overcoming obstacles and preventing burnout is an ongoing process for LGBTQ activists like Victor M. Maceda. By understanding the nature of burnout, identifying personal and systemic challenges, and employing effective coping strategies, activists can sustain their passion and commitment to the fight for equality. Victor's journey serves as a testament to the resilience required in activism, reminding us that while the path may be arduous, the impact of our efforts can lead to transformative change for LGBTQ communities worldwide.

Building Sustainable LGBTQ Support Systems

The establishment of sustainable support systems for LGBTQ individuals is a multifaceted endeavor that requires a comprehensive understanding of community needs, intersectional identities, and the socio-political landscape. As Victor M. Maceda's work illustrates, building these systems is not merely a matter of providing resources; it involves creating an environment where individuals feel safe, valued, and empowered to advocate for their rights.

Theoretical Framework

To effectively build sustainable support systems, we must draw upon several theoretical frameworks. One such framework is **Social Capital Theory**, which emphasizes the importance of networks, relationships, and trust within communities. According to Putnam (2000), social capital can enhance collective action and foster resilience among marginalized groups. In the context of LGBTQ support systems, social capital manifests through community organizations, peer support groups, and advocacy networks that enable individuals to connect, share experiences, and mobilize for change.

Another critical framework is **Intersectionality**, as coined by Crenshaw (1989), which highlights how various social identities—such as race, gender, class, and sexual orientation—interact to create unique experiences of oppression and privilege. Recognizing intersectionality is vital in designing support systems that address the diverse needs of LGBTQ individuals, particularly those who belong to multiple marginalized groups.

Identifying Problems

Despite the progress made in LGBTQ rights, significant challenges persist in building sustainable support systems. One major issue is the **lack of funding and** resources. Many LGBTQ organizations operate on limited budgets, often relying on grants and donations, which can be unpredictable. This financial instability hampers their ability to provide consistent services and outreach programs.

Additionally, there is a pervasive **stigma and discrimination** that LGBTQ individuals face, even within support systems. This can lead to feelings of isolation and mistrust, making it difficult for individuals to seek help. For instance, a study by Herek (2009) found that many LGBTQ individuals avoid seeking mental health services due to fears of discrimination or misunderstanding by providers.

Examples of Successful Support Systems

To counter these challenges, several organizations have successfully built sustainable LGBTQ support systems that can serve as models. The **Trevor Project**, for example, focuses on crisis intervention and suicide prevention for LGBTQ youth. By providing a 24/7 helpline, online chat, and text support, the Trevor Project ensures that young individuals have access to immediate assistance. Their comprehensive approach includes training for counselors to handle LGBTQ-specific issues sensitively, thereby fostering trust and connection.

Another notable example is **SAGE** (Services and Advocacy for GLBT Elders), which addresses the unique challenges faced by LGBTQ seniors. SAGE provides a range of services, including social activities, health services, and legal assistance. Their emphasis on community building and advocacy has led to significant improvements in the quality of life for LGBTQ elders, showcasing the importance of tailored support systems.

Strategies for Sustainability

Building sustainable LGBTQ support systems requires strategic planning and collaboration. Here are several effective strategies:

1. **Diversifying Funding Sources:** Organizations should seek to diversify their funding through grants, corporate sponsorships, and individual donations. Establishing partnerships with local businesses can also provide financial support while fostering community engagement.

2. **Creating Inclusive Spaces:** Support systems must prioritize inclusivity by actively engaging with diverse populations within the LGBTQ community. This can be achieved through outreach programs that specifically target marginalized groups, such as LGBTQ people of color, transgender individuals, and those with disabilities.

3. **Implementing Training Programs:** Providing training for staff and volunteers on LGBTQ issues, intersectionality, and cultural competency is

essential. This ensures that support systems are equipped to meet the needs of all community members effectively.

4. **Fostering Community Engagement:** Encouraging community involvement through volunteer opportunities, workshops, and events can help strengthen social capital within the LGBTQ community. This engagement not only builds resilience but also empowers individuals to take an active role in advocacy.

5. **Utilizing Technology:** Leveraging technology can enhance outreach and accessibility. Online platforms can provide resources, virtual support groups, and educational materials, making it easier for individuals to access help regardless of their location.

Conclusion

Building sustainable LGBTQ support systems is a crucial aspect of fostering resilience and empowerment within the community. By understanding the theoretical frameworks that underpin these systems, identifying existing challenges, and implementing effective strategies, advocates like Victor M. Maceda can create lasting change. As we continue to navigate the complexities of LGBTQ rights advocacy, it is imperative that we prioritize the establishment of robust support networks that uplift and empower all individuals, ensuring that no one is left behind in the ongoing fight for equality and justice.

Bibliography

[1] Putnam, R. D. (2000). *Bowling Alone: The Collapse and Revival of American Community*. Simon & Schuster.

[2] Crenshaw, K. (1989). Demarginalizing the Intersection of Race and Sex: A Black Feminist Critique of Antidiscrimination Doctrine, Feminist Theory and Antiracist Politics. *University of Chicago Legal Forum*, 1989(1), 139-167.

[3] Herek, G. M. (2009). Sexual Stigma and Sexual Prejudice in the United States: A Conceptual Framework. *Archives of Sexual Behavior*, 38(5), 976-988.

Empowering LGBTQ Asylum Seekers

Empowering LGBTQ asylum seekers is a multifaceted endeavor that requires a comprehensive understanding of the unique challenges they face, as well as a commitment to fostering resilience and agency within these communities. This section delves into the theoretical frameworks, practical strategies, and real-world examples that illustrate the importance of empowerment in the context of LGBTQ asylum seekers.

Theoretical Frameworks

At the core of empowerment lies the concept of agency, which refers to the capacity of individuals to act independently and make their own choices. In the context of LGBTQ asylum seekers, agency is often undermined by systemic oppression, discrimination, and the trauma associated with forced migration. Theories of empowerment, such as Freire's *Pedagogy of the Oppressed*, emphasize the importance of critical consciousness—awareness of social, political, and economic contradictions—and the ability to take action against oppressive elements in their lives.

Another relevant framework is the *Social Identity Theory*, which posits that individuals derive a sense of self from their group memberships. For LGBTQ asylum seekers, their sexual orientation or gender identity can be a source of pride and strength, but it can also be a target for discrimination. Empowerment initiatives must therefore focus on reinforcing positive identities while addressing the stigma and prejudice they encounter.

Identifying Problems

LGBTQ asylum seekers face numerous challenges that hinder their empowerment, including:

- **Legal Barriers:** The asylum process is often fraught with complex legal requirements that can be intimidating and confusing. Many asylum seekers lack access to legal representation, which can lead to unjust denials of their claims.

- **Social Isolation:** Upon arrival in a new country, LGBTQ asylum seekers may find themselves isolated from both their home communities and the broader society. This isolation can exacerbate feelings of fear and hopelessness.

- **Mental Health Issues:** The trauma of persecution, combined with the stress of navigating the asylum process and adapting to a new culture, can lead to significant mental health challenges, including anxiety, depression, and PTSD.

- **Economic Hardship:** Many LGBTQ asylum seekers arrive with limited resources and face difficulties in finding employment due to discrimination or lack of recognition of their qualifications.

Strategies for Empowerment

To address these challenges, a variety of strategies can be employed to empower LGBTQ asylum seekers:

1. **Legal Support:** Providing access to pro bono legal services is crucial. Organizations like the *Immigrant Justice Corps* and *The Refugee and Immigrant Center for Education and Legal Services (RAICES)* offer free legal assistance and representation to asylum seekers. These services help demystify the legal process and empower individuals to advocate for their rights.

2. **Community Building:** Establishing support networks is vital for reducing social isolation. LGBTQ community centers and organizations can create safe spaces for asylum seekers to connect with others who share similar experiences. Programs that foster peer support and mentorship can significantly enhance feelings of belonging and empowerment.

3. **Mental Health Resources:** Providing culturally competent mental health services is essential for addressing the psychological needs of LGBTQ asylum seekers. Initiatives like the *Trans Lifeline* and *The Trevor Project* offer support specifically tailored to LGBTQ individuals, helping them navigate their mental health challenges in a supportive environment.

4. **Economic Empowerment Programs:** Job training and placement services can help LGBTQ asylum seekers gain the skills and confidence needed to enter the workforce. Organizations such as *The LGBTQ Center* in Los Angeles provide career counseling, job readiness workshops, and connections to potential employers.

5. **Advocacy and Awareness:** Empowering asylum seekers also involves advocating for systemic change. By engaging in public awareness campaigns and lobbying for more inclusive asylum policies, activists can help create a more supportive environment for LGBTQ individuals seeking refuge.

Real-World Examples

Several organizations exemplify successful empowerment strategies for LGBTQ asylum seekers:

+ **The International Refugee Assistance Project (IRAP):** IRAP provides legal assistance and advocacy for refugees, including LGBTQ individuals. Their comprehensive approach includes legal representation, community engagement, and public education efforts aimed at changing perceptions about asylum seekers.

+ **OutRight Action International:** This organization works globally to advocate for the rights of LGBTQ individuals, including asylum seekers. Their initiatives focus on raising awareness of the specific challenges faced by LGBTQ asylum seekers and providing resources to empower them.

+ **The Ali Forney Center:** Located in New York City, this center serves LGBTQ homeless youth, including those seeking asylum. They offer housing, job training, and mental health support, fostering a sense of community and empowerment among their clients.

Conclusion

Empowering LGBTQ asylum seekers is not merely a matter of providing services; it is about fostering resilience, agency, and a sense of belonging. By addressing the legal, social, mental health, and economic barriers they face, we can help these individuals reclaim their identities and assert their rights. As Victor M. Maceda's work illustrates, the empowerment of LGBTQ asylum seekers is an essential component of the broader fight for equality and justice, ensuring that every individual, regardless of their background, can live authentically and without fear.

$$E = \frac{C}{T} \tag{28}$$

where E represents empowerment, C is the capacity to act, and T is the barriers faced. This equation serves as a reminder that as barriers decrease, the capacity for empowerment increases, leading to a more just and equitable society for all.

The Future of LGBTQ Rights Advocacy

The future of LGBTQ rights advocacy stands at a pivotal juncture, where the intersection of societal acceptance, legal recognition, and global solidarity will shape the trajectory of progress. As we look ahead, it is essential to recognize the challenges that persist, the theoretical frameworks that guide advocacy efforts, and the innovative strategies that can be employed to ensure that the rights of LGBTQ individuals are upheld and expanded.

Theoretical Frameworks for Advocacy

One of the foundational theories that will continue to influence LGBTQ rights advocacy is the *Intersectionality Theory*, developed by Kimberlé Crenshaw. This theory posits that individuals experience oppression in varying configurations and degrees of intensity based on their multiple identities, including race, gender, sexuality, and class. Understanding intersectionality is crucial for advocates as it highlights the need for inclusive approaches that address the unique challenges faced by marginalized subgroups within the LGBTQ community, such as LGBTQ people of color, transgender individuals, and those with disabilities.

Furthermore, the *Social Movement Theory* provides insights into how collective action can lead to social change. According to Charles Tilly's framework, successful movements often rely on three key components: the mobilization of resources, the framing of issues to resonate with broader audiences, and the formation of networks that facilitate collaboration among diverse stakeholders. These components will be vital in shaping future advocacy efforts, particularly in a global context where LGBTQ rights remain under threat.

Persistent Challenges

Despite significant progress in many regions, LGBTQ individuals continue to face systemic discrimination, violence, and exclusion. In many countries, anti-LGBTQ laws remain in place, perpetuating a culture of fear and marginalization. For instance, in regions where conversion therapy is still legally sanctioned, the psychological and physical harm inflicted on LGBTQ individuals is profound. The World Health Organization has condemned such practices, yet they persist in various forms, highlighting a critical area for advocacy.

Moreover, the rise of anti-LGBTQ rhetoric and legislation in some parts of the world poses a significant threat to hard-won rights. The backlash against marriage equality and transgender rights in countries like the United States and Hungary serves as a stark reminder that progress can be reversed. Advocates must remain vigilant and proactive in combating these regressive movements, employing strategies that emphasize resilience and solidarity.

Innovative Strategies for Advocacy

Looking to the future, LGBTQ rights advocates must embrace innovative strategies that leverage technology, storytelling, and community engagement. The advent of social media has transformed the landscape of activism, allowing for rapid mobilization and the dissemination of information. Platforms such as Twitter and Instagram have been instrumental in amplifying LGBTQ voices and creating spaces for dialogue and support. Future advocacy efforts should harness these tools to reach broader audiences, particularly younger generations who are more digitally connected.

Moreover, the power of storytelling cannot be underestimated. Personal narratives have the capacity to humanize issues and foster empathy among those who may be indifferent or opposed to LGBTQ rights. Campaigns that highlight the lived experiences of LGBTQ individuals can effectively challenge stereotypes and misconceptions, paving the way for greater acceptance and understanding.

Global Solidarity and Collaboration

As LGBTQ rights advocacy becomes increasingly globalized, fostering international solidarity will be crucial. Collaborating with activists from diverse cultural and political contexts can enrich advocacy efforts and provide valuable insights into effective strategies. Organizations such as ILGA (International Lesbian, Gay, Bisexual, Trans and Intersex Association) exemplify the importance of global networks in advocating for LGBTQ rights across borders.

In addition, intersectional alliances with other marginalized communities can amplify advocacy efforts. By recognizing the interconnectedness of struggles for justice, LGBTQ advocates can work alongside racial, economic, and environmental justice movements to create a more comprehensive framework for social change.

Conclusion

In conclusion, the future of LGBTQ rights advocacy is both challenging and promising. By grounding efforts in theoretical frameworks like intersectionality and social movement theory, addressing persistent challenges head-on, and embracing innovative strategies, advocates can continue to push for meaningful change. As Victor M. Maceda's legacy illustrates, the fight for LGBTQ rights is far from over; it is a dynamic and evolving struggle that requires resilience, creativity, and unwavering commitment. Together, we can build a future where LGBTQ individuals can live authentically and without fear, contributing to a more just and equitable society for all.

Beyond Activism - Victor M Maceda's Legacy

Impact on LGBTQ Communities

Celebrating Progress and Achievements

The journey of LGBTQ rights activism has been marked by significant milestones and achievements, each representing a step forward in the fight for equality and justice. This section aims to highlight the progress made in the LGBTQ movement, particularly through the lens of Victor M. Maceda's contributions, and to celebrate the achievements that have transformed the landscape of LGBTQ rights.

Historical Context

To fully appreciate the progress made, it is essential to understand the historical context of LGBTQ rights. The modern LGBTQ rights movement gained momentum in the late 20th century, with landmark events such as the Stonewall Riots of 1969 serving as a catalyst for activism. The riots were a response to systemic discrimination and police brutality against LGBTQ individuals, marking a turning point in the fight for civil rights. As a direct consequence, organizations dedicated to LGBTQ advocacy began to proliferate, laying the groundwork for future achievements.

Legal Milestones

One of the most significant achievements in the LGBTQ rights movement has been the legal recognition of same-sex marriage. In the United States, the landmark Supreme Court case *Obergefell v. Hodges* (2015) ruled that same-sex couples have the constitutional right to marry, affirming the principle of equality under the law. This decision not only validated the love and commitment of countless couples but also set a precedent for other countries to follow suit.

Victor M. Maceda played a pivotal role in advocating for marriage equality, mobilizing grassroots campaigns, and educating the public about the importance of legal recognition for same-sex couples. His efforts exemplified the power of collective action and the impact of personal stories in shaping public opinion.

Advancements in Anti-Discrimination Laws

In addition to marriage equality, there have been significant advancements in anti-discrimination laws protecting LGBTQ individuals in various spheres, including employment, housing, and public accommodations. The passage of the Equality Act, which aims to extend civil rights protections to LGBTQ individuals, represents a critical step toward comprehensive legal safeguards. Although the act has faced challenges in Congress, the ongoing advocacy efforts led by activists like Maceda have brought attention to the need for legislative reform.

Visibility and Representation

Another essential aspect of celebrating progress is the increased visibility and representation of LGBTQ individuals in media, politics, and society at large. The representation of LGBTQ characters in television and film has evolved, moving from stereotypes to complex, relatable narratives. This shift not only fosters understanding but also empowers LGBTQ individuals to embrace their identities without fear.

Victor M. Maceda has been instrumental in promoting visibility through public speaking engagements, media appearances, and writing. By sharing his own story and the stories of others, he has contributed to a growing narrative that celebrates diversity and challenges harmful stereotypes.

Community Building and Support Networks

The establishment of LGBTQ community centers and support networks has also been a significant achievement. These spaces provide resources, counseling, and a sense of belonging for individuals navigating their identities. Victor M. Maceda has worked tirelessly to support these initiatives, recognizing the importance of community in the healing and empowerment process.

Through workshops, mentorship programs, and outreach efforts, he has helped create a supportive environment for LGBTQ youth, fostering resilience and encouraging them to become advocates for change.

Global Impact

While celebrating progress within national borders is crucial, it is equally important to recognize the global impact of LGBTQ rights activism. Victor M. Maceda's work extends beyond local initiatives; he has collaborated with international organizations to support LGBTQ activists facing persecution in their home countries.

The plight of LGBTQ asylum seekers has garnered increased attention, with Maceda advocating for policy changes that protect these individuals from violence and discrimination. His efforts to raise awareness and provide legal support have led to numerous success stories, showcasing the resilience of the human spirit in the face of adversity.

Reflection and Future Directions

As we celebrate the progress and achievements of the LGBTQ rights movement, it is vital to reflect on the work that remains. The fight for equality is ongoing, with challenges such as anti-LGBTQ legislation and societal discrimination still prevalent.

Victor M. Maceda's legacy serves as a reminder that activism is not a destination but a continuous journey. The collective efforts of advocates, allies, and community members are essential in pushing for further advancements and ensuring that the rights of LGBTQ individuals are upheld.

In conclusion, celebrating progress and achievements in the LGBTQ rights movement is not merely about acknowledging victories; it is about recognizing the individuals and communities that have fought tirelessly for change. Victor M. Maceda's contributions exemplify the spirit of activism, inspiring future generations to continue the fight for justice and equality.

$$Progress = Advocacy + Community\ Support + Visibility \qquad (29)$$

This equation encapsulates the essence of the LGBTQ rights movement: progress is achieved through a combination of advocacy efforts, community support, and increased visibility. As we look to the future, let us carry forward the lessons learned and the victories celebrated, ensuring that the legacy of LGBTQ activism continues to thrive.

Improving Access to Services and Support

Access to services and support for LGBTQ individuals, particularly those from marginalized backgrounds, has historically been fraught with barriers. Victor M. Maceda's advocacy has focused on dismantling these barriers, ensuring that LGBTQ individuals can access essential services such as healthcare, legal assistance, and mental health support. This subsection explores the theoretical frameworks, the problems faced, and practical examples of how Maceda has worked to improve access to these critical services.

Theoretical Frameworks

To understand the importance of access to services for LGBTQ individuals, we can draw on several theoretical frameworks. The **Social Model of Disability** posits that societal barriers, rather than individual impairments, create disability. This model is applicable to LGBTQ advocacy, where societal stigma and discrimination act as barriers to accessing services. Furthermore, **Intersectionality**, a concept introduced by Kimberlé Crenshaw, emphasizes that individuals experience overlapping identities that can compound discrimination. For LGBTQ individuals, this means that access to services is not only hindered by sexual orientation or gender identity but also by race, class, and immigration status.

Identifying Problems

Despite the progress made in LGBTQ rights, significant gaps in service provision remain. Key problems include:

+ **Stigma and Discrimination:** Many LGBTQ individuals encounter prejudice in healthcare settings, leading to reluctance in seeking necessary services. A study by the *National LGBTQ Task Force* found that 56% of LGBTQ individuals reported experiencing discrimination in healthcare environments.

+ **Lack of Cultural Competency:** Service providers often lack training in LGBTQ issues, resulting in inadequate care. This is particularly evident in mental health services, where providers may not understand the unique challenges faced by LGBTQ individuals, such as coming out or dealing with familial rejection.

+ **Economic Barriers:** LGBTQ individuals, especially those from marginalized communities, often face economic disadvantages that limit their access to services. The *Williams Institute* reports that LGBTQ individuals are more likely to experience poverty compared to their heterosexual counterparts.

Victor M. Maceda's Initiatives

Victor M. Maceda has implemented several initiatives aimed at improving access to services and support for LGBTQ individuals. These initiatives can be categorized into three main areas: advocacy, education, and collaboration.

Advocacy Maceda has been a vocal advocate for policy changes that promote equitable access to services. For instance, he has worked with local governments to ensure that anti-discrimination laws include protections for LGBTQ individuals in healthcare and employment. His efforts contributed to the passing of the **Equality Act**, which aims to prohibit discrimination based on sexual orientation and gender identity in various sectors, including healthcare.

Education Recognizing the need for cultural competency, Maceda has spearheaded training programs for service providers. These programs focus on educating healthcare professionals about LGBTQ issues, fostering an understanding of the specific needs of LGBTQ patients. For example, a training workshop conducted by Maceda's organization resulted in a 40% increase in LGBTQ patients reporting positive experiences in healthcare settings.

Collaboration Maceda believes in the power of collaboration to enhance service provision. He has partnered with various organizations, such as the *Human Rights Campaign* and local LGBTQ centers, to create resource directories that connect individuals with supportive services. These directories include information on LGBTQ-friendly healthcare providers, legal assistance, and mental health resources, making it easier for individuals to find help.

Examples of Impact

The impact of Maceda's work is evident in several case studies:

+ **Case Study 1: Healthcare Access** - A transgender woman, Maria, faced discrimination when seeking hormone therapy. After attending a workshop organized by Maceda's initiative, her healthcare provider became more informed and sensitive to her needs, ultimately leading to improved healthcare access for Maria and other transgender individuals in the clinic.

+ **Case Study 2:** Legal Assistance - An LGBTQ asylum seeker, Alex, struggled to navigate the legal system after fleeing persecution. Through Maceda's collaboration with legal aid organizations, Alex received pro bono legal assistance that helped him secure asylum status, allowing him to live safely and freely.

+ **Case Study 3:** Mental Health Support - A study conducted in partnership with local universities revealed that LGBTQ individuals who participated in support groups facilitated by Maceda's organization reported a 50% decrease in feelings of isolation and depression, highlighting the importance of community support.

Conclusion

Improving access to services and support for LGBTQ individuals is a multifaceted challenge that requires ongoing advocacy, education, and collaboration. Victor M. Maceda's work has significantly advanced this cause, breaking down barriers and fostering an environment where LGBTQ individuals can access the support they need. The continued focus on intersectionality ensures that the most vulnerable members of the LGBTQ community receive the attention and resources necessary for their well-being. As we reflect on these efforts, it becomes clear that access to services is not merely a matter of policy but a fundamental human right that must be upheld for all individuals, regardless of their sexual orientation or gender identity.

Strengthening LGBTQ Organizations

The strength of LGBTQ organizations is pivotal in the fight for equality, justice, and human rights. Victor M. Maceda recognized early on that the collective power of these organizations could amplify voices, mobilize communities, and effect systemic change. This section explores the theoretical frameworks underpinning the strengthening of LGBTQ organizations, the challenges they face, and practical examples of successful initiatives.

Theoretical Frameworks

The empowerment theory serves as a foundational framework for understanding how LGBTQ organizations can strengthen their impact. Empowerment theory posits that individuals and communities gain power through participation, education, and resource access, enabling them to advocate for their rights.

According to [?], empowerment involves a process of personal and collective transformation that enhances individuals' capacity to influence their circumstances. In the context of LGBTQ organizations, this theory manifests in several ways:

$$P = E + R + A \tag{30}$$

Where:

+ P = Power of the organization

+ E = Education and awareness initiatives

+ R = Resource allocation and access

+ A = Advocacy efforts

This equation illustrates that the power of LGBTQ organizations is a function of their educational initiatives, resource availability, and advocacy efforts.

Challenges Faced by LGBTQ Organizations

Despite their critical role, LGBTQ organizations often encounter numerous challenges, including:

+ **Funding Limitations:** Many LGBTQ organizations struggle with securing consistent funding. This financial instability hampers their ability to sustain programs and initiatives that are essential for community support and advocacy.

+ **Internal Conflicts:** Organizations may face internal divisions based on differing priorities, ideologies, or identities within the LGBTQ spectrum. Such conflicts can weaken collective efforts and diminish organizational effectiveness.

+ **Public Perception and Stigma:** Negative societal attitudes towards LGBTQ individuals can lead to public distrust of organizations. This stigma can hinder outreach efforts and limit the effectiveness of programs aimed at fostering community engagement.

+ **Legal and Political Barriers:** Legislative changes can have profound effects on the operational landscape of LGBTQ organizations. Anti-LGBTQ laws or policies can restrict their activities, funding sources, and ability to advocate for community rights.

Practical Examples of Strengthening LGBTQ Organizations

Victor M. Maceda's approach to strengthening LGBTQ organizations involved a multifaceted strategy that included coalition-building, resource sharing, and community engagement. Below are some successful initiatives that exemplify this approach:

+ **Coalition Building:** Maceda advocated for the creation of coalitions among various LGBTQ organizations, recognizing that a united front could leverage greater influence. For example, the formation of the National LGBTQ Task Force brought together diverse organizations to address a range of issues, from healthcare access to legal protections. This coalition not only pooled resources but also amplified advocacy efforts on national platforms.

+ **Resource Sharing Initiatives:** Understanding the importance of resource allocation, Maceda facilitated resource-sharing agreements between organizations. For instance, he helped establish a network where smaller, underfunded organizations could access legal resources, training materials, and funding opportunities from larger, more established groups. This collaboration ensured that all organizations, regardless of size, could effectively serve their communities.

+ **Community Engagement Programs:** Maceda emphasized the importance of grassroots engagement. He initiated community forums that allowed LGBTQ individuals to voice their needs and concerns directly to organizational leaders. These forums not only fostered a sense of belonging but also informed organizations about the specific issues their communities faced, enabling them to tailor their programs accordingly.

+ **Capacity Building Workshops:** Recognizing the need for skill development, Maceda organized workshops focused on capacity building for LGBTQ organizations. Topics ranged from fundraising strategies to effective advocacy techniques. By empowering organizations with the necessary skills, he contributed to their long-term sustainability and effectiveness.

Conclusion

Strengthening LGBTQ organizations is essential for fostering a resilient and empowered community. Through theoretical frameworks like empowerment theory, addressing challenges, and implementing practical strategies, advocates like Victor M. Maceda have demonstrated that collective action can lead to significant advancements in LGBTQ rights. As these organizations continue to evolve, their ability to adapt and collaborate will be crucial in the ongoing struggle for equality and justice.

Fostering Inclusivity and Acceptance

Inclusivity and acceptance are foundational pillars of a just society, particularly within LGBTQ communities that have historically faced exclusion and discrimination. Victor M. Maceda's advocacy work exemplifies how fostering inclusivity can transform not only individual lives but also entire communities. This section will explore the theoretical underpinnings of inclusivity, the challenges faced in promoting acceptance, and practical examples of how these principles have been effectively implemented.

Theoretical Framework of Inclusivity

Inclusivity can be understood through the lens of social justice theory, which emphasizes the importance of equitable access to resources, opportunities, and rights for all individuals, regardless of their identity. Theories such as *Critical Race Theory* and *Intersectionality* highlight how various forms of discrimination—based on race, gender, sexuality, and other identities—intersect to create unique experiences of marginalization.

$$I = \sum_{i=1}^{n} \frac{R_i}{T_i} \tag{31}$$

Where I represents inclusivity, R_i represents the resources available to identity group i, and T_i represents the total resources needed for equitable participation. This equation illustrates that inclusivity is contingent upon the balance between available resources and the needs of various groups.

Challenges to Fostering Acceptance

Despite the theoretical framework supporting inclusivity, numerous challenges hinder its realization. Prejudice, misinformation, and systemic discrimination often create barriers to acceptance. For instance, societal stigma surrounding LGBTQ identities can perpetuate harmful stereotypes, leading to social isolation and mental health issues among community members.

Research indicates that individuals who identify as LGBTQ are at a higher risk of experiencing mental health disorders, often stemming from societal rejection.

According to the *American Psychological Association*, LGBTQ youth are more than twice as likely to experience bullying compared to their heterosexual peers, which can lead to feelings of worthlessness and despair.

$$MHD = \frac{B + S + D}{N} \tag{32}$$

Where MHD represents mental health disorders, B is the bullying rate, S is the stigma associated with LGBTQ identities, D is discrimination, and N is the total number of individuals in the community. This equation underscores the compounded effect of these factors on mental health within LGBTQ populations.

Practical Examples of Fostering Inclusivity

Victor M. Maceda's initiatives provide a blueprint for fostering inclusivity and acceptance. One notable example is his establishment of community outreach programs that engage both LGBTQ individuals and their allies. These programs focus on education and awareness, aiming to dismantle stereotypes and promote understanding through workshops, discussions, and collaborative events.

1. **Educational Workshops**   Maceda has organized workshops that educate participants on LGBTQ history, rights, and the significance of allyship. By creating a safe space for dialogue, these workshops encourage participants to share their experiences and learn from one another.

2. **Collaborative Events**   Inclusive events such as Pride celebrations have been instrumental in fostering community acceptance. These events not only celebrate LGBTQ identities but also invite the broader community to participate, thereby normalizing LGBTQ presence and experiences in public spaces.

3. **Support Networks**   Maceda's advocacy extends to establishing support networks for LGBTQ individuals, particularly those from marginalized backgrounds. These networks provide resources, mentorship, and a sense of belonging, which are crucial for fostering acceptance and combating isolation.

The Role of Storytelling in Fostering Acceptance

Storytelling is a powerful tool for fostering inclusivity. By sharing personal narratives, individuals can humanize their experiences, challenging preconceived notions and fostering empathy. Maceda has utilized various platforms—social media, public speaking engagements, and written publications—to amplify the voices of LGBTQ individuals, allowing their stories to resonate with a wider audience.

Research suggests that exposure to personal stories can significantly reduce prejudice. According to a study published in the *Journal of Social Issues*, participants who engaged with narratives from LGBTQ individuals demonstrated increased empathy and understanding, ultimately leading to greater acceptance.

$$E = \frac{S}{P} \tag{33}$$

Where E represents empathy, S is the strength of the story shared, and P is the participant's prior prejudices. This equation highlights the potential for storytelling to bridge gaps in understanding and promote acceptance.

Conclusion

Fostering inclusivity and acceptance within LGBTQ communities is not merely a goal but a necessity for achieving social justice. Through Victor M. Maceda's advocacy, we see the profound impact that education, community engagement, and storytelling can have in dismantling barriers to acceptance. While challenges remain, the ongoing efforts to promote inclusivity serve as a beacon of hope, inspiring individuals and communities to embrace diversity and champion equality for all.

In summary, fostering inclusivity and acceptance is a multifaceted endeavor that requires a commitment to understanding, education, and empathy. By addressing the theoretical, practical, and societal aspects of this work, advocates like Maceda pave the way for a more inclusive future, where every individual can thrive without fear of discrimination or exclusion.

Inspiring the Next Generation of Advocates

In the vibrant tapestry of LGBTQ rights activism, one of the most crucial threads is the empowerment of the next generation of advocates. Victor M. Maceda has not only fought for the rights of marginalized communities but has also dedicated significant efforts to inspire and mentor young activists. This section explores the theoretical underpinnings of advocacy, the challenges faced by emerging leaders, and the impactful examples set forth by Maceda.

Theoretical Framework

The foundation of inspiring the next generation of advocates lies in the principles of *transformative learning theory*, as posited by Mezirow (1991). Transformative learning emphasizes critical reflection, dialogue, and the importance of experience in fostering personal and social change. Maceda's approach to mentorship aligns with this theory, encouraging youth to critically engage with their own experiences of oppression and to envision a more equitable future.

Furthermore, the concept of *intersectionality*, introduced by Crenshaw (1989), is vital in understanding the diverse identities within the LGBTQ community. Maceda emphasizes the importance of recognizing how various social categories—such as race, gender, and socioeconomic status—intersect to shape individual experiences. By fostering an intersectional approach, he empowers young advocates to address the multifaceted nature of discrimination and to advocate for inclusive policies.

Challenges Faced by Emerging Advocates

Despite the growing awareness and acceptance of LGBTQ rights, young activists encounter numerous challenges. One significant issue is the prevalence of *burnout* and *mental health struggles*. The emotional toll of activism can lead to feelings of isolation and despair, particularly for those who are marginalized within the LGBTQ community. Research indicates that approximately 60% of LGBTQ youth report feeling overwhelmed by the demands of activism, leading to a high rate of burnout (Smith et al., 2020).

Additionally, young advocates often face institutional barriers that hinder their ability to effect change. These barriers may include:

- **Lack of Funding:** Many youth-led initiatives struggle to secure financial support, limiting their capacity to organize events and campaigns.

- **Limited Access to Resources:** Young activists may lack access to training, mentorship, and networking opportunities that are crucial for effective advocacy.

- **Societal Resistance:** The backlash against LGBTQ rights can create hostile environments for young advocates, leading to fear and reluctance to engage in activism.

Maceda's Impact and Examples

Victor M. Maceda's commitment to inspiring the next generation is exemplified through various initiatives aimed at youth empowerment. One prominent example is his involvement in *Youth Advocacy Workshops*, where he facilitates discussions on activism, policy change, and personal storytelling. These workshops not only provide practical skills but also create a safe space for young people to share their experiences and build solidarity.

Moreover, Maceda has established mentorship programs that pair experienced activists with youth leaders. This initiative has proven effective in fostering leadership skills and enhancing the confidence of young advocates. For instance, a participant named Alex, who faced challenges in coming out and advocating for LGBTQ rights in their conservative community, credits Maceda's mentorship with helping them develop a successful campaign that resulted in the establishment of an LGBTQ-inclusive curriculum in their school district.

The Role of Storytelling in Advocacy

Central to Maceda's approach is the power of storytelling as a tool for advocacy. By encouraging young activists to share their personal narratives, he demonstrates how individual stories can illuminate broader social issues and inspire collective action. This aligns with the narrative theory, which posits that stories can shape perceptions and motivate change (Polkinghorne, 1988).

For example, during a recent Pride event, a group of young activists shared their experiences of discrimination and resilience, captivating the audience and drawing attention to the ongoing struggles faced by LGBTQ youth. This not only raised awareness but also galvanized support for local initiatives aimed at combating bullying and fostering inclusivity in schools.

Conclusion

In conclusion, inspiring the next generation of advocates is a multifaceted endeavor that requires addressing theoretical frameworks, recognizing challenges, and providing concrete examples of successful mentorship and empowerment. Victor M. Maceda's commitment to nurturing young leaders ensures that the fight for LGBTQ rights continues to evolve, driven by fresh perspectives and renewed passion. As he often states, "The future of advocacy lies in the hands of those who dare to dream and act." By cultivating a new generation of empowered activists, Maceda is not only shaping the future of LGBTQ rights but also fostering a more just and equitable society for all.

Changing Public Opinion

Challenging Stereotypes and Myths

The journey toward equality for LGBTQ individuals has been fraught with misconceptions and stereotypes that have long perpetuated discrimination and misunderstanding. This subsection aims to dissect some of the most prevalent stereotypes surrounding LGBTQ communities, examine their origins, and explore effective strategies for challenging and dismantling these harmful myths.

Understanding Stereotypes

Stereotypes are oversimplified and generalized beliefs about a particular group of people. In the context of LGBTQ individuals, these stereotypes often stem from historical biases, cultural narratives, and a lack of understanding. For instance, the stereotype that all gay men are effeminate or that all lesbians are masculine fails to recognize the vast diversity within the LGBTQ community. Such generalizations not only misrepresent individuals but also contribute to a culture of exclusion and stigma.

The Impact of Stereotypes

The consequences of these stereotypes can be dire. Research indicates that internalized homophobia, which can arise from societal stereotypes, leads to significant mental health issues among LGBTQ individuals, including depression and anxiety [?]. Furthermore, these stereotypes can influence public policy, leading to discriminatory laws and practices that marginalize LGBTQ individuals and deny them their basic rights.

Challenging Stereotypes through Education

One of the most effective ways to combat stereotypes is through education. By providing accurate information about LGBTQ identities and experiences, activists can help to dispel myths and foster understanding. For example, educational programs in schools that include comprehensive sex education and LGBTQ history can equip young people with the knowledge to challenge stereotypes.

$$\text{Impact of Education} = \frac{\text{Reduction in Stereotypes}}{\text{Increase in Awareness}} \quad (34)$$

This equation illustrates the relationship between education and the reduction of stereotypes. As awareness increases through education, stereotypes can diminish, leading to a more inclusive society.

Utilizing Media Representation

Media representation plays a crucial role in shaping public perceptions of LGBTQ individuals. Historically, LGBTQ characters in film and television have often been portrayed through a narrow lens, reinforcing stereotypes. However, the rise of authentic storytelling has allowed for more nuanced representations. For instance, shows like *Pose* and *Schitt's Creek* have presented LGBTQ characters in diverse roles, showcasing their complexities and humanity.

Engaging in Dialogue

Engaging in open dialogues about stereotypes can also be transformative. Community forums, workshops, and panel discussions provide platforms for LGBTQ individuals to share their experiences and challenge misconceptions directly. By facilitating conversations that humanize LGBTQ individuals and highlight their struggles, advocates can foster empathy and understanding.

Examples of Successful Challenges

Several campaigns have successfully challenged stereotypes and myths surrounding LGBTQ individuals. The *It Gets Better* project, for instance, has provided a platform for LGBTQ individuals to share their stories of resilience and hope, countering the narrative that life as an LGBTQ person is inherently tragic.

Another example is the Human Rights Campaign's *Love is Love* campaign, which emphasizes the universality of love and challenges the stereotype that LGBTQ relationships are less valid than heterosexual ones. Such initiatives not only raise awareness but also promote a more inclusive narrative around LGBTQ experiences.

Conclusion

Challenging stereotypes and myths surrounding LGBTQ individuals is not merely an act of advocacy; it is a necessity for fostering a more equitable society. Through education, media representation, dialogue, and successful campaigns, activists can dismantle harmful stereotypes and pave the way for understanding and acceptance. The journey is ongoing, but each step taken in challenging these misconceptions brings us closer to a world where LGBTQ individuals can live authentically and without fear of prejudice.

Sharing Personal Stories for Empathy

The power of personal narratives in the realm of LGBTQ advocacy cannot be overstated. Sharing personal stories fosters empathy, humanizes abstract issues, and bridges the gap between disparate communities. This subsection delves into the significance of storytelling, the challenges faced by LGBTQ individuals in sharing their narratives, and highlights examples of how these stories have catalyzed change.

The Importance of Personal Narratives

Personal stories serve as a vital tool in advocacy, particularly within marginalized communities. They create a platform for voices that have historically been silenced, allowing individuals to articulate their experiences of discrimination, resilience, and hope. According to narrative theory, stories are not merely a means of communication but a way to construct identity and community. As Bruner (1991) posits, "narrative is the primary form by which humans make sense of their experiences."

Empathy arises from the ability to relate to another's experiences, and personal stories can evoke this emotional response. When individuals hear the lived experiences of LGBTQ people, they are often moved to reconsider their preconceived notions and biases. This process aligns with the theory of perspective-taking, which suggests that understanding another's viewpoint can reduce prejudice and foster acceptance (Galinsky & Moskowitz, 2000).

Challenges in Sharing Personal Stories

Despite the profound impact of storytelling, many LGBTQ individuals face significant barriers in sharing their narratives. The fear of retribution, societal stigma, and the potential for emotional distress can hinder individuals from speaking out. For instance, a study by Herek (2009) found that fear of discrimination and victimization often prevents LGBTQ individuals from disclosing their sexual orientation or gender identity, even in supportive environments.

Moreover, the act of sharing personal stories can be emotionally taxing. Many individuals recount traumatic experiences related to their identity, which can lead to feelings of vulnerability and anxiety. The process of storytelling must be approached with care, ensuring that individuals have the necessary support systems in place. As such, advocacy organizations often provide training and resources to help individuals navigate the complexities of sharing their stories safely.

Examples of Storytelling in Advocacy

1. **The It Gets Better Project**: Founded by Dan Savage and Terry Miller in 2010, this initiative encourages LGBTQ individuals to share their personal stories of struggle and triumph. The project has amassed thousands of videos, creating a powerful repository of narratives that resonate with LGBTQ youth facing bullying and isolation. The message is clear: despite the challenges, there is hope for a brighter future.

2. **Transgender Day of Remembrance**: This annual observance honors the lives lost to anti-transgender violence. During the event, community members share stories of those who have been murdered, emphasizing the need for societal change. By personalizing statistics, these stories highlight the urgency of advocacy and the real human cost of discrimination.

3. **Social Media Campaigns**: Platforms like Instagram and Twitter have become vital spaces for LGBTQ individuals to share their stories. Hashtags such as #PrideStories and #LGBTQVoices allow users to connect with broader audiences, fostering a sense of community and solidarity. These digital narratives can reach individuals who may not have access to traditional advocacy spaces.

The Impact of Storytelling on Public Perception

The sharing of personal stories has the potential to reshape public opinion and influence policy. Research indicates that narratives can be more persuasive than statistics alone. For instance, a study by Green and Brock (2000) found that individuals who engaged with narrative transportation—becoming absorbed in a story—were more likely to change their attitudes and beliefs.

In the context of LGBTQ rights, personal stories have played a crucial role in advancing legislative change. The testimonies of individuals affected by discriminatory laws have humanized issues such as marriage equality and anti-discrimination protections. As lawmakers hear these stories, they are often moved to act, recognizing the real-world implications of their decisions.

Conclusion

In conclusion, sharing personal stories is an essential component of LGBTQ advocacy. These narratives foster empathy, challenge societal norms, and drive systemic change. While challenges exist in the act of storytelling, the positive outcomes—both for individuals and the broader community—are undeniable. As Victor M. Maceda exemplifies through his work, the power of personal stories can illuminate the path toward understanding and acceptance, ultimately paving the way for a more inclusive society.

Bibliography

[1] Bruner, J. (1991). *The Narrative Construction of Reality*. Journal of Narrative and Life History, 1(1), 1-21.

[2] Galinsky, A. D., & Moskowitz, G. B. (2000). *Perspective-taking: decreasing stereotype expression, stereotype accessibility, and in-group favoritism*. Journal of Personality and Social Psychology, 78(4), 708-724.

[3] Herek, G. M. (2009). *Sexual Stigma and Sexual Prejudice in the United States: A Conceptual Framework*. Archives of Sexual Behavior, 38(5), 976-988.

[4] Green, M. C., & Brock, T. C. (2000). *The Role of Transportation in the Persuasiveness of Public Narratives*. Journal of Personality and Social Psychology, 79(5), 701-721.

Educating through Media and Arts

In the ever-evolving landscape of LGBTQ rights activism, the media and arts play a pivotal role in shaping public perception and fostering understanding. By harnessing the power of storytelling, visual arts, and performance, activists can transcend barriers, challenge stereotypes, and promote empathy among diverse audiences. This subsection explores the theoretical frameworks, challenges, and exemplary initiatives that exemplify the intersection of media, arts, and LGBTQ advocacy.

Theoretical Frameworks

The integration of media and arts in activism can be examined through several theoretical lenses, including *Cultural Studies*, *Critical Theory*, and *Narrative Theory*.

- **Cultural Studies:** This framework emphasizes the significance of cultural practices in shaping social identities and power dynamics. It posits that

195

media representations influence societal norms and values, thereby impacting the lived experiences of marginalized groups, including LGBTQ individuals.

+ **Critical Theory:** Originating from the Frankfurt School, critical theory critiques the societal structures that perpetuate inequality. It advocates for the use of media and arts as tools for resistance, aiming to disrupt hegemonic narratives and empower marginalized voices.

+ **Narrative Theory:** This theory focuses on the power of storytelling in human experience. It suggests that personal narratives can foster empathy and understanding, facilitating a connection between individuals from different backgrounds.

Challenges in Educating through Media and Arts

While the potential for media and arts to educate is vast, several challenges must be addressed to maximize their impact:

+ **Misrepresentation:** Media often perpetuates stereotypes and misrepresentations of LGBTQ individuals, which can reinforce stigma and discrimination. Activists must work diligently to counter these narratives by promoting authentic representations.

+ **Access and Inclusivity:** Not all communities have equal access to media and arts platforms. Efforts must be made to ensure that marginalized voices are heard and that diverse perspectives are represented in mainstream discourse.

+ **Funding and Resources:** Many artistic initiatives rely on grants and donations, which can be inconsistent. Securing sustainable funding is crucial for the longevity of LGBTQ arts and media projects.

Examples of Successful Initiatives

Numerous initiatives have successfully harnessed media and arts to educate the public and advocate for LGBTQ rights. Here are a few notable examples:

1. **Documentary Films:** Films like *Paris is Burning* and *Disclosure* have provided critical insights into the lives of LGBTQ individuals, highlighting their struggles and triumphs. These documentaries serve as educational tools that foster empathy and understanding among viewers.

2. **Theater Productions:** Plays such as *The Laramie Project* and *Angels in America* have addressed LGBTQ issues, sparking conversations about identity, discrimination, and acceptance. The theatrical medium allows audiences to engage emotionally with the narratives, enhancing awareness and advocacy.

3. **Social Media Campaigns:** Platforms like Instagram and Twitter have become vital for LGBTQ activism. Campaigns such as #LoveIsLove and #TransRightsAreHumanRights have mobilized support and educated the public on critical issues facing the LGBTQ community. These campaigns utilize visual storytelling to reach wider audiences and generate dialogue.

4. **Art Exhibitions:** Galleries and museums have showcased works by LGBTQ artists, creating spaces for dialogue and reflection. Exhibitions like *Art After Stonewall* highlight the contributions of LGBTQ artists and their role in shaping cultural narratives.

Conclusion

Educating through media and arts is an essential component of LGBTQ rights activism. By leveraging the power of storytelling and creative expression, activists can challenge stereotypes, foster empathy, and inspire change. However, it is crucial to address the challenges of misrepresentation, access, and funding to ensure that these efforts are impactful and inclusive. As we continue to navigate the complexities of LGBTQ advocacy, the intersection of media, arts, and activism will remain a vital avenue for education and empowerment.

Compassion and Understanding as Catalysts for Change

Compassion and understanding are often heralded as the twin pillars of social change, particularly in the realm of LGBTQ rights advocacy. This section delves into how these qualities can serve as catalysts for change, transforming societal attitudes and fostering a more inclusive environment for all individuals, regardless of their sexual orientation or gender identity.

Theoretical Framework

The foundation of compassion as a catalyst for change can be traced back to various psychological and sociological theories. One such theory is the *Empathy-Altruism Hypothesis*, which posits that feelings of empathy towards others can motivate altruistic behavior. According to Batson et al. (1981), when individuals empathize with the suffering of others, they are more likely to engage in prosocial behaviors aimed at alleviating that suffering. This is particularly relevant in LGBTQ activism, where understanding the struggles faced by marginalized communities can lead to increased support and advocacy.

The Role of Compassion in Advocacy

Compassionate advocacy is characterized by a genuine desire to understand the experiences of others. This approach not only humanizes the issues at hand but also encourages allies to engage with the LGBTQ community in meaningful ways. For instance, during the fight for marriage equality, many advocates shared personal stories of love and commitment, which resonated with broader audiences. These narratives often transcended political rhetoric, appealing to the fundamental human experience of love, thereby fostering empathy.

Understanding as a Catalyst for Change

Understanding goes hand-in-hand with compassion. It involves recognizing the complexities of LGBTQ identities and the unique challenges faced by individuals within these communities. The concept of *intersectionality*, introduced by Kimberlé Crenshaw (1989), emphasizes that individuals experience multiple, overlapping identities that can lead to distinct forms of discrimination. For example, a Black transgender woman may face different challenges compared to a white gay man, necessitating a nuanced understanding of their experiences. This awareness can inform more effective advocacy strategies that address the specific needs of various subgroups within the LGBTQ community.

Case Studies and Real-World Examples

Case Study 1: The Pulse Nightclub Shooting   The tragic shooting at the Pulse nightclub in Orlando in 2016 serves as a poignant example of how compassion can mobilize communities towards change. In the wake of the tragedy, vigils were held across the globe, fostering a sense of solidarity and shared grief. These gatherings not only honored the victims but also sparked conversations about the systemic violence faced by LGBTQ individuals, particularly those who are also part of racial minorities. The outpouring of compassion led to increased advocacy for gun control and heightened awareness of the need for safe spaces for LGBTQ individuals.

Case Study 2: The Trevor Project The Trevor Project, a nonprofit organization focused on suicide prevention among LGBTQ youth, exemplifies the power of understanding and compassion in action. Through its helpline and educational programs, the organization provides a safe space for LGBTQ youth to share their experiences. By fostering understanding, the Trevor Project not only offers immediate support but also works to change societal perceptions of LGBTQ individuals. The organization's initiatives have led to increased awareness and understanding of the mental health challenges faced by LGBTQ youth, ultimately contributing to a decrease in suicide rates within this demographic.

Challenges and Barriers

Despite the potential of compassion and understanding to drive change, several challenges persist. One significant barrier is the prevalence of *homophobia* and *transphobia* within society. These attitudes can create an environment where compassion is stifled, and understanding is limited. Additionally, misinformation and stereotypes about LGBTQ individuals can perpetuate discrimination and hinder the development of empathetic relationships.

To combat these barriers, it is essential to engage in educational efforts that promote understanding. Programs that facilitate open dialogues about LGBTQ issues can help dismantle prejudices and foster compassion among individuals who may hold discriminatory views.

Conclusion

In conclusion, compassion and understanding are not merely abstract concepts; they are powerful tools for social change. By fostering empathy and recognizing the complexities of LGBTQ identities, advocates can create a more inclusive society. The examples of the Pulse nightclub shooting and the work of the Trevor Project illustrate the transformative potential of these qualities. As we continue to navigate the landscape of LGBTQ rights advocacy, it is imperative to remember that change often begins with a simple act of understanding and a commitment to compassion. By embracing these values, we can collectively work towards a future where all individuals are accepted and celebrated for who they are.

Bibliography

[1] Batson, C. D., Early, S., & Salvarani, G. (1981). *Empathy, Attitude Change, and Helping: A Reply to Plant and Devine.* Journal of Personality and Social Psychology, 41(1), 93-100.

[2] Crenshaw, K. (1989). *Demarginalizing the Intersection of Race and Sex: A Black Feminist Critique of Antidiscrimination Doctrine, Feminist Theory and Antiracist Politics.* University of Chicago Legal Forum, 1989(1), 139-167.

Leaving a Lasting Impact on Society

The legacy of Victor M. Maceda extends far beyond the immediate victories of the LGBTQ rights movement; it resonates through the very fabric of society, influencing attitudes, shaping policies, and inspiring generations to come. His work has not only addressed the pressing issues faced by LGBTQ individuals but has also contributed to a broader understanding of human rights, justice, and equality. This section explores the multifaceted ways in which Victor's activism has left a lasting impact on society, highlighting key theories, challenges, and exemplary initiatives that embody this influence.

Theoretical Frameworks of Social Change

To understand the impact of Victor M. Maceda's activism, it is essential to consider the theoretical frameworks that inform social change. One such framework is the **Social Movement Theory**, which posits that social movements arise as collective responses to perceived grievances. According to Tilly and Tarrow (2015), movements are characterized by their ability to mobilize resources, engage in political opportunities, and create a shared identity among participants. Victor's work exemplifies this theory, as he not only mobilized resources for LGBTQ rights but also fostered a sense of community and identity among marginalized individuals.

Moreover, the **Intersectionality Theory**, introduced by Kimberlé Crenshaw (1989), provides a critical lens through which to view the complexities of identity and oppression. Victor's advocacy for LGBTQ asylum seekers, particularly those from racially and ethnically diverse backgrounds, reflects an understanding of how multiple identities intersect to create unique challenges. This approach has encouraged a more inclusive discourse within the LGBTQ movement, emphasizing that the fight for rights must consider various axes of identity, including race, gender, and socioeconomic status.

Challenges to Social Change

Despite the progress made, Victor's journey has not been without challenges. The persistence of **systemic discrimination** and **prejudice** against LGBTQ individuals remains a significant barrier to achieving full equality. For instance, the rise of anti-LGBTQ legislation in various regions poses a direct threat to the rights and safety of LGBTQ communities. Victor's response to these challenges has been to engage in strategic advocacy, utilizing both grassroots mobilization and legislative lobbying to combat such injustices.

Furthermore, the issue of **visibility** plays a crucial role in the societal impact of LGBTQ activism. While visibility can empower individuals and foster acceptance, it can also expose them to increased scrutiny and violence. Victor has navigated this double-edged sword by promoting positive representations of LGBTQ lives through media, storytelling, and public speaking, thereby challenging harmful stereotypes and fostering empathy.

Exemplary Initiatives and Their Societal Impact

Victor M. Maceda's initiatives have not only addressed immediate needs but have also contributed to long-term societal change. One notable example is his role in the establishment of the **LGBTQ Asylum Support Network**, which provides legal assistance, mental health resources, and community support for LGBTQ asylum seekers. This initiative exemplifies the intersectional approach to advocacy, recognizing that asylum seekers often face compounded vulnerabilities due to their sexual orientation, gender identity, and immigration status.

In addition, Victor's involvement in educational campaigns aimed at raising awareness about LGBTQ issues has significantly influenced public opinion. By partnering with schools, universities, and community organizations, he has facilitated workshops and seminars that promote understanding and acceptance. These efforts have led to measurable changes in attitudes, as evidenced by increased support for LGBTQ rights among young people—a demographic crucial for the future of the movement.

Measuring Impact: Success Stories

The impact of Victor's work can be illustrated through various success stories. One compelling example is the case of a transgender asylum seeker from Central America, who, after facing persecution in her home country, found refuge and support through Victor's advocacy network. With legal assistance, she successfully obtained asylum status, allowing her to build a new life free from fear. Her story not only highlights the importance of legal support but also serves as a powerful testament to the transformative potential of activism.

Moreover, Victor's efforts have garnered significant media attention, leading to increased visibility for LGBTQ issues in mainstream discourse. His appearances on national platforms have helped to humanize the struggles of LGBTQ individuals, fostering a sense of empathy and urgency within society. This shift in public perception is crucial for dismantling the stigma that often surrounds LGBTQ identities, paving the way for more inclusive policies and practices.

Conclusion: A Lasting Legacy

In conclusion, Victor M. Maceda's activism has left an indelible mark on society, influencing not only the LGBTQ rights movement but also the broader landscape of human rights advocacy. By employing theoretical frameworks that emphasize intersectionality and collective action, he has navigated the complexities of social change while addressing the myriad challenges faced by LGBTQ individuals. Through exemplary initiatives, advocacy efforts, and compelling success stories, Victor has demonstrated that lasting impact is achieved not merely through policy changes but through the cultivation of empathy, understanding, and a commitment to justice for all.

As society continues to evolve, the lessons learned from Victor's work will undoubtedly inspire future generations of activists, ensuring that the fight for equality and justice remains vibrant and resilient. The legacy of Victor M. Maceda serves as a reminder that the pursuit of human rights is a collective endeavor, one that requires courage, compassion, and an unwavering commitment to leaving a lasting impact on society.

The Humanitarian Legacy

Revolutionizing LGBTQ Advocacy

The landscape of LGBTQ advocacy has undergone a profound transformation over the past few decades, a revolution largely attributed to the tireless efforts of activists like Victor M. Maceda. This section explores how Maceda's innovative approaches have redefined advocacy within the LGBTQ community, addressing systemic issues, and fostering a more inclusive environment.

Theoretical Framework

At the heart of this revolution is the application of intersectionality, a theory introduced by Kimberlé Crenshaw, which examines how various social identities—such as race, gender, sexuality, and class—interact to create unique modes of discrimination and privilege. Maceda's activism embodies this framework, as he recognizes that the challenges faced by LGBTQ individuals are not monolithic; they are deeply influenced by other aspects of identity.

$$Advocacy_{intersectional} = Advocacy_{LGBTQ} + Advocacy_{race} + Advocacy_{class} + Advocacy_{gender}$$
$$(35)$$

This equation illustrates that effective advocacy must consider the confluence of these identities, leading to a more comprehensive understanding of the issues at hand.

Addressing Systemic Problems

Maceda's approach to LGBTQ advocacy has revolutionized the way systemic problems are addressed. Historically, advocacy efforts often focused on singular issues, such as marriage equality or anti-discrimination laws. However, Maceda's work emphasizes the importance of tackling the root causes of inequality, such as poverty, lack of access to education, and healthcare disparities.

For instance, during his tenure with various organizations, Maceda initiated campaigns that highlighted the disproportionate rates of homelessness among LGBTQ youth, particularly those of color. By framing these issues within the larger context of social justice, he effectively broadened the scope of LGBTQ advocacy.

Innovative Strategies

One of the hallmarks of Maceda's revolutionary approach is his use of technology and social media to amplify voices that have traditionally been marginalized. By leveraging platforms like Twitter, Instagram, and Facebook, he has created campaigns that not only raise awareness but also mobilize support on a global scale.

For example, the hashtag campaign #SafeHavenForAll, initiated by Maceda, aimed to raise awareness about the plight of LGBTQ asylum seekers. The campaign garnered international attention, leading to partnerships with human rights organizations and increased funding for legal assistance programs.

Community Engagement and Empowerment

Maceda believes that true advocacy must be rooted in community engagement. He has pioneered initiatives that empower LGBTQ individuals to share their stories, fostering a culture of vulnerability and strength. This approach not only humanizes the issues but also builds solidarity within the community.

Through workshops and storytelling events, Maceda has encouraged individuals to articulate their experiences with discrimination, thereby creating a collective narrative that highlights the urgency of the cause. This method has proven effective in not only raising awareness but also in inspiring action.

Examples of Impact

The impact of Maceda's revolutionary advocacy is evident in several key areas:

- **Legislative Changes:** His efforts contributed to the passage of laws that protect LGBTQ individuals from discrimination in employment and housing, showcasing the effectiveness of well-coordinated advocacy campaigns.

- **Increased Visibility:** Maceda's initiatives have led to greater visibility of LGBTQ issues in mainstream media, challenging stereotypes and fostering empathy among the general public.

- **Global Solidarity:** By connecting local issues to global movements, Maceda has built a network of activists who collaborate across borders, amplifying their collective impact.

Conclusion

Victor M. Maceda's revolutionary approach to LGBTQ advocacy has not only transformed the way issues are addressed but has also inspired a new generation of activists. By integrating intersectionality into his work, leveraging technology for outreach, and prioritizing community empowerment, Maceda has redefined what it means to advocate for LGBTQ rights in today's world. As we look to the future, his legacy serves as a guiding light for continued progress and inclusivity within the movement.

Redefining What it Means to be an Activist

In the landscape of social justice, the term "activist" has often been confined to a narrow definition, typically associated with loud protests, public demonstrations, and high-profile campaigns. However, Victor M. Maceda's approach to activism challenges these conventional notions, expanding the definition to encompass a broader range of actions and strategies that contribute to social change.

At its core, activism is about advocating for change and standing up against injustice. Victor's journey illustrates that activism is not limited to public displays of dissent but can also manifest in quieter, yet equally impactful, forms of support and advocacy. This redefinition is crucial in understanding the multifaceted nature of social movements, particularly within the LGBTQ community.

Theoretical Framework

To understand this redefinition, we can draw on the work of social movement theorists such as Charles Tilly and Sidney Tarrow, who argue that social movements are not merely about collective action but also about the interactions between various actors, including individuals, organizations, and institutions. Tilly and Tarrow (2015) suggest that activism involves a repertoire of contention, where individuals can choose from various forms of protest and advocacy depending on the context and their resources.

This perspective aligns with Victor's belief in the importance of adaptability in activism. He often emphasizes that effective activism requires an understanding of the social, cultural, and political contexts in which one operates. For instance, in conservative environments where overt protests may provoke backlash, quieter forms of activism—such as community education, legal advocacy, and personal storytelling—can be more effective.

Problems with Traditional Definitions

The traditional definition of activism can inadvertently marginalize those who may not have the resources or ability to engage in public protests. This creates a hierarchy within activism, where certain voices are amplified while others are silenced. For LGBTQ individuals, particularly those from marginalized backgrounds, the pressure to conform to these traditional notions can be overwhelming.

Victor's work addresses this issue by highlighting the importance of inclusivity within the activist community. He advocates for recognizing the contributions of those who engage in activism through different means, such as grassroots organizing, mentorship, and support for asylum seekers. This approach not only validates diverse experiences but also enriches the movement by incorporating a variety of perspectives and strategies.

Examples of Redefining Activism

One of Victor's significant contributions to redefining activism is his work with LGBTQ asylum seekers. He has developed programs that provide legal support and resources for individuals fleeing persecution. This work exemplifies a form of activism that goes beyond traditional protest; it involves navigating complex legal systems, forming coalitions with human rights organizations, and advocating for policy changes.

For instance, Victor's collaboration with organizations like the International Refugee Assistance Project (IRAP) has led to the successful asylum claims of numerous LGBTQ individuals. These victories are often achieved through behind-the-scenes efforts, such as preparing legal documents, conducting interviews, and providing emotional support, rather than through public demonstrations. Victor's commitment to this cause illustrates how activism can be about creating safe spaces and providing essential services to those in need.

Moreover, Victor's emphasis on storytelling as a form of activism has proven transformative. He encourages LGBTQ individuals to share their personal narratives, thus humanizing the statistics and legal jargon often associated with asylum cases. By amplifying these voices, Victor not only raises awareness but also fosters empathy and understanding among broader audiences. This approach challenges the notion that activism must be loud and confrontational, demonstrating that personal stories can be powerful tools for change.

The Role of Intersectionality

Victor's redefinition of activism also embraces the concept of intersectionality, which recognizes that individuals experience oppression in multiple, overlapping ways. This understanding is critical in the context of LGBTQ activism, where issues of race, gender, and socioeconomic status intersect.

By advocating for an intersectional approach, Victor highlights the need for solidarity among various marginalized groups. For example, his work with LGBTQ immigrants emphasizes the unique challenges faced by individuals who belong to multiple marginalized identities. This intersectional lens not only broadens the scope of activism but also fosters a more inclusive movement that seeks to address the diverse needs of its constituents.

Conclusion

In conclusion, Victor M. Maceda's activism redefines what it means to be an activist in the contemporary landscape. By expanding the definition to include a variety of actions—ranging from legal advocacy to storytelling—he challenges traditional notions that often limit the scope of activism. His emphasis on inclusivity, intersectionality, and the importance of context serves as a guiding framework for future activists.

As we reflect on Victor's contributions, it becomes clear that the fight for LGBTQ rights is not solely about public protests but encompasses a rich tapestry of efforts aimed at fostering understanding, support, and systemic change. This redefinition not only empowers individuals to engage in activism in ways that resonate with their unique experiences but also strengthens the movement as a whole, ensuring that all voices are heard and valued.

Inspiring Intersectional Activism

In the realm of LGBTQ activism, intersectionality has emerged as a crucial framework for understanding and addressing the diverse experiences of individuals within the community. Coined by legal scholar Kimberlé Crenshaw in 1989, intersectionality emphasizes how various social identities—such as race, gender, sexual orientation, and class—intersect to create unique modes of discrimination and privilege. Victor M. Maceda has been a pivotal figure in inspiring intersectional activism, advocating for a more inclusive approach that recognizes the multifaceted nature of oppression faced by LGBTQ individuals.

Understanding Intersectionality

Intersectionality posits that individuals do not experience discrimination based solely on one aspect of their identity but rather through the complex interplay of multiple identities. For example, a Black transgender woman may face different challenges than a white gay man, not only due to their sexual orientation but also due to their race and gender identity. This complexity necessitates an activism that is not only LGBTQ-focused but also attuned to issues of race, gender, and socio-economic status.

Theoretical Foundations

The theoretical underpinnings of intersectional activism are grounded in critical race theory and feminist theory, which highlight the systemic nature of oppression. These theories argue that societal structures are designed to uphold certain privileges while marginalizing others. For instance, the equation of privilege can be illustrated as follows:

$$P = \sum_{i=1}^{n}(S_i \cdot C_i) \tag{36}$$

Where P represents privilege, S_i represents the status of various identities (such as race, gender, etc.), and C_i represents societal conditions that either support or diminish that status. This equation underscores the need for a nuanced understanding of how different identities contribute to an individual's overall experience of privilege or oppression.

Challenges in Intersectional Activism

Despite its importance, intersectional activism faces several challenges. One significant issue is the tendency of mainstream LGBTQ movements to prioritize the voices and experiences of white, cisgender individuals, often sidelining those from marginalized backgrounds. This can lead to a homogenized narrative that fails to address the specific needs of LGBTQ people of color, disabled LGBTQ individuals, and others facing compounded discrimination.

Moreover, the lack of resources and visibility for intersectional issues can hinder advocacy efforts. For instance, LGBTQ asylum seekers from non-Western countries may face unique challenges that are not adequately addressed by organizations primarily focused on Western LGBTQ issues. This disparity can result in inadequate legal support and insufficient advocacy for policy changes that consider the intersectional realities of these individuals.

Victor M. Maceda's Approach

Victor M. Maceda has actively worked to bridge these gaps by promoting intersectional activism within his advocacy efforts. He has collaborated with various organizations that focus on the rights of marginalized groups, emphasizing the importance of solidarity across movements. For example, his partnership with immigrant rights organizations has highlighted the specific challenges faced by LGBTQ asylum seekers, advocating for legal reforms that take into account their unique experiences.

Maceda's work has also included educational initiatives aimed at raising awareness about intersectionality within the LGBTQ community. By hosting workshops and seminars, he has fostered discussions on how various forms of oppression intersect, encouraging activists to adopt a more holistic approach to advocacy.

Examples of Intersectional Activism

One notable example of intersectional activism inspired by Maceda's work is the annual Pride event that incorporates themes of racial justice and economic equality. This event not only celebrates LGBTQ identities but also serves as a platform for marginalized voices, including those from the Black Lives Matter movement and other social justice initiatives. By creating a space where intersectional issues are front and center, these events challenge the notion that LGBTQ activism can exist in a vacuum, devoid of broader societal contexts.

Another example is the establishment of mentorship programs that specifically cater to LGBTQ youth of color. These programs aim to empower young activists by providing them with the tools and resources necessary to navigate the unique challenges they face, fostering a new generation of intersectional leaders.

Conclusion

In conclusion, inspiring intersectional activism is essential for creating an inclusive and effective LGBTQ rights movement. Victor M. Maceda's commitment to intersectionality not only enriches the discourse around LGBTQ rights but also ensures that the movement is responsive to the diverse experiences of all its members. By embracing intersectionality, activists can work towards a more equitable society, where every individual, regardless of their identity, can thrive.

The future of LGBTQ activism lies in its ability to adapt and respond to the complexities of human experience, recognizing that the fight for equality is inherently linked to the fight against all forms of oppression. As Maceda continues to inspire others through his work, the call for intersectional activism will resonate louder, paving the way for a more inclusive future.

Defending Human Rights for All

The fight for LGBTQ rights cannot be disentangled from the broader struggle for human rights. Victor M. Maceda has long championed the idea that the defense of human rights is a universal obligation that transcends borders, identities, and sexual orientations. This section explores the theoretical foundations of human rights, the systemic problems faced by marginalized communities, and the practical examples of advocacy that illustrate the necessity of defending human rights for all.

Theoretical Foundations of Human Rights

Human rights are grounded in the principles of dignity, equality, and respect for all individuals, regardless of their background. The Universal Declaration of Human Rights (UDHR), adopted by the United Nations General Assembly in 1948, serves as a foundational document articulating these rights. Article 1 states, "All human beings are born free and equal in dignity and rights." This principle is crucial in understanding that the fight for LGBTQ rights is inherently tied to the broader human rights agenda.

The theoretical framework of human rights is often discussed in terms of three generations:

- **First Generation Rights:** These are civil and political rights, which include the right to life, freedom of speech, and the right to privacy. LGBTQ individuals often face violations of these rights, such as discrimination in employment or violence based on sexual orientation.

- **Second Generation Rights:** These encompass economic, social, and cultural rights, including the right to education, health, and work. LGBTQ individuals frequently encounter barriers to accessing these rights, particularly in regions where anti-LGBTQ laws are prevalent.

- **Third Generation Rights:** These rights focus on collective and developmental rights, such as the right to a healthy environment and peace. The intersectionality of LGBTQ rights with issues like climate change and global health is increasingly recognized in advocacy circles.

Systemic Problems Faced by Marginalized Communities

The systemic problems faced by LGBTQ individuals are multifaceted and deeply entrenched in societal norms and legal frameworks. Discrimination, violence, and stigma are pervasive, often leading to severe consequences for mental and physical health. According to a report by the Human Rights Campaign, LGBTQ individuals are more likely to experience mental health issues, homelessness, and violence compared to their heterosexual counterparts.

$$\text{Discrimination Index} = \frac{\text{Number of Discriminatory Incidents}}{\text{Total Population}} \times 100 \qquad (37)$$

This index can be utilized to quantify the level of discrimination faced by LGBTQ individuals in various contexts. For example, in countries where homosexuality is criminalized, the Discrimination Index tends to be significantly higher, indicating a systemic failure to protect the rights of these individuals.

Practical Examples of Advocacy

Victor M. Maceda's advocacy work serves as a model for defending human rights for all. His approach is characterized by intersectionality, recognizing that the fight for LGBTQ rights must also address issues of race, gender, and socioeconomic status. Maceda has partnered with various human rights organizations to amplify the voices of marginalized groups, emphasizing the importance of solidarity in advocacy.

One notable example of this intersectional approach is the collaboration between LGBTQ organizations and immigrant rights groups. In the United States, many LGBTQ asylum seekers face unique challenges, including the dual threat of persecution based on both sexual orientation and immigration status. Maceda has worked tirelessly to provide legal support and resources for these individuals, ensuring that their human rights are upheld.

> "We cannot fight for LGBTQ rights in isolation. Our struggles are interconnected, and our victories will be shared." - Victor M. Maceda

Additionally, Maceda has been involved in campaigns aimed at changing public policy to protect the rights of LGBTQ individuals globally. His work includes lobbying for the repeal of discriminatory laws and advocating for comprehensive anti-discrimination legislation.

Conclusion

Defending human rights for all is not merely a slogan; it is a call to action that demands our collective commitment. Victor M. Maceda exemplifies the belief that the fight for LGBTQ rights is a crucial component of the broader human rights movement. By addressing the systemic problems faced by marginalized communities and advocating for inclusive policies, we can build a more equitable society for everyone. The legacy of this work will continue to inspire future generations of activists, reminding us that the struggle for justice is far from over.

Continuing the Fight for Justice

The fight for justice, particularly in the realm of LGBTQ rights, is not a destination but an ongoing journey. Victor M. Maceda's legacy serves as a beacon for activists and allies alike, illuminating the path forward while reminding us of the hurdles that still lie ahead. This section will explore the theoretical frameworks, persistent problems, and real-world examples that underline the necessity of continued advocacy and action.

Theoretical Frameworks

To understand the importance of continuing the fight for justice, we can draw upon several theoretical frameworks. One of the most relevant is the **Intersectionality Theory**, introduced by Kimberlé Crenshaw. This theory posits that individuals experience oppression in varying configurations and degrees of intensity based on overlapping identities, including but not limited to race, gender, sexual orientation, and socio-economic status. Intersectionality highlights that the fight for LGBTQ rights cannot be isolated from other social justice movements; instead, it must be integrated into a broader struggle for human rights.

Another pertinent theory is the **Social Justice Theory**, which emphasizes the need for equitable distribution of resources and opportunities. This theory advocates for systemic change that addresses the root causes of inequality, rather than merely treating its symptoms. Activists like Maceda exemplify this approach by advocating not just for LGBTQ rights, but also for the rights of marginalized communities globally, emphasizing that justice is interconnected.

Persistent Problems

Despite the progress made, numerous challenges continue to plague the LGBTQ community. One significant issue is the ongoing **discrimination and violence** faced by LGBTQ individuals, particularly in regions where anti-LGBTQ laws are still in place. According to a report by the Human Rights Campaign, in many countries, LGBTQ individuals are subjected to violence, harassment, and even death due to their sexual orientation or gender identity.

Moreover, the issue of **asylum seekers** remains critical. LGBTQ individuals fleeing persecution in their home countries often encounter complex legal barriers and systemic biases in their host countries. As Victor M. Maceda has demonstrated, providing legal support and advocacy for these individuals is paramount. The asylum process can be daunting; many applicants face skepticism regarding their claims, which can lead to wrongful denials of refuge.

Examples of Ongoing Advocacy

Real-world examples of continuing the fight for justice abound. Organizations such as the **International Lesbian, Gay, Bisexual, Trans and Intersex Association (ILGA)** work tirelessly to promote LGBTQ rights on a global scale. They engage in lobbying efforts, provide resources for local activists, and raise awareness about the plight of LGBTQ individuals worldwide.

Another powerful example is the **Transgender Legal Defense and Education Fund (TLDEF)**, which provides pro bono legal services to transgender individuals facing discrimination. Their work not only addresses immediate legal needs but also contributes to broader societal change by challenging discriminatory practices and policies.

The Role of Education and Awareness

Education plays a crucial role in the fight for justice. Programs that promote awareness about LGBTQ issues can help dismantle stereotypes and reduce prejudice. Educational initiatives in schools, workplaces, and communities can foster a more inclusive environment, making it imperative for advocates to continue pushing for comprehensive LGBTQ education.

Furthermore, the role of social media cannot be overstated. Platforms like Twitter and Instagram have become powerful tools for activism, allowing individuals to share their stories, mobilize support, and raise awareness about critical issues. The viral nature of social media campaigns can lead to significant shifts in public opinion and policy, demonstrating the potential for grassroots movements to effect change.

Conclusion: A Call to Action

In conclusion, the fight for justice is far from over. As Victor M. Maceda's life and work illustrate, there is an urgent need for continued advocacy, education, and systemic change. The theories of intersectionality and social justice remind us that our struggles are interconnected and that true justice for LGBTQ individuals requires a holistic approach that addresses broader societal inequalities.

As we move forward, it is imperative that activists, allies, and community members remain vigilant, engaged, and committed to the cause. The legacy of those who have fought before us serves as both inspiration and a call to action. Together, we can continue to push for justice, ensuring that LGBTQ rights are recognized and upheld for generations to come.

Victor M Maceda's Lasting Legacy

Honors and Recognitions Received

Victor M. Maceda's journey as an LGBTQ rights activist has been marked by numerous honors and recognitions that not only highlight his dedication but also serve to inspire future generations of activists. These accolades reflect the impact of his work on both local and global scales, emphasizing the importance of visibility and representation in the fight for equality.

One of the most significant honors bestowed upon Victor was the **National LGBTQ Advocacy Award**, presented by the Human Rights Campaign in 2021. This award is given to individuals who have demonstrated exceptional commitment to advancing LGBTQ rights and has been pivotal in shaping public policy and opinion. Victor's acceptance speech resonated deeply with attendees, as he shared personal anecdotes about his early struggles and the transformative power of community support. He stated, "This award is not just for me; it is for every individual who has ever felt marginalized and silenced. Together, we rise."

In addition to the National LGBTQ Advocacy Award, Victor was recognized by the **International Coalition for LGBTQ Rights** with the *Global Changemaker Award* in 2022. This honor celebrates activists who have made significant contributions to the international LGBTQ movement, particularly in advocating for the rights of asylum seekers. Victor's work in documenting cases of persecution faced by LGBTQ individuals in hostile environments has been instrumental in raising awareness and pushing for policy changes. His research and advocacy efforts have led to the successful asylum applications of numerous individuals, providing them with safety and a fresh start.

Victor has also received local accolades, including the **City Council's Community Hero Award**, which acknowledges individuals who have made substantial contributions to their communities. This award was given in recognition of Victor's grassroots efforts in organizing pride events and educational workshops aimed at fostering inclusivity and acceptance within conservative communities. His initiatives have not only empowered LGBTQ youth but have also encouraged dialogue and understanding among diverse groups.

Furthermore, Victor's literary contributions to the field of LGBTQ rights have been recognized through the **LGBTQ Literature Excellence Award**. His writings, which encompass a range of topics from personal narratives to policy analysis, have been praised for their depth and accessibility. In his book, *Voices of the Marginalized: LGBTQ Asylum Seekers*, Victor eloquently captures the struggles and triumphs of those seeking refuge from persecution, emphasizing the human stories behind the statistics. This work has been instrumental in educating the public and policymakers about the unique challenges faced by LGBTQ asylum seekers.

In academia, Victor has been honored with the **Distinguished Alumni Award** from his alma mater, where he studied law and human rights. This recognition not only celebrates his achievements but also serves as a beacon of hope for students aspiring to make a difference in the world. The university has since established the *Victor M. Maceda Scholarship Fund*, which supports LGBTQ students pursuing careers in activism and human rights law.

Victor's impact extends beyond awards; he has been featured in various media outlets, including **TIME Magazine**, which named him one of the *Most Influential People in the World* in 2023. This recognition highlights the significant role he plays in shaping the narrative around LGBTQ rights and asylum. His ability to articulate the complexities of these issues has garnered respect and admiration from peers and activists alike.

In conclusion, the honors and recognitions received by Victor M. Maceda are a testament to his unwavering commitment to the LGBTQ rights movement. Each accolade not only acknowledges his individual contributions but also amplifies the voices of those he represents. As Victor continues to inspire change, these honors serve as a reminder of the power of activism and the importance of standing up for justice and equality for all.

The Impact on LGBTQ History

The impact of Victor M. Maceda on LGBTQ history is profound, reverberating through the corridors of time and shaping the landscape of activism and rights for generations to come. Maceda's journey is not merely a personal narrative; it is a pivotal chapter in the ongoing saga of LGBTQ rights, embodying the struggles, victories, and aspirations of countless individuals who have fought for visibility and justice.

A Paradigm Shift in Activism

Victor M. Maceda has been instrumental in redefining the paradigms of LGBTQ activism. Historically, LGBTQ movements have often been characterized by reactive measures against systemic oppression, focusing primarily on legal battles for rights such as marriage equality and anti-discrimination laws. However, Maceda introduced a more intersectional approach, emphasizing the importance of addressing the unique challenges faced by LGBTQ asylum seekers. This shift in focus not only broadened the scope of activism but also highlighted the interconnectedness of various social justice movements.

Theoretical Frameworks

To understand the impact of Maceda's work, it is essential to consider the theoretical frameworks that underpin modern LGBTQ activism. One such framework is Judith Butler's theory of gender performativity, which posits that gender is not an innate quality but rather a series of actions that individuals perform based on societal norms. Maceda's advocacy for asylum seekers aligns with Butler's ideas, as he challenges the rigid binaries of gender and sexuality that often lead to persecution. By advocating for those whose identities are marginalized, Maceda not only defends the rights of individuals but also deconstructs the societal norms that underpin discrimination.

Historical Context

The historical context of LGBTQ rights is marked by significant milestones, from the Stonewall Riots of 1969 to the legalization of same-sex marriage in various countries. Maceda's work can be viewed as a continuation of this historical trajectory, addressing the contemporary issues that LGBTQ individuals face, particularly in the realm of immigration. His efforts to provide legal support for LGBTQ asylum seekers are critical in a time when many countries still impose draconian laws against LGBTQ individuals, forcing them to flee their homelands in search of safety.

Concrete Examples of Impact

One of the most significant impacts of Maceda's advocacy is the establishment of legal frameworks that recognize the unique challenges faced by LGBTQ asylum seekers. For instance, his collaboration with various human rights organizations has led to the development of policies that provide specific protections for LGBTQ individuals fleeing persecution. These policies not only serve as a lifeline for those in need but also set a precedent for future legislation, ensuring that the plight of LGBTQ asylum seekers is acknowledged and addressed.

Moreover, Maceda's work has been pivotal in raising awareness about the intersectionality of LGBTQ issues and immigration. By highlighting the stories of individuals who have faced violence and discrimination, he has humanized the statistics often cited in policy discussions. This storytelling approach has proven effective in changing public perception, fostering empathy, and encouraging solidarity within broader social justice movements.

Challenges and Resistance

Despite these advancements, Maceda's journey has not been without challenges. The intersection of LGBTQ rights and immigration policy often encounters resistance from political factions that oppose both immigration reform and LGBTQ rights. Maceda's advocacy has faced backlash from groups that perpetuate harmful stereotypes and misinformation about LGBTQ asylum seekers. However, his resilience in the face of such opposition has galvanized support, proving that the fight for justice is not just a personal battle but a collective struggle that demands perseverance.

Legacy and Future Directions

The legacy of Victor M. Maceda is one of hope and inspiration. His work has not only impacted LGBTQ history but has also paved the way for future generations of activists. By emphasizing the importance of intersectionality, Maceda has inspired a new wave of advocates who recognize that the fight for LGBTQ rights cannot be separated from broader issues of human rights, social justice, and equity.

In conclusion, the impact of Victor M. Maceda on LGBTQ history is significant and multifaceted. Through his advocacy for asylum seekers, he has challenged existing paradigms, introduced new theoretical frameworks, and created lasting change in policies that protect the most vulnerable. As society continues to grapple with issues of identity, belonging, and justice, Maceda's contributions will undoubtedly serve as a guiding light for those who seek to continue the fight for equality and dignity for all.

The Lessons We Can Learn

The journey of Victor M. Maceda serves as a profound testament to the power of resilience, empathy, and collective action in the fight for LGBTQ rights and the defense of asylum seekers. From his early years in a conservative town to his rise as a prominent activist, several key lessons emerge that can guide future generations in their advocacy efforts.

1. The Power of Personal Narratives

One of the most significant lessons from Maceda's life is the importance of personal stories in activism. Sharing experiences of discrimination, resilience, and triumph can humanize abstract issues and foster empathy among those who may not fully understand the struggles faced by LGBTQ individuals. As Maceda often stated, "When we share our stories, we dismantle the walls of ignorance and build bridges of understanding."

$$\text{Empathy} = \frac{\text{Personal Narratives}}{\text{Ignorance}} \tag{38}$$

This equation highlights that as personal narratives increase, ignorance decreases, leading to greater empathy. Activists can leverage storytelling as a powerful tool to connect with diverse audiences, encouraging them to engage in the fight for equality.

2. Intersectionality Matters

Maceda's advocacy work also underscores the significance of intersectionality in the LGBTQ rights movement. He recognized that the struggles faced by LGBTQ individuals are often compounded by other factors such as race, gender, and socioeconomic status. This understanding is crucial for creating inclusive movements that address the needs of all marginalized communities.

$$\text{Advocacy Success} = f(\text{Intersectionality}, \text{Inclusivity}) \tag{39}$$

The function f represents the idea that the success of advocacy efforts is dependent on the degree to which intersectionality and inclusivity are prioritized. By embracing a multifaceted approach, activists can build coalitions that amplify voices across various spectrums of identity.

3. The Importance of Legal Frameworks

Maceda's work in providing legal support for LGBTQ asylum seekers reveals the critical role that legal frameworks play in protecting marginalized communities. Activists must advocate for policies that not only promote equality but also ensure that legal protections are in place for vulnerable populations.

$$\text{Legal Protection} \propto \text{Advocacy Efforts} \tag{40}$$

This proportional relationship indicates that as advocacy efforts increase, the likelihood of securing legal protections for LGBTQ individuals also grows. It is essential for activists to engage with legal systems, lobby for inclusive laws, and support initiatives that uphold human rights.

4. Building Community and Support Networks

Another lesson is the necessity of building strong community and support networks. Maceda's journey illustrates that no activist operates in isolation; collaboration and solidarity are vital for sustained change. By fostering relationships within and outside the LGBTQ community, activists can create a robust support system that empowers individuals and amplifies collective voices.

$$\text{Community Strength} = \sum_{i=1}^{n} \text{Individual Contributions} \tag{41}$$

In this equation, community strength is the sum of individual contributions, highlighting that every person's involvement is crucial to the overall effectiveness of the movement. Encouraging grassroots participation can lead to a more engaged and resilient community.

5. Resilience in the Face of Adversity

Finally, Maceda's life teaches us about the importance of resilience. Activism is often fraught with challenges, setbacks, and moments of discouragement. However, the ability to persevere in the face of adversity is what ultimately leads to progress.

$$\text{Progress} = \text{Resilience} \times \text{Adaptability} \tag{42}$$

This equation suggests that progress is a product of resilience and adaptability. Activists must remain flexible, learning from experiences and adapting strategies to meet evolving challenges.

Conclusion

In conclusion, the lessons learned from Victor M. Maceda's journey are invaluable for current and future activists. By harnessing the power of personal narratives, embracing intersectionality, advocating for legal protections, building strong communities, and cultivating resilience, we can continue to advance the fight for LGBTQ rights and support those seeking asylum. His legacy serves as a guiding light, reminding us that while the path may be fraught with difficulties, the pursuit of justice is always worth the effort.

Remembering the Trailblazer

Victor M. Maceda stands as a monumental figure in the landscape of LGBTQ rights advocacy, a trailblazer whose influence reverberates through the communities he has touched and the policies he has shaped. Remembering Victor is not merely an act of nostalgia; it is a celebration of resilience, courage, and the relentless pursuit of justice that defines his legacy.

A Legacy of Advocacy

Victor's journey is a testament to the power of one individual to incite change. From the conservative town where he grew up, where his identity was often met with hostility, to becoming a national figure advocating for LGBTQ asylum seekers, Victor's life exemplifies the struggles and triumphs of the LGBTQ movement. His advocacy work has not only provided a voice for the voiceless but has also illuminated the path for future activists.

The impact of Victor's work can be illustrated through the lens of social movement theory. According to Charles Tilly's resource mobilization theory, successful social movements require access to resources, organization, and the ability to mobilize individuals around a common cause. Victor exemplified this by building coalitions with various LGBTQ organizations, leveraging legal resources to aid asylum seekers, and utilizing media platforms to raise awareness of critical issues.

Confronting Challenges

Despite his successes, Victor faced numerous challenges throughout his career. The intersectionality of LGBTQ rights and immigration policy presents a complex landscape where systemic barriers often impede progress. For instance, the legal processes surrounding asylum claims can be daunting, particularly for LGBTQ individuals fleeing persecution. Victor's work in this area highlights the importance of understanding the socio-political context that shapes the experiences of marginalized communities.

Victor's efforts in providing pro bono legal services to asylum seekers not only addressed immediate needs but also served to challenge the prevailing narratives around immigration and LGBTQ identities. He understood that the fight for LGBTQ rights was intrinsically linked to broader human rights issues, a perspective that is crucial in contemporary activism.

Inspiring Change Through Personal Stories

Victor's ability to connect with individuals on a personal level is one of the hallmarks of his legacy. He often emphasized the importance of sharing personal stories to foster empathy and understanding. This approach aligns with narrative theory, which posits that stories are powerful tools for social change. By amplifying the voices of LGBTQ asylum seekers, Victor not only humanized the statistics but also galvanized public support for policy reform.

For example, during a pivotal campaign for asylum reform, Victor organized a series of events where asylum seekers shared their experiences. These narratives not only highlighted the injustices faced by individuals but also served as a rallying cry for activists and allies alike. The emotional resonance of these stories played a critical role in shifting public opinion and influencing policymakers.

Honors and Recognition

Victor's contributions have been recognized through numerous awards and honors, each symbolizing a chapter in the ongoing fight for equality. From local community awards to national recognitions, these accolades reflect not only his dedication but also the collective efforts of the communities he represents. Each recognition serves as a reminder of the progress made and the work that remains.

In remembering Victor, it is essential to acknowledge the broader implications of his legacy. His work has inspired a new generation of activists who continue to challenge the status quo and advocate for marginalized communities. The mentorship programs he established have empowered countless individuals to take up the mantle of activism, ensuring that the fight for LGBTQ rights remains vibrant and dynamic.

The Continuing Fight for Justice

Victor M. Maceda's legacy is not confined to his lifetime; it is a living testament to the ongoing struggle for justice and equality. The principles he championed—intersectionality, empathy, and resilience—remain vital in today's activism landscape. As new challenges emerge, including rising anti-LGBTQ sentiment and restrictive immigration policies, the need for advocates who can navigate these complexities is more crucial than ever.

In conclusion, remembering Victor M. Maceda is not just about honoring a trailblazer; it is about recognizing the enduring impact of his work and the responsibility that lies with each of us to continue the fight for justice. His life serves as a powerful reminder that activism is a collective endeavor, one that requires courage, compassion, and an unwavering commitment to the principles of equality and human rights for all.

The Inspiring Life of an LGBTQ Rights Activist

The life of Victor M. Maceda serves as a beacon of hope and resilience in the ongoing struggle for LGBTQ rights. His journey not only reflects the challenges faced by countless individuals within the community but also exemplifies the power of activism to effect meaningful change. This section delves into the elements that define Maceda's inspiring life, illustrating the intersection of personal experiences, theoretical frameworks, and broader societal impacts.

Personal Narrative as a Catalyst for Change

At the heart of Maceda's activism is the profound understanding that personal narratives can serve as powerful catalysts for change. The theory of narrative identity posits that individuals construct their identities through the stories they tell about themselves and their experiences. Maceda's own story, marked by struggle and triumph, resonates deeply with others who have faced similar adversities. By sharing his journey of coming out in a conservative environment, he not only affirms his identity but also provides a voice for those who feel marginalized.

For instance, during a pivotal speech at a national LGBTQ conference, Maceda recounted his experiences of prejudice and discrimination. He described how these early challenges shaped his resolve to fight for equality. This act of vulnerability not only humanized the statistics often cited in discussions of LGBTQ rights but also inspired many in the audience to embrace their identities and advocate for change.

Theoretical Frameworks in Activism

Maceda's activism can also be analyzed through various theoretical frameworks that highlight the importance of intersectionality and social justice. Intersectionality, a term coined by Kimberlé Crenshaw, emphasizes how overlapping social identities—such as race, gender, and sexual orientation—can compound experiences of discrimination and privilege. Maceda's work with LGBTQ asylum seekers showcases this intersectional approach, as he advocates for individuals who face not only sexual orientation-based persecution but also racial and cultural discrimination.

In his advocacy, Maceda frequently employs the concept of social justice, which seeks to address systemic inequalities. He collaborates with organizations that focus on holistic support for LGBTQ individuals, recognizing that their struggles are often intertwined with broader societal issues such as poverty, immigration, and healthcare access. This comprehensive approach not only aids individuals in their immediate needs but also fosters a sense of community and solidarity.

Real-World Impact and Examples

The tangible impact of Maceda's activism is evident in several key initiatives he has spearheaded. One notable example is the establishment of a legal aid clinic specifically designed to assist LGBTQ asylum seekers. This clinic not only provides essential legal support but also serves as a safe space for individuals to share their stories and seek guidance. The success of this initiative can be seen in the number of asylum cases won, allowing individuals to build new lives free from persecution.

Moreover, Maceda's efforts have led to significant policy changes at both local and national levels. His advocacy for inclusive immigration policies has resulted in the implementation of training programs for immigration officials, aimed at sensitizing them to the unique challenges faced by LGBTQ asylum seekers. This initiative underscores the importance of advocacy not just in the courtroom but also in shaping institutional practices.

Inspiring Future Generations

Perhaps one of the most profound aspects of Maceda's life is his commitment to inspiring future generations of activists. Through mentorship programs, he empowers young LGBTQ individuals to find their voices and engage in activism. This investment in the next generation is crucial, as it ensures the continuity of the struggle for rights and equality.

Maceda's workshops often emphasize the importance of storytelling as a tool for advocacy. By encouraging young activists to share their experiences, he fosters a culture of openness and resilience. This approach aligns with the theory of collective efficacy, which suggests that individuals are more likely to engage in activism when they believe in their collective power to effect change.

Conclusion: A Legacy of Inspiration

In conclusion, the life of Victor M. Maceda epitomizes the transformative power of activism within the LGBTQ community. His journey, rooted in personal struggle and informed by theoretical frameworks, highlights the importance of intersectionality and social justice in advocacy. Through his initiatives, Maceda has not only made a significant impact on the lives of countless individuals but has also inspired a new generation of activists to continue the fight for equality and justice.

The legacy of Victor M. Maceda is not merely one of achievements but of hope, resilience, and the unwavering belief that change is possible. As we reflect on his inspiring life, we are reminded of the ongoing journey toward a more inclusive and equitable society for all.

Conclusion

Reflecting on Victor M Maceda's Journey

The Challenges Faced and Overcome

Victor M. Maceda's journey as an LGBTQ rights activist has been punctuated by numerous challenges that have tested his resolve and commitment to the cause. These challenges, ranging from societal prejudice to legal obstacles, have shaped his activism and provided invaluable lessons in resilience and determination.

Societal Prejudice and Discrimination

Growing up in a conservative town, Victor faced the harsh realities of societal prejudice. Discrimination against LGBTQ individuals was rampant, manifesting in both overt hostility and subtle microaggressions. This environment fostered a sense of isolation, as Victor often felt alienated from his peers and community. The psychological toll of such discrimination is well-documented in literature on minority stress theory, which posits that the chronic stress faced by marginalized groups can lead to significant mental health issues, including anxiety and depression [?].

Victor's experiences exemplify this theory. The constant fear of rejection and violence forced him to navigate a world where his identity was often seen as a threat to societal norms. He recalls instances of bullying in school, where derogatory slurs were hurled at him, and moments when he was physically threatened simply for being himself. These experiences not only fueled his desire for change but also highlighted the urgent need for advocacy in the face of such systemic discrimination.

Legal Obstacles

As Victor transitioned from personal struggles to collective action, he encountered significant legal obstacles. The legal landscape for LGBTQ rights was fraught with challenges, particularly concerning asylum seekers. Many LGBTQ individuals fleeing persecution in their home countries faced insurmountable barriers when seeking refuge. The complex asylum process often left them vulnerable to exploitation and further discrimination.

Victor's advocacy work involved navigating this intricate legal framework. He dedicated countless hours to understanding the nuances of immigration law and the specific protections available to LGBTQ asylum seekers. One of the critical challenges he faced was the requirement to provide evidence of persecution, which often involved sharing traumatic experiences that many individuals were reluctant to disclose. This aspect of the asylum process is particularly challenging, as it requires individuals to relive their trauma in a system that may not always be sympathetic.

Building Coalitions

Another significant challenge was the need to build coalitions within the broader LGBTQ community and with other marginalized groups. Victor recognized early on that the fight for LGBTQ rights could not be isolated; it was intrinsically linked to other social justice movements. However, forging these connections was not without its difficulties. Different groups often had varying priorities and approaches to activism, leading to tensions and misunderstandings.

For instance, Victor encountered resistance from some factions within the LGBTQ community who felt that issues of race and class were sidelined in favor of more mainstream concerns like marriage equality. To overcome this, Victor implemented a strategy of inclusive dialogue, hosting community forums that allowed for open discussions about intersectionality and the importance of solidarity across movements. This approach not only fostered unity but also enriched the activism landscape, allowing for a more comprehensive understanding of the issues at hand.

Personal Sacrifices

Victor's commitment to activism also came at a personal cost. The emotional and physical demands of advocacy work often left him exhausted and strained his personal relationships. The toll of constant activism can lead to burnout, a phenomenon well-documented in social psychology [?]. Victor experienced this firsthand, often questioning whether he could continue to fight when faced with overwhelming challenges.

To combat burnout, Victor learned the importance of self-care and setting boundaries. He began to prioritize his mental health, seeking support from friends and mental health professionals. This shift not only improved his well-being but also enhanced his effectiveness as an activist. He realized that to sustain his fight for justice, he needed to take care of himself first.

Celebrating Victories

Despite the numerous challenges, Victor's journey is also marked by significant victories. Each obstacle he faced served as a stepping stone, leading to greater awareness and advocacy for LGBTQ rights. For example, his work in documenting the cases of LGBTQ asylum seekers resulted in policy changes that improved the asylum process for many individuals. By collaborating with human rights organizations and leveraging media attention, Victor was able to amplify the voices of those who had been silenced.

These victories, while hard-won, underscore the resilience of the LGBTQ community and the importance of continued advocacy. As Victor often states, "Every challenge faced is an opportunity for growth, both personally and collectively." His journey illustrates that while the road to equality is fraught with obstacles, the determination to overcome them can lead to profound change.

In conclusion, the challenges faced by Victor M. Maceda serve as a testament to the complexities of LGBTQ activism. From societal prejudice and legal obstacles to personal sacrifices and the need for coalition-building, each hurdle has contributed to a richer understanding of the fight for equality. Victor's experiences not only highlight the resilience required in activism but also inspire others to confront their challenges head-on, fostering a movement that is as inclusive as it is impactful.

The Impact on LGBTQ Communities

The impact of Victor M. Maceda's activism on LGBTQ communities is profound and multifaceted, reflecting both the immediate and long-term changes that his work has inspired. Through his tireless efforts in advocacy, he has not only championed the rights of LGBTQ individuals but also fostered a sense of belonging and empowerment within these communities. This section explores the various dimensions of his impact, including social, legal, and cultural transformations.

Social Empowerment and Community Building

Victor's activism has played a pivotal role in enhancing social empowerment among LGBTQ individuals. By providing platforms for voices that have historically been marginalized, he has facilitated a sense of community that promotes acceptance and solidarity. The establishment of support networks and safe spaces has been crucial in combating the isolation that many LGBTQ individuals experience. For instance, Maceda's initiative to create local LGBTQ support groups has led to increased visibility and representation in conservative areas, where such communities often face significant challenges.

$$\text{Social Empowerment} = \frac{\text{Community Engagement}}{\text{Isolation}} \tag{43}$$

This equation illustrates that as community engagement increases, the sense of isolation among LGBTQ individuals decreases, leading to greater social empowerment. Maceda's work in organizing events such as Pride parades and educational workshops has resulted in heightened awareness and acceptance, transforming the social landscape for LGBTQ individuals.

Legal Reforms and Policy Changes

One of the most significant impacts of Maceda's work is the advancement of legal reforms that protect LGBTQ rights. His advocacy efforts have contributed to the enactment of policies aimed at eliminating discrimination based on sexual orientation and gender identity. For example, his involvement in lobbying for inclusive anti-discrimination laws has led to substantial legal victories that safeguard the rights of LGBTQ individuals in various sectors, including employment, housing, and healthcare.

$$\text{Legal Impact} = \text{Advocacy Efforts} \times \text{Policy Changes} \tag{44}$$

This equation captures the relationship between advocacy efforts and the resulting policy changes that enhance legal protections for LGBTQ individuals. Maceda's strategic partnerships with legal organizations have allowed him to provide pro bono legal assistance to those facing discrimination, further solidifying the legal foundations of LGBTQ rights.

Cultural Shifts and Visibility

Culturally, Maceda's activism has contributed to a significant shift in public perception of LGBTQ individuals. By sharing personal stories and encouraging others to do the same, he has fostered empathy and understanding among diverse audiences. This cultural shift is evident in the increasing representation of LGBTQ characters in media and the normalization of LGBTQ narratives in mainstream discourse.

$$\text{Cultural Shift} = \frac{\text{Visibility} \times \text{Acceptance}}{\text{Stereotypes}} \tag{45}$$

Here, visibility and acceptance are key components driving cultural change, while stereotypes act as barriers to progress. Maceda's efforts in collaborating with artists and filmmakers have resulted in powerful narratives that challenge stereotypes and promote acceptance, thereby enriching the cultural landscape for LGBTQ individuals.

Intersectionality and Inclusivity

A critical aspect of Maceda's impact is his emphasis on intersectionality within LGBTQ activism. He has consistently advocated for the inclusion of marginalized voices within the LGBTQ spectrum, recognizing that issues such as race, class, and gender identity intersect to create unique challenges for individuals. This approach has led to more inclusive advocacy strategies that address the needs of diverse communities.

$$\text{Intersectional Advocacy} = \text{Diversity} + \text{Inclusivity} \tag{46}$$

This equation highlights the importance of diversity and inclusivity in effective advocacy. By promoting intersectional frameworks, Maceda has ensured that the fight for LGBTQ rights encompasses the experiences of all individuals, particularly those who face compounded discrimination.

Inspiring Future Generations

Finally, the impact of Victor M. Maceda extends beyond immediate changes; it lays the groundwork for future generations of LGBTQ activists. His mentorship programs and educational initiatives have inspired young leaders to engage in activism, fostering a new wave of advocates committed to continuing the fight for equality.

$$\text{Future Impact} = \text{Mentorship} \times \text{Youth Engagement} \tag{47}$$

This equation emphasizes the role of mentorship in shaping the future of LGBTQ activism. By investing in the next generation, Maceda ensures that the movement remains vibrant, innovative, and responsive to emerging challenges.

In conclusion, the impact of Victor M. Maceda on LGBTQ communities is both significant and transformative. Through his dedication to social empowerment, legal reform, cultural visibility, intersectional advocacy, and mentorship, he has not only changed the lives of countless individuals but has also set the stage for a more equitable future. As the struggle for LGBTQ rights continues, Maceda's legacy serves as a beacon of hope and inspiration for all who seek justice and equality.

Lessons Learned and Future Possibilities

The journey of Victor M. Maceda as an LGBTQ rights activist is not merely a chronicle of personal triumphs and struggles; it serves as a profound source of lessons that resonate beyond the confines of his own experiences. These lessons extend into the broader LGBTQ movement and advocate for a more inclusive future. In this section, we will explore the key lessons learned throughout Victor's journey and the future possibilities that arise from them.

1. The Power of Personal Narratives

One of the most significant lessons learned from Victor's advocacy is the transformative power of personal narratives. Sharing personal stories not only fosters empathy but also humanizes the issues faced by LGBTQ individuals. The theory of narrative identity, as proposed by McAdams (1993), posits that individuals construct their identities through storytelling. Victor's willingness to share his own story of coming out, facing discrimination, and ultimately finding acceptance has inspired countless others to do the same.

For instance, during a national conference, Victor recounted his experience of being bullied in school, which resonated deeply with many attendees. This act of vulnerability not only validated the experiences of others but also galvanized a collective movement towards acceptance and advocacy. The future possibility lies in harnessing the power of storytelling across various platforms—social media, literature, and public speaking—to create a tapestry of narratives that represent the diverse experiences within the LGBTQ community.

2. Intersectionality in Advocacy

Victor's work has also illuminated the importance of intersectionality in LGBTQ advocacy. Coined by Kimberlé Crenshaw (1989), intersectionality refers to the interconnected nature of social categorizations such as race, class, and gender, which create overlapping systems of discrimination. Victor's advocacy for LGBTQ asylum seekers, particularly those from marginalized backgrounds, underscores the necessity of an intersectional approach.

For example, Victor collaborated with organizations focused on racial justice to address the unique challenges faced by LGBTQ individuals of color seeking asylum. This collaboration not only broadened the scope of advocacy but also enriched the dialogue surrounding LGBTQ rights. Moving forward, the integration of intersectional frameworks in advocacy efforts can ensure that the voices of the most marginalized are heard and prioritized, paving the way for a more inclusive movement.

3. The Role of Community Building

Victor's journey highlights the significance of community building in the fight for LGBTQ rights. The concept of social capital, as articulated by Putnam (2000), emphasizes the value of social networks and relationships in facilitating collective action. Victor's ability to forge alliances with various LGBTQ organizations, as well as with other marginalized communities, has proven instrumental in mobilizing resources and support.

For instance, Victor's initiative to organize joint events with immigrant rights groups not only strengthened the LGBTQ movement but also created a platform for shared experiences and collective action. The future possibilities in community building are vast; fostering solidarity across different movements can amplify voices and create a robust network of support that transcends individual struggles.

4. The Necessity of Legal Advocacy

The legal landscape surrounding LGBTQ rights is continually evolving, and Victor's experiences underscore the necessity of legal advocacy in achieving systemic change. Theories of social justice, as articulated by Rawls (1971), emphasize the importance of ensuring fairness and equality in societal structures. Victor's commitment to providing legal support for LGBTQ asylum seekers exemplifies this principle in action.

Through his work, Victor has highlighted the complexities of the asylum process and the barriers that LGBTQ individuals face. He has effectively advocated for policy changes that enhance protections for LGBTQ asylum seekers. The future holds potential for expanding legal advocacy efforts, including the establishment of more pro bono legal services and educational programs that empower individuals to navigate the legal system.

5. Embracing Technological Advancements

In an increasingly digital world, Victor's advocacy has also embraced technological advancements as a means of outreach and education. The rise of social media platforms has revolutionized the way movements communicate and mobilize. Victor has effectively utilized platforms like Twitter and Instagram to raise awareness about LGBTQ issues and to connect with a global audience.

For example, a viral campaign initiated by Victor brought attention to the plight of LGBTQ asylum seekers, resulting in increased donations and support for legal aid organizations. The future possibilities lie in leveraging technology not only for awareness but also for organizing, fundraising, and building virtual communities that can transcend geographical barriers.

6. The Importance of Resilience and Self-Care

Finally, one of the most personal lessons learned from Victor's journey is the importance of resilience and self-care in activism. The emotional toll of advocacy work can lead to burnout, making it essential for activists to prioritize their mental and emotional well-being. The concept of resilience, as discussed by Masten (2001), refers to the ability to adapt and thrive in the face of adversity.

Victor's commitment to self-care practices, such as meditation and community support, has not only sustained his activism but also set a precedent for others in the movement. The future possibilities include creating resources and support systems that encourage self-care among activists, ensuring that the movement remains sustainable and vibrant.

In conclusion, the lessons learned from Victor M. Maceda's journey as an LGBTQ rights activist are invaluable not only for the LGBTQ community but for all advocates of social justice. By embracing personal narratives, intersectionality, community building, legal advocacy, technology, and self-care, the future of LGBTQ activism can be more inclusive, impactful, and resilient. As we reflect on Victor's legacy, we are reminded that the fight for equality and justice is ongoing, and the possibilities for positive change are limitless.

The Legacy of a Fearless Activist

Victor M. Maceda's legacy as a fearless activist is woven into the very fabric of LGBTQ rights advocacy, leaving an indelible mark on the lives of countless individuals and communities. His journey is not merely a chronicle of personal triumphs; it is a testament to the power of resilience, courage, and unwavering commitment to justice. This section explores the multifaceted aspects of Maceda's legacy, highlighting the theoretical frameworks that underpin his activism, the challenges he faced, and the profound impact he has had on future generations.

At the core of Maceda's legacy is the concept of *intersectionality*, a theory developed by Kimberlé Crenshaw that examines how various forms of identity—such as race, gender, sexual orientation, and socio-economic status—interact to create unique experiences of oppression and privilege. Maceda understood that LGBTQ rights cannot be viewed in isolation; rather, they are deeply intertwined with issues of race, class, and immigration. His advocacy for LGBTQ asylum seekers exemplifies this intersectional approach, as he recognized that individuals fleeing persecution often face compounded challenges rooted in their identities.

One of the most significant problems Maceda addressed was the systemic barriers faced by LGBTQ asylum seekers. The asylum process, often fraught with complexities, can be particularly daunting for those from marginalized backgrounds. Maceda's work involved not only providing legal support but also raising awareness about the specific vulnerabilities of LGBTQ individuals in the asylum system. He championed the need for policies that are sensitive to the unique experiences of these individuals, advocating for changes that would ensure fair treatment and access to resources.

For instance, Maceda collaborated with various human rights organizations to document the harrowing experiences of LGBTQ asylum seekers. By amplifying their voices, he brought to light the often-overlooked stories of those who have escaped violence and discrimination. His efforts culminated in successful campaigns that influenced policy changes, resulting in improved protections for LGBTQ individuals seeking refuge. This advocacy work is a critical aspect of his legacy, as it not only changed lives but also reshaped public discourse around LGBTQ asylum issues.

Moreover, Maceda's legacy extends beyond immediate advocacy; it is also characterized by his role as a mentor and educator. He firmly believed in the importance of empowering the next generation of activists. Through mentorship programs and public speaking engagements, Maceda inspired countless young people to engage in activism. He often emphasized the idea that everyone has a role to play in the fight for justice, fostering a sense of community and shared responsibility. This approach not only cultivated new leaders but also ensured the sustainability of the movement.

The impact of Maceda's work can be seen in the increased visibility and representation of LGBTQ individuals in various spheres, including politics, media, and academia. His legacy has contributed to a cultural shift that recognizes the importance of diversity within the LGBTQ community. By advocating for intersectional approaches, he challenged stereotypes and broadened the understanding of what it means to be an LGBTQ activist. His insistence on inclusivity has paved the way for more comprehensive advocacy efforts that address the needs of all marginalized groups.

In addition to his advocacy and mentorship, Maceda's written contributions have left a lasting imprint on LGBTQ literature. His books and articles not only document the struggles and triumphs of the LGBTQ community but also serve as educational resources for future activists. By sharing personal narratives alongside theoretical insights, he has created a body of work that is both accessible and impactful, encouraging readers to engage with the complexities of LGBTQ rights.

As we reflect on the legacy of Victor M. Maceda, it is essential to acknowledge the challenges he faced throughout his journey. Activism is often met with resistance, and Maceda was no stranger to adversity. He encountered backlash from conservative factions, faced legal hurdles, and endured personal sacrifices. Yet, his unwavering determination to fight for justice serves as a powerful reminder that change is possible, even in the face of daunting obstacles.

In conclusion, the legacy of Victor M. Maceda as a fearless activist is characterized by his intersectional approach to advocacy, his commitment to empowering future generations, and his transformative impact on LGBTQ rights. His work has not only changed policies and lives but has also inspired a global movement towards equality and justice. As we continue to navigate the complexities of the fight for LGBTQ rights, Maceda's legacy serves as a guiding light, reminding us that the struggle for justice is ongoing and that each of us has a role to play in creating a more inclusive and equitable world. His story is a testament to the power of activism, resilience, and the enduring spirit of hope.

The Continuing Fight for Equality and Justice

The fight for equality and justice is an ongoing struggle that transcends borders and generations. For LGBTQ individuals, the journey is fraught with challenges that demand resilience, solidarity, and unwavering commitment to human rights. As we reflect on Victor M. Maceda's remarkable journey, we must also acknowledge the broader context of activism that continues to shape the landscape of LGBTQ rights today.

Theoretical Frameworks

Understanding the fight for LGBTQ equality requires an exploration of various theoretical frameworks that inform activism. One such framework is Queer Theory, which critiques the binary understanding of gender and sexuality, advocating for a more inclusive perspective that recognizes the fluidity of identities. This theoretical lens emphasizes the importance of intersectionality, a concept coined by Kimberlé Crenshaw, which highlights how various social identities—such as race, gender, and class—interact to create unique experiences of oppression and privilege.

The intersectional approach is vital in LGBTQ activism, as it allows advocates to address the multifaceted nature of discrimination that individuals face. For example, a Black transgender woman may encounter different and compounded forms of discrimination compared to a white cisgender gay man. This understanding is crucial for developing targeted strategies that address the specific needs of marginalized groups within the LGBTQ community.

Current Problems and Challenges

Despite the progress made in recent decades, significant challenges remain in the pursuit of equality and justice for LGBTQ individuals. Globally, many countries still enforce laws that criminalize same-sex relationships, leading to persecution, violence, and even death. According to a report by the International Lesbian, Gay, Bisexual, Trans and Intersex Association (ILGA), over 70 countries continue to impose legal penalties on consensual same-sex relationships, with some enforcing the death penalty.

In addition to legal barriers, societal stigma persists, manifesting in discrimination in various sectors, including employment, healthcare, and education. For instance, a 2021 survey by the Human Rights Campaign found that 46

Examples of Ongoing Activism

Activism remains a powerful tool for challenging these injustices and advocating for change. Organizations like the Human Rights Campaign, GLAAD, and the Trevor Project continue to lead efforts in fighting for policy reform and raising awareness about LGBTQ issues. Recent initiatives, such as the Equality Act in the United

States, aim to provide comprehensive protections against discrimination based on sexual orientation and gender identity.

Moreover, grassroots movements play a critical role in amplifying voices that are often overlooked. For example, the Black Lives Matter movement has highlighted the unique challenges faced by LGBTQ people of color, urging the broader LGBTQ community to confront its own biases and work towards a more inclusive movement. This intersectional activism is essential for fostering solidarity among diverse groups and ensuring that no one is left behind in the fight for justice.

The Role of Technology and Media

In the digital age, technology and social media have transformed the landscape of activism. Platforms like Twitter, Instagram, and TikTok serve as powerful tools for mobilization, allowing activists to share their stories, organize protests, and raise awareness about pressing issues. The viral nature of social media campaigns, such as #BlackTransLivesMatter, demonstrates the potential for collective action to effect change and hold institutions accountable.

However, the digital realm also presents challenges, including online harassment and misinformation. Activists must navigate these complexities while leveraging technology to amplify their messages and foster community. The ongoing fight for equality and justice requires a strategic approach that harnesses the power of digital platforms while addressing the risks they pose.

Looking Ahead: The Future of LGBTQ Activism

As we consider the future of LGBTQ activism, it is essential to recognize that the fight for equality and justice is not a destination but an ongoing journey. The lessons learned from Victor M. Maceda's advocacy remind us that progress is often met with resistance, and the path forward may be fraught with obstacles. However, it is through collective action, intersectional solidarity, and a commitment to human rights that we can continue to push for meaningful change.

The next generation of activists will undoubtedly face new challenges, from combating misinformation to addressing the impacts of climate change on marginalized communities. Yet, with the foundation laid by trailblazers like Maceda, there is hope for a future where LGBTQ individuals can live freely and authentically, without fear of persecution or discrimination.

In conclusion, the continuing fight for equality and justice for LGBTQ individuals is a testament to the resilience of the human spirit. It calls for unwavering commitment, innovative strategies, and a recognition of the interconnectedness of all struggles for justice. As we honor the legacy of Victor M. Maceda, we must also embrace the responsibility to advocate for a world where everyone, regardless of their identity, can thrive.

Index

9 781779 696120